LISTENING TO OTHERS

Joyce Huggett

HODDER AND STOUGHTON

LONDON SYDNEY AUCKLAND TORONTO

Bible quotations are from the New International Version,
Copyright © 1973, 1978, 1984 by
International Bible Society

The author and publisher have endeavoured to trace all copyright
holders for the material used, but apologise for any inadvertent
omissions which will be rectified in any reprint.

For permission to use copyright material they are grateful to the
following sources:
David Ausburger, extract from *Caring Enough to Hear and Be
Heard*, Regal Books, Ventura, CA 93006.
Michael Jacobs, extract from *Swift to Hear*, © 1985 Michael
Jacobs, SPCK
Francis MacNutt, extract from *Healing*, © 1974 Ave Maria Press,
Notre Dame, IN 46557. All rights reserved.
Henri Nouwen, extract from *Compassion*, © 1982 by Darton,
Longman & Todd.
John Powell, extract from *Will the Real Me Please Stand Up*, ©
1985 by John Powell, S.J. Printed by Tabor Publishing in the
United States of America. Used with permission.
John Stott, extract from *Issues Facing Christians Today*, © 1984
John Stott, Marshall Pickering.

British Library Cataloguing in Publication Data

Huggett, Joyce, 1937–
   Listening to others.
   1. counselling – Manuals – For christians
   I. Title
   253.5

   ISBN 0 340 42590 3

For

Anne

to whom I owe so much

Contents

	Preface	7
	Acknowledgements	13
1	Catching Compassion	17
2	Coping with Crises	33
3	A Rabbit-hole Christian	52
4	People Matter More than Meetings	69
5	Learning to Listen	89
6	The Listening Heart	108
7	Listening to the Bereaved	129
8	Listening to Past Pain	149
9	Making Peace with the Past	172
10	Listening to the Depressed	197
11	One Spoke of the Wheel	218
12	Listening to Joy	241
	Notes	251
	Recommended Resources	255
	Recommended Reading	259

Preface

Throw-away sentences often contain far more truth than we recognise when first we hear them. A throw-away sentence sowed the seed which has since germinated in my mind and given rise to this book. And Jeremy is the person I have to thank for the pertinent question which prompted me to put pen to paper once more.

Jeremy used to be the producer of religious broadcasts at BBC Radio Nottingham. He read my *Listening to God* with obvious interest and, shortly after the book was published, came to interview me for local radio.

After the interview we talked about my personal pilgrimage of prayer and Jeremy's own appreciation of silence. It was then that he said, 'Joyce! I'm interested that there's no reference to social justice in *Listening to God*. Yet, surely, prayer and social justice go together? *Maybe that'll be the subject of your next book?'*

This comment caught me off my guard and I was glad that we were no longer on the air. My rather feeble response was: 'I suppose it receives no mention because I'm only just beginning to see for myself where the two disciplines of prayer and care fit into one another and overlap.' I doubted whether I would ever tackle the proposed book.

But this throw-away suggestion lodged in my mind and bothered me. 'Jeremy's right,' I admitted to myself. The art form of listening to God is only one side of a two-sided coin. The flip side of that coin is care for others. Listening to God will always remain incomplete until I have shown how it affects our ordinary everyday lives. I am not qualified to show how listening to God works in the world of politics or involvement in the inner city because I have never worked in these deprived areas. What I can do is to place the spotlight on a different aspect of social concern – people-helping in general.

During my summer holiday that year, while I was listening to God, the realisation dawned more clearly than ever before, that my counselling and my attentive listening to God belong to each other. I saw too that my upbringing had prepared me not simply for one-ness with God, it had also given me an acute awareness of people.

These twin truths excited me. I was still reeling from readers' response to *Listening to God*. That book seemed to have struck a chord in the heart of a large number of people. Many had taken the trouble to write to tell me how God had been drawing them into a deeper awareness of himself and his love. At the same time, through conferences and conventions, I was encountering Christians who were expressing the desire, not simply to listen to God, but to listen to people in pain also: couples in crisis, the bereaved, the depressed, those at a low spiritual ebb.

'Maybe there's scope for a book entitled *Listening to Others*?' I said to myself as I walked along the beach in Greece. It would underline the truth of a claim once made by St Teresa of Avila that those who listen to God most will love others most: 'They will love others much more than they did, with a more genuine love, with greater passion and with a love which brings more profit.'[1]

I sat in the sun that holiday sketching an outline for this book. When I returned home I showed it to my editor, who encouraged me to clothe this skeleton with flesh.

Seven months elapsed before I could create enough space to begin to write in earnest. During those months all kinds of people with all kinds of needs crowded into my life so that I found myself with less time to pray than ever before and scarcely any time to write.

At first this baffled me. I had written a book describing my pilgrimage of prayer. It was selling well. Now the

pattern of my prayer seemed to be changing. Frequently I
was being forced to sacrifice the structures which safe-
guarded my stillness so that I could be more available and
attentive to the desperation of those in need.

Little by little the realisation dawned that, yet again,
God was moving me on; challenging me to let go of all I
held dear so that my hands were free to receive the new
gift he held out to me. This gift came in the form of the
awareness that, sometimes, to stay alongside people in
their pain is a more authentic form of prayer than retreating into silence mentally to lift these people into the
healing hands of God. As Peter Dodson rightly reminds
us, contemplation is paying rapt attention to God and his
world.[2] Or, as St Benedict has put it, the activity of true
prayer is both vertical and horizontal. Vertical in that the
person praying is united with God and horizontal in that
the pray-er unites himself with the world of which he is a
part.

Even so, holding two things in tension – my ongoing
need to be still before God so that I can be effective in my
contact with people and the challenge to be so caught up
with people that I am prepared, when necessary, to let go
of my sacred space to be one hundred per cent available
to them – was a problem which seemed to have no easy
answer.

I see now that, in many ways, God was writing this
book on the parchment of my experience. On the day
when I had planned to begin the writing in earnest, my
husband came into my study carrying a letter. 'You'd
better sit down before you read it,' he advised. 'It'll be
quite hard for you to take.'

The letter was from a nun:

I wonder if you have heard the happy-sad news of
Sister Rachel Mary? If it had to be, thanks be to God –
she went downhill at a gallop and died on the evening
of February 7th. She accepted and suffered with immense dignity . . . just continuing her vocation of
prayer and moving towards our Lord.

I was glad I was sitting down. I was stunned. Sister Rachel Mary dead? It was she who had taught me so much about prayer. It was she who stayed alongside me in much of the darkness I had experienced from time to time in my prayer pilgrimage. It was she who had listened and cared and cheered me on.

Later that evening I replied to the letter the nun had written. And I tried to express some of the emotions which were tumbling round in my heart:

> I am trying to hold all kinds of things in tension: the emptiness of trying to come to terms with the fact that she isn't here; gratitude for all that she's given me and envy of her spiritual stature . . . she always seemed to have the right book or the right word for the right occasion.

Here it was again: the two-sided coin. This friend of mine who was dearer to me than a sister, was so anchored in God and filled with love for me that, intuitively, she knew when to write, what to say and how to pray. Because she prayed much (in a silent, attentive, unobtrusive way), she cared much – and her caring was pure and selfless. It was as though, through her prayer, she touched God with one hand and through the depth of her care touched me with the other.

There had been occasions, I knew, when Sister Rachel Mary had sacrificed times earmarked for prayer so that she could stay alongside me in the desperation of my need. I wanted to follow her example; to help others like that.

Sister Rachel Mary would be the first to admit that she was no counsellor. She sought no such grandiose title. Yet she became what every would-be listener to God can become: a person used by him to share the sufferings and successes of others without seeking to possess or smother the people with whom she became involved.

My original plan was to write a book for those who, like

Sister Rachel Mary, having started on the lifelong adventure of listening to God, find themselves drawn into the task of listening to others also. It was to have been for those who are asking, How can I become better equipped to listen to people effectively?

I was aware that, in all probability, such readers would not have the opportunity to become specialists – to train as counsellors. What they will have is something far more vital, opportunity after opportunity to sit with people in pain, to listen to them with patience and concern and to stretch out a sensitive helping hand when the boat of their life is tempest-tossed.

But as I wrote I found myself addressing not only people who fall into this category, but another group also: those who have not yet caught a vision of what it means to 'be merciful, just as your Father is merciful' (Luke 6:36) and the challenge of St Paul, to bear one another's burdens and so fulfil the law of Christ (Gal. 6:2). They may be full of evangelistic zeal or pride themselves on being ardent students of God's word, or even value highly the warmth of a supportive Christian fellowship, but they have never discovered either the urgency or joyful privilege of serving others in this way.

Now this book embraces all these groups. Its autobiographical nature is deliberate and it is my prayer that as this further piece of my personal history unfolds, readers may so identify with the joy and the pain I describe that they go on from there to discover how they can best reach out a rescuing hand to the men, women and children God brings across their path – especially the hundreds who are hurting.

JOYCE HUGGETT

Acknowledgements

'Who we are, what we become, depends largely on those who love us.' This claim of John Powell's took on new meaning for me as I wrote this book and realised more fully than ever before just how much I owe to certain people. I am glad to be able to express in public my thanks to a few of those who have shaped my life by caring for me at cost to themselves.

The first accolade must go to my husband, David, for honouring his wedding vows and loving me through the worst as well as the joyful times. And the second to Anne Long who, on so many occasions, allowed herself to be God's instrument of healing to me. Without the dedicated love and ongoing care of these two people, I might never have been rescued from my brokenness; might never have reached the degree of maturity I enjoy today.

I would like to thank my brother, Ray, too, for all the love he showered on me, his 'baby sister' both in Roberts Road days and more recently in Perth, Australia. His memory of our childhood is so much better than mine. Without his help I would not have recalled the names of some of our neighbours.

I am also indebted to those who prayed for me while I was giving birth to this book. This particular 'labour' was prolonged and, at times, painful. But these faithful friends refused to give up praying. One family even provided me with a place where I could 'duck under', be fed and press on with the praying and the writing in peace. I know no adequate words to sum up just how much I appreciate their co-operation, concern and care.

Among those who gave practical help and advice were my editor, Tim Anderson, and my personal assistant,

Charlotte Swan. Tim is a great encourager. Talking with him so sharpens my thinking that I have grown to value this editor-author partnership more and more. Charlotte, too, believed in the book even when it was gestating. She read and re-read the manuscript, made shrewd suggestions, and relieved me of mundane, time-consuming tasks like proof reading, compiling the bibliography and checking references – behind-the-scenes work which she does so faithfully and efficiently.

I would have loved to be able to thank personally each member of the Roberts Road community for the rich start in life which they gave me. Alas, this has not been possible. What I have been able to do is to make contact with Arthur and Doreen Drowley again and I thank them for inspiring David and me to offer for the full-time ministry.

My final thanks go to Elaine, the secretary who once worked with us and who unwittingly triggered off so much of the pain I describe in this book. When the manuscript was finished, I wrote to ask her permission to make public our once-strained relationship and her reply was heart-warming: 'You have more than my permission or goodwill. If there can be one word spoken, one song sung, one word written to bring wholeness to our broken world then may God richly be served and praised.'

This forgiving, reconciling letter, full of undeserved love, humbled me – and amazed me. Elaine records that her lasting memories of her year with us are: 'Your wonderful, smiling, intelligent son and daughter and your laughter in the house.'

She sent me a photograph of herself and her husband and her lovely children. They now smile at me from my study wall.

Reaching Out

I feel your pain
and long to touch the hurt
and make it melt away.
Yes, I know
that I can't really see
the breadth
and depth
of this dark valley you're in.
I can't truly know
just how sharp the knife is
in your soul –
for it is you in its path,
not me.
But I have known other valleys,
and in my heart
still bear knife-wound scars.
Even so,
I would walk your road
and take your pain
if I could.
I cannot.
And yet, perhaps
in some way
I can be a hand to hold
in the darkness;
in some way, try to blunt
the sharpness of pain.
But if not –
it may help a little
just to know I care.

(Christine Rigden)

1

Catching Compassion

The shiny black Daimler seemed to slip slowly and silently between number 24 Roberts Road, where I lived, and the red-brick church hall immediately opposite. I followed its progress as it inched its way past Webber's quaint and poky grocery shop which graced the corner of Roberts Road and Franklin Street, past Bolt's the butchers which stood at the junction of Roberts Road and Temple Road and past the undistinguished dairy where Mrs Hart did most of her shopping. Mrs Hart, with her husband and small son Barry, lived almost opposite the dairy. And it was outside their tiny terraced house – number 5 – that the Daimler stopped on the dot of 2 p.m.

When the car purred past number 24 no one in the street below would have known that the bedroom of our house was being used as a lookout. Heavy lace curtains concealed my mother and me. Even so, since my mother lifted the curtains away from the window ever so slightly, we had a grandstand view of the limousine, the man-in-black driving it, and his companion who was also dressed in black.

Full of four-year-old curiosity I crept under the curtain, pressed my nose against the window-pane and waited.

No one in Roberts Road owned a car, so when one was parked in the road it attracted a flurry of interest. This one was no exception. Within seconds, it seemed, a small knot of women had congregated outside the church hall and were now standing near the scarlet telephone box staring at the Harts' house like newspaper reporters scenting a scoop.

My mother showed no sign of leaving her post, so I lingered beside her, equally eager to discover what would happen next. Several minutes ticked by before she pulled me away from the window, dropped the curtain, and contented herself with peeping through one of the larger holes formed by the lace pattern. I copied her. And again we saw the shiny black Daimler drive past our house. But this time it was being driven up the steep hill towards Radford Road and this time, behind the men-in-black sat a polished box which was overlaid with sprays of flowers of every size, shape, texture and colour – blues, yellows, whites, crimsons, pinks, purples, reds. I had never seen so many flowers before. And I had never seen a beautiful box like that before, so naturally I demanded to know what it was.

While the gaggle of housewives took a long last look at the cortège, my mother explained that Barry Hart had gone to be with Jesus.

I do not remember how my four-year-old mind wove together the multi-coloured strands of that day: the solemn black strands of the funeral proceedings, the mute shades of the child-size coffin, the brightly-coloured hues of the wreaths and floral tributes, the colourless strands of the sudden silence which seemed to have enshrouded our normally busy and happy street. Nor do I remember how I coped with the fact that so much strange sorrow should surround such a potentially joyful occasion as a visit to Jesus, the friend we had come to love in Sunday School. What I do remember is the effect this tragic and sudden death had on my mother and the Roberts Road community.

For the rest of the day my mother withdrew into herself and seemed sad. It was the way she used to behave some Sunday afternoons when I would be sitting at the kitchen table thumbing through the old photographs which were kept in a St Bruno tobacco tin in the side-board cupboard. The routine was always the same. I would examine each picture in turn, ask 'Who's that?' and listen while one of my parents patiently retold the tale behind the picture which I had heard so often before.

One photograph in particular fascinated me. It was of a tiny grass mound which my parents called a grave.

'What's that?' I would ask.

'That's where Maurice is now,' my father would reply.

'Who's Maurice?' I would persist.

'Maurice would have been your brother but he died before you were born.'

'Why did he die?'

'Because he was born a "blue baby".'

This explanation always silenced my insensitive interrogation and I would turn to the next photograph, which was equally brown with age and curled up at the corners through much handling. Young though I was, I understood the term 'blue baby' because that was the term the grown-ups in Roberts Road used to describe Barry Hart. It was an accurate description. Sometimes I would meet him in the dairy with his mother, and would notice that his lips and face and fingertips were tinged with an inky blue – a sharp contrast to the rosy cheeks with which my own healthy face usually glowed.

With the wisdom of adulthood I can now understand why sadness descended on my mother like a snow cloud that day . . . Barry and Maurice must have been a similar age when they died: just three years old. No wonder I overheard my mother admit to the greengrocer when he called later that afternoon: 'My heart really went out to them.' For her, many painful memories had been buried alive. The sight of another child's funeral brought them surging to the surface once more.

But my mother was not the only person in Roberts Road to be affected by Barry's death. It made an impact on the entire Roberts Road community.

Like Coronation Street, two rows of monotonous redbrick terraced houses provided homes for the residents of Roberts Road. The proximity of one house to the next ensured that no one could keep secrets from the neighbourhood even if they tried. The disadvantage of this was that even private pain soon became public property. The advantage was that problems were shared. People cared. It was care and concern which was being expressed by the group of women outside the street's only telephone kiosk. Everyone understood that this was their way of communicating: 'If there's anything we can do let us know.'

Another advantage was that if one person was in pain the whole of Roberts Road seemed to respect that fact and behave accordingly. On this occasion a hush descended on the neighbourhood which was not unlike the gloom that accompanies fog in February. For several days after the funeral no children played in the street outside our house as they usually did. No ball bounced in the back yards which were the Roberts Road substitute for gardens. No youths whistled on their way home from work as they did on happier days. No one dared even to laugh or to turn up the volume on their radio. To do so would have seemed the height of insensitivity and disrespect. Mourners were mourners. When death visited one home in Roberts Road, it visited them all. When tragedy struck we were in it together. We belonged to one another.

No one had taught these people that the word compassion comes from two Latin words *pati* and *cum* which put together mean 'to suffer with'. No one had taught them that 'compassion asks us to go where it hurts, to enter into places of pain, to share in brokenness, fear, confusion, and anguish'. No one had taught them that 'compassion challenges us to cry out with those in misery, to mourn with those who are lonely, to weep with those in tears . . . to be weak with the weak, vulnerable with the vulnerable, and powerless with the powerless'. No one had taught them that 'compassion means full immersion in the condition of being human'.[1] Yet compassionate was what these people were. For them, compassion was instinctive: doing what comes naturally.

It was into this sensitive compassionate community that I was born. It was deeper into this caring community that I was drawn when war ravaged our historic city. And it was from this caring community that I discovered that concern for others is an essential part of being human. No one ever *taught* me that fact. In Roberts Road caring for others was not taught but caught. And I cottoned on to the concept at a very early age.

Mother's example

Though I failed to recognise it at the time, people's reactions to Barry's death made a big impact on my sensitive personality. When the Second World War disturbed the happy equilibrium of Roberts Road even more, my apprenticeship in compassion and caring took a new turn. As many people who lived through those turbulent years have observed, ties with family and friends were strengthened under the impetus of impending crises.

Our next-door neighbour in Roberts Road was an elderly lady called Mrs Langmead. She was overweight, riddled with rheumatism and hard of hearing. Her body aroused my child's curiosity because, as she hobbled from room to room in her home, her entire form seemed to creak. It was years later that I discovered that it was not her body but her corsets that made this curious sound. My brothers and their friends accused her of being bossy because she would spend hours standing on her doorstep watching them play in the street and if a ball bounced too near her windows or if the level of noise rose above her threshold of tolerance, she would wave her stick angrily and shout at them to go and play elsewhere.

But she was not always cantankerous. Occasionally she would be in gentler mood. On such occasions she would invite my mother and me into her home and I would perch on her black leather pouffe, feel the furry texture of the black velveteen cloth which covered her big round table and gaze at the black-lead hearth which formed the focus of her otherwise cheerless living room. That hearth was the home of an equally black kettle which always seemed to sing and sometimes spewed blobs of water on to the flames, turning them blue. Above the stove, on the mantelpiece, a pair of black and white china dogs with black china chains round their necks stared down at us. Between them stood an antique clock which marked every hour with a pretty chime and which delighted me so much that, when I heard its preparatory whirr, I would put my finger to my lips and say 'Shh!' to the adults who insisted on talking through the chime. When Laing (as I nicknamed her) invited us in on winter afternoons my cup of happiness would be full because then I would watch her reach for a long wax taper and light the gas lights which were the only form of lighting she would allow in this home cluttered with Victoriana.

When war broke out my mother worried about Laing. One clap of thunder was enough to worry the old lady out of her wits and send her into hiding in the coal cupboard under the stairs. How was she to cope with the constant wail of sirens and the heart-chilling scream of dive-bombers?

To quieten my mother's fears and to guarantee Laing's safety, we worked out a way of communicating through the cardboard-thin walls which separated her house from ours. As soon as the whine of the sirens built up to its stomach-churning crescendo, our entire family would wedge themselves into the cupboard under our stairs: the only place which was considered safe to protect us from the danger of falling debris. Likewise Laing would manouevre her stiff over-size body into *her* cupboard. When we were all in position we would knock on the wall and Laing would make three raps in response. Then we would rest assured that she was safe, and in number 24 we would remain huddled together in our hidey-hole until the 'all clear' was given. As soon as that welcome sound was heard one of us would go into number 26 to check that Laing was unharmed.

I loved to take upon myself the responsibility of caring for Laing in this way. Before the moan of the siren had died away I would rush into the cupboard under our stairs, push past the gas masks which hung on improvised hooks, press myself against the far wall where the gas meter ticked loudly and banging on the wall as loudly as I could, I would shout at the top of my voice: 'Laing! Laing! Can you hear me?'

One memorable day, when the customary warning pierced the peace of the neighbourhood, I leapt into the cupboard as usual, knocked on the wall with my right fist and though I knocked and knocked until my knuckles were red and sore, Laing did not reply. Clearly she had not heard, I would have to go and *tell* her the siren had gone.

By this time our family had acquired a Morrison shelter which had been erected in the front room – the best room which was only used at Christmas and on Sundays in peacetime but which had to double as a refuge during these troubled days. While my father and brothers crept into this shelter I darted towards the front door. Reading my mind, my mother chased after me but I was more nimble than she was and I reached the street first. As I ran out of the bottle-green door I was greeted by the terrifying scream of approaching aircraft. I sped to number 26 but, even as I ran, I could see aeroplanes almost brushing with their bellies the slates of the Roberts Road houses opposite our home. All the more reason for ignoring my mother's shouts and running in to make sure that Laing was safe.

I found Laing shuffling her bulky body towards her cupboard. She had been asleep in her rocking chair and had not heard me knocking but had been startled by the sudden scream of the engines.

'Go back home quickly,' she urged me, waving her stick in the direction of my home. 'Tell them Laing's all right.'

Something about the tone of her voice frightened me so much that I scuttled back to number 24 as quickly as I could.

My mother was outside our house leaning against the neatly-pointed red-brick wall, her face deathly white. And she was angry.

'Go inside at once,' she scolded in a voice I dared not defy. 'You nearly had your mummy killed.' And she dragged me into our house slamming the door behind her.

While she had been pursuing me a curtain of bullets had been fired from one of the aeroplanes. A piece of shrapnel had missed her by a fraction of an inch, smashed the front-room window and fallen on the steel roof of the Morrison shelter where my father and brothers were huddled.

Whenever my mother told this story to relatives and neighbours, showing them the jagged piece of shrapnel to add spice to her story, I would blush with shame. It filled me with horror to discover that my recklessness had almost caused my mother's death. But it did nothing to dampen my desire to help others. By this time the seam of compassion seemed to have been deeply ingrained in my heart.

Father's example

That is hardly surprising since my father was just as compassionate as my mother. After he had read the newspaper and the Bible in the evening, we would often hear him say: 'I think I'll go and visit old Mrs Davey.' Or, 'I'm going over to see Mrs Jones. Shan't be long.' And he would go and while away his free time with one of these housebound old ladies. And we would accept that life for these women would become more bearable because my father had visited them.

If news reached us that someone had lost his job or had tried to commit suicide or had just come out of hospital or had lost a loved one, it was my father who would visit them. He was one of the world's wonderful carers. Though he had never read a book about compassion, he was so full of that Christ-like characteristic that instinctively he knew that what really counts in moments of pain and suffering is that someone is prepared to stay alongside us, not necessarily providing us with solutions but offering us the consolation and comfort which comes through a supporting presence.

This caring embraced children as well as adults. Indeed it was his concern for working-class children that pushed him into accepting the invitation to become first the lieutenant and then the captain of the 7th Exeter Boys' Brigade Company which met in the church hall opposite our home.

The houses in Roberts Road had no gardens. The pocket-handkerchief-size yards which backed on to the neighbouring streets were too small for the games of boisterous children. Sometimes we would play in the nearby park. But usually we played in the street. For such children organisations like the Boys' Brigade for boys and Brownies and Guides for girls fulfilled a very real need. They provided an outlet for our energy and creativity. And they were character-trainers.

My father threw himself into training the boys in his charge. He took them to camp in the summer and encouraged them to learn to play bugles and drums and cymbals in winter. The band flourished. He always tried to point away from himself as captain to the captain he served: Jesus. Because of the fine work he was doing he earned the respect and affection of many in the neighbourhood including the headmaster of the residential school for the severely deaf near our home.

In the 1940s this headmaster, Mr Kettlewell, approached my father to ask his co-operation in an experiment he was wanting to make. All the children in his school had been born deaf. Since they had little useful residual hearing they had been unable to pick up speech from their parents as hearing children do. One of the chief tasks the teachers in the school faced was to teach these children to speak in a way which would enable them to communicate with hearing people. He believed that one way to hasten the learning process was to encourage them to mix with hearing children. He asked my father if he would be prepared for a group of deaf boys to join the Boys' Brigade Company with this aim in mind. Father agreed.

When the deaf boys began to be integrated into the group, their love for my father became obvious. On Saturdays, when they came to Roberts Road to spend their pocket money in the post office or the newsagent's at the bottom of the road, they would pop in to see us because they knew that they would always find a welcome in our home.

'How d'you understand what they're saying?' I would ask my father.

The boys could pronounce vowels easily enough but most of their words lacked consonants. So when they called my father by his name they would call him '*i-er oo-oo*' instead of Mr Duguid (pronounced Do-good). And that confused me. Most of the time their voices had a nasal quality which I found as distracting and unpleasant as the flat intonation of their speech.

'You get used to it if you're patient and listen carefully,' my father would reply.

'And how d'you talk to them?' I persisted.

Then my father would teach me some of the rules: 'Make sure that the light falls on your face so that they can lip-read. Speak slowly but naturally and carefully and don't mind if they stare at you because they are listening with their eyes instead of their ears.' I would watch him put this theory into practice.

Sometimes even he failed to understand what was being communicated. In this event the boys would 'talk' to each other through sign language before deciding what to 'say' to my father on paper.

My early initiation

Children love to imitate their parents and I was no exception. So when girls from the deaf school joined the Brownie Pack I attended, I did my best to communicate with them by imitating my father. To my delight – and theirs – I found that if I spoke clearly I could make myself

understood and if I listened carefully to the sounds they
made and to the context of the sentences, I could usually
decipher what they were saying. These girls became my
trusted friends and it was one of the highlights of my
young life when Mr Kettlewell invited me to go to the
school on the hill to play with them.

Some Brownies also came from Dr Barnardo's Home.
My mother explained to me that this meant that they had
no parents or homes of their own so they all had to live
together in one big house without a mother and a father. I
could think of nothing more terrible than being without
a mother or father or brothers. So when 'Brown Owl'
asked whether any of us could invite some of these
children to our homes for tea from time to time, I
volunteered.

We were always cramped for space in our house. It
boasted only four rooms: two bedrooms upstairs and two
rooms downstairs. Each of these rooms was only nine
foot square. There were few creature comforts: no bath-
room, no hot running water and the toilet was outside in
the back yard. We had little money. Though my father
was a master-baker he earned very little and my mother
supplemented his income by taking a job as a waitress in
a café in the centre of town. Even then their joint salary
left nothing for buying luxuries. But once a month, on
Sunday afternoons, girls from the Dr Barnardo's Home
would be invited for tea and the front room would be
filled with people, fun and laughter. The little we had to
offer was all we could share. The war was still on and
food was rationed, but somehow there was always
enough. We all loved it. And the experience showed me
that compassionate people live a compassionate lifestyle.
They refuse to grasp the little they have but share it gladly
with those who need it most. Compassionate people
continue to care even when such caring costs. In counting the cost and paying it, true joy is experienced.
Though I did not appreciate it at the time, I was learning a
profound lesson about compassion. Henri Nouwen puts
it well:

Compassion is not a bending toward the under-privileged from a privileged position; it is not a reaching out from on high to those who are less fortunate below; it is not a gesture of sympathy or pity for those who fail to make it in the upward pull. On the contrary, compassion means going directly to those people and places where suffering is most acute and building a home there.[2]

'Going directly to those people and places where suffering is most acute and building a home there.' My parents had done that. It was not that they had searched for suffering and found it. Rather, they found tragedy on their doorstep – the tragedy of bereavement, deafness, homelessness and the helplessness of old age – and they did what they could to touch it with the love of God. Because they were poor, my parents could minister effectively to the poor. Because they had suffered deprivation themselves, they could touch the deprived also. Because their compassion was genuine, it communicated and drew fellow sufferers to itself. And because I was a part of them, I found myself caring from an early age without ever giving it the glamorous name-tag 'ministry'.

The community's example

But I am conscious that my background gave me, not only a vision of how to live compassionately, but the ability to feel compassion. Such an ability seems rare even in some Christian circles today. But in Roberts Road, if people felt an emotion they expressed it. When I was little I saw grown-ups cry quite frequently, particularly during the war years.

I had never seen Mrs Tolman cry until the spring of 1941. Mrs Tolman was a dumpy, cheerful lady who wore high heels and smelt of perfume during the week and who squeezed herself into Salvation Army uniform on Sundays. She had no children of her own but seemed fond of other people's and I loved her because in winter she wore a fox fur round her neck which I was encouraged to stroke. She was a skilled furrier and worked in a shop in Holloway Street. Most days on her way home from work she would wave to me and call 'coo-ee' or my pet name 'Joycee' in a high-pitched, cheery voice.

One morning in May 1941 I was sitting on our doorstep sharing a small patch of warm sun with Snowy, our white fluffy cat, when suddenly I heard the tell-tale sound of Mrs Tolman's high-heeled shoes tapping the pavement. She was hurrying towards her home, her head bowed low. And she was crying. I called out to her expecting the normal greeting. But there was no cheerful wave on this occasion. Instead the sight of me seemed to upset her even more. She let out a loud sob and hurried on without speaking.

Later that day I learned from my father the reason for her distress. In the blitz of the night before a landmine had dropped on Holloway Street, the road adjacent to Roberts Road, and Mrs Tolman had arrived at work that morning to find, not the customary parade of high-class fashionable shops of which their owners were so proud, but a pile of rubble and smouldering ruins. She had lost everything she possessed.

My father did not hide his distress. When the war started, he had volunteered as an air raid warden whose responsibility it was to patrol the warren of streets that backed on to Roberts Road, Franklin Street and Temple Road. Because there had been enemy activity the night before he had been up all night making sure that no chink of light escaped through the blackout which covered people's windows, and searching for leaking gas and hidden bombs. And because he was a baker he had had an early start that morning. Now he held his lined and weary face in his hands while the tears flowed. Like Jesus, he was unashamed to weep openly with those who wept.

I did not know then that, in expressing this anguish, he was giving me a glimpse of the compassion Jesus used to feel when he was faced with similar pain. But now I see certain parallels. Henri Nouwen describes Jesus' reaction to human suffering powerfully:

> There is a beautiful expression in the Gospels that appears only twelve times and is used exclusively of Jesus or his Father. That expression is 'to be moved with compassion'. The Greek verb *splangchnizomai* reveals to us the deep and powerful meaning of this expression. The *splangchna* are the entrails of the body or as we might say today, the guts. They are the place where our most intimate and intense emotions are located . . . When Jesus was moved to compassion, the source of all life trembled, the ground of all love burst open, and the abyss of God's immense, inexhaustible, and unfathomable tenderness revealed itself. . .
>
> When Jesus saw the crowd harassed and dejected like sheep without a shepherd, he felt with them in the center of his being (Mt 9:36). When he saw the blind, the paralysed, and the deaf being brought to him from all directions, he trembled from within and experienced their pains in his own heart (Mt 14:14). When he noticed that the thousands who had followed him for days were tired and hungry, he said, I am moved with compassion (Mk 8:2). And so it was with the two blind men who called after him (Mt 9:27), the leper who fell to his knees in front of him (Mk 1:41), and the widow of Nain who was burying her only son (Lk 7:13). They moved him, they made him feel with all his intimate sensibilities the depth of their sorrow. He became lost with the lost, hungry with the hungry, and sick with the sick. In him, all suffering was sensed with a perfect sensitivity.[3]

Jesus was full of compassion for people. When people suffered, he suffered with them. Jesus reacted to pain in this way because God reacts to human suffering in this way. Jesus' solidarity with our suffering reveals his Father's identification with the depth of our need. This, as Henri Nouwen reminds us, is wonderful news: 'The truly good news is that God is not a distant God, a God to be feared and avoided, a God of revenge, but a God who is moved by our pains and participates in the fullness of the human struggle.'[4]

In their own way, and in so far as they were able, my parents were like that too. They incarnated the love of Christ to the chimney sweep and the window cleaner, the pilot and the insurance agent, the grocer and the butcher, the greengrocer, the newsagent and the coalman, the policeman, the nurse and the housewives who lived, cheek by jowl, alongside them in Roberts Road. They were not icon saints. They were ordinary working-class people struggling to make a living and, at the same time, trying to live a Christ-like life in the only home they could afford: a rented two up, two down, back-to-back terraced house in a run-down area of Exeter.

Even so they were effective for God in touching the lives of ordinary people. 'Wonderful people,' recalls one of the boys in the Boys' Brigade who is now in his sixties. If anyone had told them that they were reflecting the love of God to the people in our street or that they had a ministry of helping, they would have made light of such labels. Yet this was what they were doing. And in doing it they were making their own response to the great commission of Christ.

In this last and great commission Jesus commands his followers to love as he loved, to care as he cared, to hurt when others hurt. Such love, he said, is the hallmark of the Christian. And such love is one of the basic requirements of anyone who would seek to stretch out a helping hand to others in the middle of life's crises.

It was such compassion that prompted Jesus to heal hurting people. He healed people for one reason only – not to impress them, nor to prove his divinity, but because their pain created such an ache within his own heart that he suffered with them. Because hurting humanity called from him this depth of concern for the sufferer, he stretched out the helping hand which rescued, restored and, in many cases, eventually healed. He was the personification of compassion.

Jesus received this ability to tune in to human anguish and identify with people's pain from his Father, and in turn passed it on to his disciples. He passed it on to Paul who, we read, was filled with tender compassion for the converts in Philippi (Phil. 1:8).

It is a quality all would-be carers and listeners need. For where such Christ-like compassion is absent, stretching out to others sometimes has a hollow ring about it. At best such help can come across as dutiful, brash or insensitive. At worst it can even seem unkind or cruel.

But compassion not duty, kindness not brashness pushed my parents and the Roberts Road community into supporting others. Because these, my relatives and neighbours, were well schooled in the art of expressing such care, this fruit of God's Spirit seeded itself in the fertile soil of my life. I neither asked for it nor expected it. It came. And it came early. On that bright May morning when I encountered Mrs Tolman silenced by the shock of the atrocities she had witnessed at work, the instinct of my young heart was to run to her to comfort her, just as my instinct was to do all in my power to protect the old lady, Laing, from impending danger.

But the desire to comfort and protect are but small and immature beginnings – signs that the seeds of com-passion have been sown but not indications that the mature fruit has yet ripened. I was to discover that if these seeds were to germinate and grow, they would require rain as well as sunshine. I was also to discover that the necessary rain clouds were gathering fast.

2

Coping with Crises

The first hint of trouble came with the end of the war. That is not to say that our family did not share in the jubilation and celebration of V Day. We did. The Roberts Road street parties were held outside our front door. Each house in the road sported its own Union Jack. Bunting was draped zig-zag fashion across the road, someone's piano was heaved on to the pavement outside our house and the trestle tables borrowed from the church hall were laden with sandwiches, iced cakes, jellies, trifles and blancmanges. The memory of the reds and oranges, the yellows and greens of the jellies and the pinks and the sweet sickly smell of the blancmanges rises before my eyes still whenever I hear the words 'street parties'.

More treats were in store. The first came in the form of a rumour which was passed round among the children: 'Mr Staddon's making ice-cream again.' Mr Staddon owned the dairy in Holloway Street and we were told that if we took a teacup to his shop he would fill it with freshly made ice-cream. 'Can I go? Can I go?' we all clamoured and since there was no road to cross between Roberts Road and Holloway Street, we were allowed to troop in convoy to Staddon's Dairy. And our mouths would water as we watched Mr Staddon dip his steel scoop into a jug of hot water, scrape a big blob of cream-coloured ice-cream out of a round tub, and plop it into the cups which we held so eagerly up to his counter.

Fresh bananas also appeared for the first time. My

mother bought some one day from Mr Major, the green-grocer who used to call at our home. He came by motor bike and we would know when he had arrived because he was the proud possessor of a rubber horn which he used to honk when he arrived at a customer's front door. When he came to our house my mother would reach for the brown leather purse she kept in the sideboard drawer and I would rush out to examine the side-car which was always laden with potatoes and cabbages, carrots and onions, apples and oranges, pears and plums, according to the season.

The first time I saw bunches of yellow crescent-shaped fruit perched on top of the side-car, I voiced my curiosity: 'What's that?' 'Try one,' invited Mr Major and placed a big ripe banana in my hands. 'How d'you eat it?' I asked. Mr Major and my mother laughed as they showed me how to unzip the skin before biting into the creamy flesh inside.

I was seven years old when I was bombarded with all these childhood delights. I was also seven when I real-ised that, though the war was over, its shadow had not left us completely. The problem was that, though the international crisis seemed to have passed, young men were still being conscripted into the armed forces. And that meant that my eldest brother Ray would soon have to leave home.

Ray was fourteen years old when he left school. He joined the Post Office and became a Telegraph boy. When call-up time drew near Ray made up his mind that, rather than allow others to determine the future for him, he would decide for himself whether he should join the army, the navy or the air-force. At the age of seventeen, therefore, he joined the Royal Navy as a volunteer.

Ray was ten years older than me – more like a favourite uncle than a brother. It was Ray who helped me polish my Brownie badge on Tuesday evenings. It was Ray who spoilt me by giving me extra pocket money. And it was Ray who protected me from the merciless teasing of my other brother, John.

When Ray started to prepare for his departure by showing me the kitbag marked with his initials R.E.D. (for Raymond Ernest Duguid), the sense of adventure filling him spilt over on to me. And when he dressed up in his naval uniform he became my hero.

But while the anticipated adventure energised Ray and while pride of my big brother inflated me, gloom descended on my mother.

We were a close-knit family living in a close-knit community. When someone left that community, they left a hole which nothing and no one could fill. And when that 'someone' was your eldest son, a mother's grief left her desolate and empty.

Bereavement and depression

My mother would have been unfamiliar with clichés like 'the empty nest syndrome' or 'grief work'. But as the train spluttered out of St David's station carrying away her kitbag-carrying son and leaving her, a forlorn figure, waving a tearful farewell to the fast-disappearing form of this uniformed young lad, a deep and terrible sadness swept over her which left her suffering an emptiness and inner turmoil that hung over her for months.

Such overwhelming time-consuming sadness is normal. Many mothers (and fathers) experience similar crippling emotions when their offspring first leave home to try life their own way. Indeed part of the high cost of loving is to suffer the searing pain which seems to pierce our heart when one we love is torn away for any reason. But coupled with the terrifying sense of loss she experienced was a paralysing sense of anxiety. The terrors of war with the atrocities suffered by the British troops were fresh in everyone's memory. They flooded into my mother's mind uninvited and lodged there. Anxiety, that inner, nagging sense of apprehension, uneasiness and dread which we all experience from time to time, seemed to hold my mother in such a vice-like grip that she lost much of her sparkle and spontaneity. At times she would be weepy and listless. Life lost much of its interest for her.

One way of coping with the sense of severance such separation brings is to keep in contact with the loved one. At first maintaining physical contact with my brother was not easy. Ray was stationed in Plymouth, some fifty miles from Exeter and most weekends his exeat permitted him to travel only twenty miles. My mother refused to be daunted by such obstacles and weekends would find us boarding the steam train at St David's station, chugging to Newton Abbot, the half-way point between Exeter and Plymouth, and making the long, tiring journey back home again.

Picnicking in a park with Ray in this way, seeing for herself that someone else could feed her son and being reassured by him that he could survive life outside the cloisters of Roberts Road seemed to revive her spirits. At least while the visit lasted. But during the journey home the tears would flow again and the black cloud of depression would descend.

Was this separation from Ray pressing on the unhealed pain of two previous severances: from Maurice, the three-year-old blue baby who died and from the loss she suffered when an earlier baby had been stillborn? I was too young to ask such questions so I shall never know the answers. What I do now know is that it often happens that there is a distinct correlation between the way a person copes with the loss of a significant person in the present with the way that person has coped with similar such separations in the past. Clearly my mother had suffered deeply when her two tiny children had died. In a similar way she was suffering now and she needed help.

Help came in a whole variety of ways. It came casually from people like Mrs Broom at number 33, Mrs Burgess at number 46 and Mrs Bellamy at number 28 Roberts Road. When they walked past our house on the way to Webber's corner shop they would see my mother vigorously polishing the brass doorstep or the matching door knobs and they would stop and enquire: 'How's

that big boy of yours?' And my mother would pass on
the latest snippets of news knowing that someone was
genuinely interested.

None of these neighbours would have dreamed that
this question was a ministry to my mother. The question
was prompted by neighbourliness; the concern the
Roberts Road community still had for one of its own. Yet
this question, lovingly, frequently and sensitively asked,
was more therapeutic for my mother than a whole series
of counselling sessions would have been. It kept the
memory of her son alive during that strange stage of
separation when, to one's horror, one can no longer
recall what the loved one looks like. It gave her permission to admit that she was hurting because she was
missing Ray; that sometimes just to see some of his
possessions lying around in his bedroom caused a pang
of pain to shoot right through her. And, of course, it
brought her into contact with people who cared so that
gradually she emerged from the darkness, came to terms
with her son's absence and re-negotiated her life on a
new set of terms: a life which no longer revolved around
Ray.

Other people came alongside my mother in a costly,
caring way as she stood at this crossroads of her life. One
outstanding carer was my father's sister, Aunt Rene.
Aunt Rene seemed to have that God-given knack of
arriving just when my mother was reaching her lowest
ebb. And Aunt Rene would listen to news of Ray with
real interest, look at photographs of him, and somehow
communicate to my mother that she understood how
hard it must be to have one's child move out of one's
immediate orbit. That is not to say Aunt Rene encouraged my mother to wallow in self-pity. On the contrary,
she helped her to avoid that pitfall simply by accepting
my mother as she was, trying to see life through my
mother's eyes and giving her the support she needed as
she learned to cope with this hole in our home. Time after
time Aunt Rene succeeded in reducing the level of my
mother's anxiety and helping her to regain hope and a

new perspective on life simply through the genuineness of her love.

This aunt of mine had never trained in counselling. But God had gifted her with one of those 'inherently helpful'[1] personalities which express with loving ease both warmth and sensitivity, understanding and concern, confidence and appropriate optimism. Because she loved my mother as Jesus loves – aching inwardly when she saw how my mother ached – a visit from Aunt Rene was always welcome.

When I took my place in this family circle and listened to this aunt and my mother talk in the intimate way two women often do, I had no idea that I was being taught some of the ground rules of good listening. But now I realised that 24 Roberts Road was one school in which I served my apprenticeship as a listener and carer; that my father's sister was my teacher. For several research studies have shown that effective listening involves not simply theory or techniques, but a personality which is characterised by empathy, warmth and genuineness.

Dr Gary Collins, a professor of psychology and author of several books on counselling, defines 'empathy' by tracing the word back to its German root *einfühlung*, which means 'feeling into', or 'feeling with'. Empathy asks: 'Why is this person so upset?' 'How does she view what is happening?' If I were in her shoes, how might I feel?' In other words, empathy seeks to view life through the troubled person's eyes, to experience another person's world as though it were our own while keeping the words *as though* in the forefront of our mind. It involves walking in the other person's moccasins until you feel where they rub. Empathy attempts to show the person in pain that their feelings are both understood and accepted.

Warmth, according to Gary Collins, is synonymous with caring. It is a non-smothering, non-possessive concern for someone which is communicated by a friendly facial expression, a gentle tone of voice, gestures and appropriate touch, posture and eye contact which communicate the clear message: 'I care about you and your well-being.'

And 'genuineness', as described by Dr Collins, is the art of being real. The genuine person is an authentic person. He has no need to pretend or to project a false superiority. Genuineness is authenticity which refuses to contemplate the playing of a superior role. It is openness without phoniness. It is sincerity, consistency and it is full of respect for others.[2]

Aunt Rene embodied each of these qualities in her own sweet and simple way and, though I did not recognise it at the time, as I watched and heard her stay alongside my troubled mother the seeds of compassion which had already been sown in me were being watered by the current crisis.

Physical pain

It has been said that helping people in pain is a skill which, like any other skills, improves with practice. Though this particular problem worked its way out of our family, another storm was brewing which was to hit our household with even greater force and give me the practice I still needed. This crisis erupted four years later – soon after I had thrilled everyone in Roberts Road by passing the Eleven Plus examination.

When Roberts Road children sat the Eleven Plus, everyone in the street became emotionally involved. It was as though the future of the entire community was at stake. It was rare for a Roberts Road child to go to grammar school but when my turn came round to sit the dreaded exam, I was tipped to make the grade. So when it was announced that I had gained a place at Bishop Blackall Grammar School the whole street seemed to celebrate what they considered to be an outstanding achievement. My godfather entered into the joy too by buying me a brand new green Raleigh bicycle, partly as a reward and partly as a means of travelling to this new school which was on the other side of the town.

But this early euphoria faded when my mother became ill. The illness manifested itself in three ways: with frequent severe attacks of asthma which left her gasping for breath, with a cough which racked her body with pain and left her weak and with a mysterious symptom we learned to call 'a turn'. At first it was feared that these turns were epileptic fits. But they were not. Neither were they strokes, though sometimes she gave the appearance of a person suffering a stroke.

When she was sickening for 'a turn', my mother would be overcome with dizziness, her speech would become slurred and eventually she would lose consciousness – sometimes for several minutes, often for several hours and occasionally for more than a day. Her condition distressed everyone who knew her yet it drew from her all the pluck which made her the determined person so many people admired.

But it meant that often my father and I would have to do everything for her. If she had had a turn during the evening we would have to carry her to bed, undress her, slip her nightdress over her and wash her. Carrying her to bed was no easy task because our staircase was narrow – the width of only one person – and there was a sharp bend towards the top which meant that my father would have to walk ahead of me, clutching the top half of my mother's body and I would follow, holding on to her legs. While we heaved her in this way we were always frightened lest we should hurt her, and well aware that in her unconscious state she would not have been able to tell us that we were inflicting hurt. My mother was stubborn too, and even when she felt a turn coming on she refused to give in to it. Consequently, sometimes she would fall and cut, burn or bruise herself and we would administer first aid.

Shortly after I entered the grammar school my mother was bedridden for several weeks. Money, as always, was in short supply so a home-help was out of the question. Before I left for school in the morning I would polish the lino in the living room and the two bedrooms, dust the skirting boards, brush the stair carpet and try to bring a shine to the dressing tables, the sideboard and the dining room table. Though she was ill, my mother was still house-proud and would give me careful instructions and surveillance from her bed.

My father too took up certain household chores. He would polish the brass doorstep every day until we could see our reflection in it as clearly as in the mirror. He would clean the oven after cooking the lunch on Sundays. And he would tackle the washing on Mondays. We had no washing machine. Sheets and pillow-cases were sent to the laundry. Smaller items including towels and tea-towels were boiled up in a galvanised bath on the gas cooker. After the clothes had been boiled and pounded with a wooden stick the bath was lifted from the cooker and carried to the sink. There the clothes were drained and rinsed by hand in cold water before being run individually through the mangle in the back yard.

These chores, which my mother usually did with skill and speed before going off to work, my father and I now master-minded with difficulty. But our efforts were rewarded when, seeing that we could cope with the practicalities, she relaxed and her health began to improve. And this taught me a salutary lesson. Sometimes compassion must be expressed practically rather than verbally. There are times when there are no words. And there are times when actions speak louder than words.

What surprised me was that, though it hurt to see my mother crippled by so much physical pain, and though it was tiring to nurse her *and* clean the house, spend the day at school, come home to homework *and* more nursing of my mother, yet the overwhelming emotion was of joy which used to rise inside me like a mysterious well-spring as I polished or pedalled up the hill to school.

Henri Nouwen offers an explanation for this inner fountain of well-being:

Wherever we see real service we also see joy, because in the midst of service a divine presence becomes

visible and a gift is offered. Therefore those who serve
as followers of Jesus discover that they are receiving
more than they are giving. Just as a mother does not
need to be rewarded for the attention she pays to her
child, because her child is her joy, so those who serve
their neighbour will find their reward in the people
whom they serve.[3]

At the early age of eleven I was given the privilege of
proving the truth of this observation. I have gone on
proving it. There have been times when my body should
have been weary with over-exertion and my emotions
wrung out with the strain of performing practical tasks
for people in pain, but instead it is as though this energis-
ing sense of well-being which seems to radiate from God
himself, has flooded every part of me: body, mind and
spirit. Looking back I think I was relieved to be able to
take the pressure off my parents by giving practical help.
I was too young to give them the emotional support they
both needed. In due course, others did that. Meanwhile I
was learning that sometimes before a person can be
brought into emotional, spiritual or physical healing,
someone needs to see life through the sick person's eyes
and to take immediate and practical action.

    Jesus did this so often. That may be one reason why he
fed the five thousand. That may be the reason why,
having healed Jairus's daughter, he reminds her parents
that having abstained from food for so long she will be
hungry. And it might explain why, on the night before he
died, in the absence of the customary slave Jesus himself
assumed this role, reached for a bowl and a towel and
washed his disciples' dirty sweaty feet. This humble
practical gesture demonstrated in an unforgettable way
that 'our God is a servant God'.[4] His compassion reveals
itself in servanthood – self-emptying. When he calls us to
incarnate his compassion and care, he invites us to
imitate his servanthood. To be carers.

    Every follower of Christ is called to care in this costly
way. The call came early to me. I responded by caring

practically and trying to be kind and gentle, but I had not yet learned the art of enabling my mother to unburden her frustrations, fear and helplessness.

Our family doctor did what he could. He would spend hours with my mother giving her professional help and endless support. And the vicar of our church helped too. He would cycle from his vicarage to our home, sit with my mother, talk to her and pray with her. But I noticed that my mother never really relaxed with either of these men. A secret smoker, she would stub out her cigarette if she suspected a knock on the door heralded a visit from either of them. And frequently I sensed that she was telling them what she felt they wanted to hear rather than the way she really felt. So although these visits were appreciated by all of us, their usefulness was limited in value.

But, as often happens, a variety of helpers each contributed their unique expression of concern: Aunt Rene again, Mrs Furseman who was a waitress in the same café as my mother, Mrs Tolman who had suffered so intolerably in the war years, Mrs Ford, a retired neighbour who had plenty of that precious commodity, time and plenty of that fruit of the Spirit, patience, who visited regularly, listened and sat with my mother for whole long afternoons while my father and I were out.

These ordinary unqualified women gave my mother what she needed: understanding and the assurance that they would not abandon her but rather would stand by her in her need. This solidarity with her suffering was self-giving which could never be rewarded but which was of inestimable value.

Some recent research suggests that times have not changed. It has shown the value of relatives, neighbours and friends as well as professional counsellors. The role of the professional is obvious. It is vital. But friends and relatives play a key part also. They live close by, are readily available, and often seem easier to talk to than someone who wears the label, 'doctor', 'clergyman', 'counsellor', or 'psychotherapist'.

Encouragingly, research has also revealed that in certain circumstances such friends and neighbours can be as competent as professional counsellors. Several reasons have been offered by way of explanation. One is that a relative or friend knows the person better and can therefore understand the problem better. Another is that the non-professional can often offer more time. And of course friends and neighbours know the person's family, their home environment and their work situation, which is a great advantage in gleaning an accurate assessment of the problem. They use the same dialect, accent or colloquialisms as the person in need so they can chat informally, be natural and lace their help with friendly humour. Perhaps the chief advantage is that helping *this* person emerge from his crisis is the friend's top priority. He is not faced with the daunting realisation that a queue of people are clamouring for his care, so the person in pain never feels like a mere name among a list of clients or patients but knows he is the subject of a sensitive person's love, care and commitment. Thousands of people are saved from emotional drowning by non-professionals. My mother was one of them.

Even so her physical problems persisted and she needed specialised help: from the doctor, the neurologist and, after she had been hospitalised, the occupational therapist. These skilled people turned every possible stone to try to unearth the reason for her 'turns'. No satisfactory diagnosis was found. At times there would be considerable and encouraging signs of improvement. But always, eventually, she would lapse back into another phase of ill health which frequently triggered off discouragement and sometimes depression.

When I left home to go to university my father felt the full brunt of the responsibility. It was a strain he bore gladly and sacrificially – one expression of his love for his wife. Nevertheless it left him tired, worried and drained. So during my vacations I tried to give whatever help I could to relieve him.

Burnout

During my first summer vacation from Southampton University I nursed my mother, tried to keep the house-cleaning up to her high standard, took on a full-time job at British Home Stores to supplement my dwindling grant *and*, most evenings, would try to tackle the academic work I had brought home with me. The result was that by the end of the vacation I was suffering from burnout.

In defining burnout, John Sanford says it is 'a word we use when a person has become exhausted with his or her profession or major life activity'. It is 'a chronic tiredness of the sort that is not repaired by sleep or ordinary rest and only temporarily alleviated by vacations.'[5]

It had never occurred to me that burnout could be caused by pouring oneself out for another while trying to keep up with a hectic schedule. But this was what had happened to me. The collapse came before the new university term. It happened in the home of a doctor.

The reason why I was in this doctor's home was that I had become Secretary of the Christian Union at Southampton University and it was a tradition that the committee spent a weekend together at the end of the summer vacation before going on to the annual Christian Union pre-term conference. Dr and Mrs Murray Webb-Peploe, who were advisers to the Christian Union, hosted this residential committee meeting in their spacious home, Woodley, London Road, Lymington, Hampshire.

This was my first visit to their home. Before term started I received the following travelling instructions from someone who had been there before: 'You'll be travelling into Lymington on the Southampton Road. Before you reach the town, get off the bus, walk down the road for fifty yards and on your right you'll find a pair of green gates with the name-plate Woodley on them. Walk through these. And you'll find yourself in Paradise: a little bit of heaven on earth.'

I don't know if we shall be overwhelmed by heaven

when we arrive there, but my first impressions of this 'little piece of heaven on earth' certainly overwhelmed me. There were no front gardens in Roberts Road. Passers-by would have been able to look straight into the front-room window if there had been no lace curtains to provide a modicum of privacy. But having found the gates of Woodley my feet scrunched up a gravel path, which led first to the cluttered garage and then snaked around the front of the huge Edwardian house separating it from its tree-secluded lawn. While the door bell clanged and I waited for someone to open the big green door, I stared incredulously at the size of the lawn, drank in the beauty of the copper beech trees which gave the garden its shade and gazed at the fruit-laden trees in the orchard. If the garden was like this, I wondered, what was I going to find inside the house.

Once inside everything seemed equally unfamiliar: the giant grandfather clock in the spacious hall which ticked its own story for visitors, the huge oak-framed family portraits in the dining room, the bulging bookcases on the landings, the enormous pine dresser complete with blue and brown Denby pottery in the kitchen and the black lacquered Chinese cabinets which seemed to fill and dominate the drawing room. While Mrs Webb-Peploe poured tea from a silver teapot I studied the Chinese scenes painted in gold on these fascinating pieces of furniture. And I retreated into my shy shell for safety.

But though the house and garden were overwhelming, our host and hostess were quite the opposite. Dr Webb-Peploe was jovial, welcoming and relaxed. He seemed to relish the thought of hosting a houseful of students for a whole weekend. He entertained us with tales and jokes throughout tea and dinner. Mrs Webb-Peploe was quieter but nonetheless welcoming. This petite lady, with her gentle aristocratic features, was dressed in a grey pleated skirt and simple white blouse. Her soft silver hair was persuaded into a pleat at the back of her head, but wavy wisps would sometimes escape from the coil and fall attractively on to her face. She beamed her shy welcome on everyone as they arrived. In her smile there was tenderness and love, and in the twinkle of her eyes I could see that she too looked forward to this weekend with child-like excitement and great anticipation, not knowing *what* God was going to do, yet sensing that something significant was about to happen. I was enchanted by her lilting continental accent. I was enchanted by her serenity. And in particular I was enchanted by the way she talked about God. It was as though her friendship with him was intimate.

On Friday evening the Webb-Peploes left us to our first committee meeting, and after the three-month vacation we enjoyed the reunion. We were full of zeal, enthusiasm and vision for the work God wanted to do through us in the university that year. At least the others were. But their energy and verve was highlighting just how exhausted I felt.

By mid-Saturday morning I began to run a temperature. Instead of tramping in the New Forest with the others on Saturday afternoon I retreated to bed. Dr Webb-Peploe summed up the situation and prescribed prolonged rest. So I missed the remainder of the committee meetings and the pre-term conference and spent the time instead with the Webb-Peploes.

In my safe home environment of Roberts Road I was a confident, outgoing person. But outside of this working-class environment I frequently felt completely out of my depth and insecure. I had learned few social graces and masked my insecurity and uncertainty with a layer of shyness which it was difficult for anyone to penetrate. The Webb-Peploes never tried to untie this mask. Instead they accepted the shy, insecure, silent me just as I was. Without demanding to know why a young and otherwise healthy student should collapse at the end of a three-month so-called vacation, they simply showed me that they cared and cared deeply.

This was Christian caring with a curious twist; a whole new pattern of servanthood for me. I was a complete stranger and yet they were taking me in. There would never be any way in which I could repay them. Yet they showered me with kindness, tenderness and under-standing love. Sensitive and skilled in helping others as they were, they must have realised that there would have been little mileage in encouraging me to talk about the pressures that had caused me to collapse. Inarticulate as I was, I would not have been able to find words to express my feelings to anyone, least of all to strangers in such an overwhelmingly new environment. Nevertheless it was in their home that the coil of tension in me slowly unwound and I relaxed sufficiently to receive the spiritual healing God gave me through them.

Not that healing was talked about. To my knowledge the word was not even mentioned. They did not even offer to pray with me and I would have been terrified if they had. What they gave me was richer and deeper, more sacrificial to them and meaningful to me than mere words. They simply provided a healing environment where I could 'just be', soaked me in prayer without threatening my equilibrium by telling me that this was what they were doing, and because of the person she was rather than anything she ever said, Mrs Webb-Peploe in particular took me by the hand, as it were, and led me to the source of healing and refreshment, Jesus himself. The result was that I received for myself the riches of God from God.

I am not saying that she talked to me about God nor that through her I turned to Christ for the first time. I had known about God as a tiny child and committed my life to him when I was in the sixth form at school. No. What I am saying is that, though I knew many people who talked about God, in Mrs Webb-Peploe I was meeting a different quality of Christian. She was someone who showed me that she knew him. She even radiated his love wherever she was and no matter what she was doing.

That transparent love was there when, still wearing her dressing gown, she would bring me my breakfast tray, complete with starched linen tray cloth and a tiny vase of flowers alongside the cereal, the prunes, the toast, the butter and the honey. That love shone through as she stood by my bed, her long silver hair still flowing round her waist and her eyes twinkling even at that time of day. That love shone through the warmth and genuineness of her smile. And that love beamed at me too as she persuaded me to stay in bed for just as long as I liked.

When eventually I sauntered downstairs, I would frequently find her in the dining room, sitting at the table either deep in prayer or reading her Bible or a devotional commentary. And I would detect a fragrance filling the room. It was not unlike the scent of the lilies of the valley which fill my study today as I write. Yet it was not the fragrance of flowers but rather the heady perfume of the sense of the presence of the living God. It sometimes seemed as though, if I had stretched out my hand, I could have touched God for myself. From the serenity which shone from her face and the stillness pervading her whole body it was clear that Mrs Webb-Peploe had enjoyed a fresh encounter with her Saviour. Indeed whenever she spoke of 'de Lord' (she had difficulty pronouncing 'th') it was as though he was closer to her than the husband she adored and whose pet name for her was 'Treasure'.

One morning when I found her deep in prayer she showed me the book she was reading. It was a devotional commentary on the twenty-third psalm by F. B. Meyer. She invited me to dip into it. That day I sat in the sun in the stillness of the garden and read:

WE ALL NEED REST. There must be pauses and parentheses in all our lives. The hand cannot ever be plying its toils. The brain cannot always be elaborating trains of thought. The faculties and senses cannot always be on the strain. To work without rest is like over-winding a watch; the main spring snaps, and the machinery stands still. There must be a pause frequently interposed in life's busy rush wherein we may recuperate exhausted nerves and lowered vitality . . . Be at rest!
. . . In all moments of peril and dread, softly murmur

His name, Jesus! Jesus! and He will at once comfort
thee by His presence and by His voice, which all the
sheep know; and this shall be His assurance: 'My
sheep shall never perish, neither shall any man pluck
them out of My hand.'[6]

I read on eagerly. The author, with his words, was doing
what the Webb-Peploes were doing with their lives –
pointing me to the Wonderful Counsellor who could
cope with my weariness, my fears for my mother, my
anxieties for my father, my guilt at leaving behind such a
sorry state of affairs for the fun-life of university, and my
yearning for friendship. And the Wonderful Counsellor,
the Shepherd, was leading me to the well-springs of life
which alone can satisfy and refresh at the deepest level,
those resources miraculously and mysteriously supplied
by his life-giving Spirit. I did not know how to ask for
these riches. I simply opened myself in the poverty of my
need to the Psalmist's shepherd, sustainer and guide and
in ways I shall never fully understand, he met me.

The only way I can describe the sustenance I enjoyed is
to liken it to the way a bee crawls into the heart of a rose
where it stays and sucks up nectar until it is satisfied.
Because peace pervaded the house and garden, the
orchard and the mini-farm which was Dr Webb-Peploe's
pride and joy, I was able to let go of the pressures,
breathe in that peace and discover for myself that still inner centre where this deep spiritual nurturing takes place.

This was God's gift to me through the Webb-Peploes.
Their ministry was powerful because it was gentle, un-
threatening, appropriate and because it was born out of
the womb of listening prayer. They had no need to prise
me apart to discover what was troubling me. As they
tuned into God, they tuned into my anguish and committed themselves to be the channels through which he
could love me and heal me. And he did. Some afternoons
Mrs Webb-Peploe and I would sit in the garden shelling
peas or just enjoying the spaciousness of God's creation
in this oasis of a home. As we sat, she would tell me
stories of the way she had seen God breaking into the

lives of needy people so that the tormented found un-expected peace and joy again.

I did not know then what I have since discovered: that Mrs Webb-Peploe was a Dutch baroness; that she had suffered greatly while she and her husband were serving God in India; that during the war years, while she was in India, she had been troubled as she thought of her parents living through the horrors of war-stricken Holland. What I did know was that all the anecdotes she told me fanned the flicker of my faith into a flame and that, in listening to her, it was as though the hurts inside me were being touched and soothed and healed by God.

Was it because she was one of God's wounded healers that she was so sensitive and wise? Or was it because she spent time tuning into the Father-heart of God each morning that she became his instrument of healing to me? I suspect it was a combination of both. Whatever it was, in this home where the silence of eternity was so elo-quently interpreted by love, energy flowed back into me.

Were these two servants of God aware, as they stood at the bus stop and waved me off on the first day of the university term, that that short stay in their home had not only healed me of burnout but had made a profound and lasting impression on me? I doubt it. I was too shy to do more than send a polite thank you note. But when we married, my husband and I were to take this couple as our model. Like them, we wanted to be stretched by God, always available to people, yet without being bowed down by the tyranny of pressure. We wanted to provide a home for people where the healing touch of Jesus could be felt. We wanted to reach out to a suffering world with the Father's unpolluted love from the security of a per-sonal relationship with Jesus. We coveted their ability to say the right thing to the right person at the right time; to be able to place the right book in the right person's hand at the right time. And though when I left them that day I would have been incapable of summarising just what it was that I had learned, I knew I wanted to be like them – always.

3

A Rabbit-hole Christian

I would like to be able to record that, having been so beautifully helped by Dr and Mrs Webb-Peploe, and having learned from the Roberts Road community the value of listening to people in pain and the need to give practical help to those in need, my final year at Southampton University stands out in my mind as the year when my growth in compassion could be measured visibly. Alas! That is not my memory of it. On the contrary, as I recall it, I was struggling inwardly, asking myself a question which seemed to have no computer-manual type answer. *What is my priority in life: to evangelise or to care for people's practical and emotional needs?*

One reason for this struggle was that from the very early days of my time at Southampton I had become a rabbit-hole Christian, to borrow John Stott's colourful phrase.

The evangelist J. John describes the rabbit-hole student as one whose closest friends share his convictions, who looks around the lecture theatre to find another Christian with whom to sit and who, even in the refectory, will again look out for a cluster of Christians with whom to enjoy lunch; one who sighs contentedly from time to time: 'Isn't it wonderful that God has brought so many of us to the same university?'[1]

The Christians in the hall of residence where I lived when I first arrived at university were like that.

On my first evening in Highfield Hall, where I was to live for the next three years, before I had finished unpacking my belongings, and while feelings of apprehension and excitement familiar to most new students vied for attention inside me, these sincere people drew me into their circle. I was away from home for the first time. I was immature and insecure. I was sharing a room with a girl who could understand neither my need for God nor my desire to make a relationship with him. I needed friendship. When these Christians offered it I received it gratefully.

Before I left home the Captain of the Girl Guide Company I attended in Roberts Road warned me against becoming 'narrow'. The warning surprised me. I had no intention of letting go of any of my four first loves: singing, cycling, studying and sport. I joined the university choir, explored Hampshire by bike, worked hard, particularly at my theological studies which fascinated me, and played for the university netball team twice a week, eventually winning my college blue. Life was rich and full and good. At the same time I joined in the weekly round of meetings organised by the Christian Union: the fellowship meeting on Saturday night when a visiting speaker would give us biblical guidelines about Christian living; the Thursday lunch-time Bible studies when one of the nearby vicars or pastors would expound a Bible passage for us; the Tuesday night meeting for Christians in Highfield Hall when we would pray and study the Bible together; the early morning prayer meetings when we would give ourselves to intercession and the after-church coffee parties which a student arranged in his room.

John Powell once made the claim that who we are and what we become is largely affected by those who love us. Perhaps it was inevitable therefore that, little by little, I should become more and more like these Christians with whom I spent most of my time. Whether it was inevitable or not, a rabbit-hole Christian was what I became.

Conviction

The main reason for this was not weakness on my part so much as conviction. These Christians most nearly resembled the ones who had supported me during the crucial months when God was reshaping my spiritual life. The key person at that time was my boy friend Gerald. He and the others had been left behind in Exeter.

Gerald and I had been friends for years. We had grown up together in the same church. He enjoyed cycling too. And we belonged to the same missionary prayer group. Unlike most students, Gerald stayed at home when he became an undergraduate and read for his degree at Exeter University. It was then that we graduated from being 'just good friends' and enjoyed instead the magic of in-loveness.

When Gerald became president of the Christian Union at Exeter University, he was invited to take a team of Christians from the university to a little town called Plympton, eight miles from Plymouth. The students were to provide back-up for the preaching and ministry of Frank Farley, an evangelist working under the auspices of Youth for Christ.

'Why don't you come too?' Gerald suggested one day.

When he explained that during the day the team would receive training from Frank, go door-to-door visiting and speak at various meetings, such as young wives' groups, I could think of no good reason why I should go. Just the thought of speaking to a group of young married women gave me sleepless nights. Nevertheless I went. On the first night a black and white film about the life of Jesus was shown. I do not remember its title. What I do remember is that the film broke down twice and the sound-track was scarcely audible in places. Even so its message winkled its way into my heart: that during the last tempestuous week of his life on earth, the very people who hailed Jesus with happy hosannas on Palm Sunday were the self-same people who clamoured for his crucifixion with their blood-curdling cries of 'Crucify! Crucify!' on Good Friday. When it came to the crunch these people chose, not Jesus, but Barabbas.

When the film broke down for the second time, Frank Farley sensitively underlined this thought: 'Tonight you have a similar choice,' he said. 'You can't sit on the fence for ever. Unless you choose Jesus as the Lord of your life, by implication you are rejecting him.' He went on to explain that Jesus longs that we should surrender our entire lives to him and urged anyone who had never done so to make a decision for Christ.

The sights and sounds of the film and now the wooing words of the preacher were finding a niche in my heart. The facts I was hearing and seeing were not new. I had been hearing them for years. What was new was the challenge to make a personal response to God's love. I had never heard anyone give that challenge before. But it made sense. If Jesus loved me enough to die for me, the least I could do was to express my thanks in an act of glad surrender. What was also new was the surge of emotion that welled up inside me, expressing more eloquently than any words the deepest desire of my heart and mind – for both were fully engaged in that moment – to place my life once and for all in the hands of the living God. When Frank Farley later invited those to come forward to the front of the church who would like to make such a commitment to Christ, I pushed my way past Gerald who was sitting at the end of the pew and stumbled up the aisle.

At first Gerald tried to stop me. He thought I had not understood. 'He's talking to the *non*-Christians,' he said in a loud whisper. But I had not misheard. I knew what I wanted to do and was determined to go through with this public abandonment of all I had and all I was to the Christ who had revealed himself to me afresh that night.

Was it the tears that streamed down my face which persuaded Gerald that I needed to go forward? I do not know. What I do know is that that moment was a turning-point in my life: a conversion experience. I meant every word of the hymn we sang:

> Just as I am, without one plea
> But that Thy Blood was shed for me,
> And that Thou bidd'st me come to Thee
> O Lamb of God, I come.

Just as I am, though tossed about
With many a conflict, many a doubt,
Fightings and fears within, without,
O Lamb of God, I come.

Just as I am, poor, wretched, blind;
Sight, riches, healing of the mind,
Yea, all I need, in Thee to find,
O Lamb of God, I come.

Just as I am, Thou wilt receive,
Wilt welcome, pardon, cleanse, relieve;
Because Thy promise I believe,
O Lamb of God, I come.

Just as I am (Thy love unknown
Has broken every barrier down),
Now to be Thine, yea, Thine alone,
O Lamb of God, I come.

Just as I am, of that free love
The breadth, length, depth and height to prove,
Here for a season, then above,–
O Lamb of God, I come.

(Charlotte Elliott)

After the service I struggled to express to Gerald a
fraction of the relief and strange joy with which I seemed
to be inebriated. At the team meeting next morning,
again I attempted to put into words the wonder of the
afterglow of the night before. I had no name for the
experience. I could not claim that I had heard about Jesus
for the first time and that, eureka! I had fallen in love with
him. On the contrary, when I accepted the invitation to
become part of the team I did so because I already
considered myself a believer. It was more like an underlining in ink of what had already been written on my
heart in pencil: the love for Christ which had been
instilled in me as a child. But it was liberating – and
life-changing none the less.

The team were ecstatic. As far as they were concerned I

was a very baby Christian and they treated me like one, teaching me all they knew, and in particular drilling me in the art of witnessing. They continued to nurture me in this way when we returned to Exeter. And as far as I was concerned I had nailed my colours to the mast and determined to discover all I could about the Bible.

The aim of the mission where I had had this un-expected encounter with God was to reach the people of Plympton for Christ – particularly those who never darkened the doors of a church. The team recognised that 'in-drag' – expecting such people to pour into a church for an evening meeting – was not the most profitable means of evangelism. They therefore organised open-air meet-ings, house-to-house visits and small meetings in people's homes so that those who would not come to a meeting in church might still be touched by God. We were also encouraged to 'gossip the gospel' – to talk about Jesus to anyone we met no matter where we met them.

Full of new-found joy in the acceptance I was receiving from Frank, the members of the team and from God, and full of evangelistic zeal I developed the art of this method of 'witnessing'. It outlasted the mission to Plympton. Wherever I went I wanted to witness. Whether the people in my orbit were interested or not, I would tell them my testimony.

My travelling companion in the compartment of the train that carried me from Plymouth to Exeter when the mission was finished heard it. My parents heard it. My scripture teacher at school heard it. My parents and my scripture teacher were thrilled. But I suspect that the stranger who was unfortunate enough to be my travel-ling companion that day was relieved when the train screeched to a halt at Exeter St David's, disgorged me and left her to continue her journey in peace. My enthusiasm and evangelistic fervour were not, I fear, laced with sensitivity and I had not yet learned the art of earn-ing one's right to speak for Christ by first making a relationship with someone.

The reason why I was so zealous was that, in Plympton, I had seen for myself that God could change people's lives. He was changing mine. He had changed Gill, another teenager who had capitulated to the love of Christ during the mission and who corresponded with me regularly. My longing was to be caught up with the commission of Christ to go into the whole world to win people for him. I wanted to go on seeing God change people's lives.

When I left Exeter to start my university career I left behind the Christians who had nurtured my newly-awakened faith. And after the first term my romantic relationship with Gerald came to an end, so I lacked the support of his twice-weekly letters and occasional visits. But members of the Christian Union in Highfield Hall filled the gap. Together we attempted to tease from the scriptures what it means to live biblically on campus and we shared the same vision. We wanted to witness for Christ in the hall and beyond. This conviction united us. 'Christ is the answer' was our slogan for people in need. Sadly we had not yet learned that until one stops to listen to a person's questions and anguish, that person is unlikely to discover *how* Christ could meet their inner-most needs and thus become the answer to them.

Occasionally people with problems would come to talk to me. There was Pat, for example, who was suffering from claustrophobia and wanted to move out of the small single room the warden had allocated to her. There was the Indian girl who was homesick and worried about the safety of her politician father. And there was the girl who wanted to talk about the problems she was having with her boyfriend. My prayer for each of these students was the same: that they would find Christ. I made the naïve assumption that if they, too, came into a conversion experience their problems would be ironed out overnight. Pat's terrible fear of being crushed or hemmed in would leave her, the Indian girl would settle down, and boyfriend troubles would melt away. So these and countless other opportunities to incarnate the love of

God to hurting people were wasted. Instead of bearing
my colleagues' burdens (Gal. 6:2) with the care and
commitment the Good Shepherd showered on the man
who fell among thieves, and in obedience to God, I
looked for an opportunity to give my stock answer, 'Turn
to Christ', and implied that Christians have no problems.
I lent them books and prayed for them but I seemed to
have forgotten the lessons I had learned at my mother's
side in Roberts Road and the resolve I had made in the
bus on the way back to Southampton from the Webb-
Peploes' – to love others in the costly compassionate way
they had loved me – to express compassion to others
simply because compassion is what my heavenly Father is.

I failed to recognise it at the time and would have been
appalled if I had even begun to detect that the God-
implanted sapling of compassion was being choked. I
was becoming more zealous than caring, more enthusias-
tic than wise. Whether I went to lectures, to choir or to
netball matches, I looked for an opportunity to speak to
someone about Christ. Indeed when I failed to manipulate the conversation to create an opportunity for such
overt witnessing, pangs of guilt would wound me. It had
been drummed into me that this was my duty – the only
valid form of witnessing. I swallowed the piece of in-
doctrination without question. It had not occurred to me
that though all of Christ's followers are commanded to
witness for him the gift of evangelism which I was aping
has been entrusted to only a few. Neither had I learned
that serving others by meeting their needs in love and
with sensitivity is as much a gift from God as the gift of
evangelism (Rom. 12:6–8); that indeed some people are
attracted to Christ, not by the paucity of people's words,
but by the loveliness of a life lived for him like that of Mrs
Webb-Peploe whose concern had touched my own hurts
so powerfully. Because other members of the Christian
Union wore similar blinkers to mine, and because we all
shared this dutiful and limited view of evangelism, we
were bound together in loyalty and a precarious kind of
love.

Persuasion

But there was another reason why I became a rabbit-hole Christian. My theological persuasions pushed me deeper and deeper into the rabbit warren.

I was reading for a theology degree. All my lecturers were liberal theologians. None accepted my evangelical standpoint. The beliefs I cherished were constantly being questioned and challenged and I needed the support of like-minded Christians.

At the same time, as Secretary of the Christian Union, I had occasion from time to time to correspond with the Secretary of the Student Christian Movement – SCM for short.

The gulf between the Christian Union and the SCM had widened over the years. When I was a student in the 1950s it seemed unbridgeable. The SCM by and large attracted students who embraced the theological liberalism which was enjoying considerable popularity at the time. These liberals believed that the essential purpose of Christianity was not to woo individuals into the kingdom of God by challenging them to change but rather to concentrate on transforming society so that the harmony of heaven could be enjoyed on earth. They sought to Christianise society by meeting the material needs of the poor, feeding the hungry and visiting the sick. Philanthropy, not proselytism, was their goal. This was the way to further God's kingdom on earth, they claimed, and they criticised the Christian Union for its evangelistic activity, which came across to them as scalp-hunting, being interested in a person for the sake of saving their soul, but which lacked compassion for the whole person.

The Christian Union (or CU, as it was affectionately known by its members) on the other hand was equally suspicious of the SCM and poured scorn on its 'social gospel' stance, which appeared to reject the clear teaching of Christ: 'I tell you the truth: no one can see the kingdom of God unless he is born again . . . no one can enter the kingdom of God unless he is born of water and the Spirit . . . For God so loved the world that he gave his one and only Son, that whoever believes in him shall not perish but have eternal life' (John 3:3,5,16).

Every now and again the SCM would invite the CU to join them in philanthropic enterprises and missions. But because their main aim seemed to be to transform society, while the CU's main aim remained unshakeable: to encourage people to allow Christ to transfigure them and to live biblically; these two groups which both wore the label 'Christian' were unable to co-operate with one another. Both groups became more deeply entrenched in their opposite and opposing viewpoints. The CU defended its view of the Bible's teaching with all the ferocity of those fighting with their back to the wall. The SCM defended its 'social gospel' interpretation of Christ's teaching with equal aggression. The CU accused the SCM of liberalism. The SCM retaliated by accusing the CU of narrow-mindedness. The gulf which separated them widened. And those of us in the CU retreated into our rabbit warren, confused, battered and bewildered, completely unable to distinguish between the 'social gospel' of the liberals and the clear challenge of Christ to involve ourselves with those in need.

Against this background perhaps it is scarcely surprising that, as a group, we were in danger of losing sight of the message embedded in Isaiah, that religion without compassion is not only useless but incurs God's wrath and disgust, that his command is clear: 'encourage the oppressed. Defend the cause of the fatherless, plead the case of the widow' (Isa. 1:17). We were in danger too of losing sight of the clear teaching of Jesus: that when we fail to come alongside the hungry, the sick and those in captivity, it is he himself we are neglecting.

We almost lost sight of Galatians 5:22: 'The fruit of the Spirit is love, joy, peace, patience, kindness, goodness, faithfulness, gentleness and self-control.' The love here, which is love-in-action, love with its sleeves rolled up to help the needy, loving until it hurts, had not yet been discovered by our group. Neither had gentleness, the ability to walk a mile in another person's moccasins, to quote the old Indian proverb, so to identify with a person's feelings that no needless pain is inflicted; the ability to pour love in where there has been little or no love. And we were not experienced enough nor wise enough to know that, in some situations, people's pain – depression, bereavement, phobias, loneliness – could not be eliminated with a well-meaning response like: 'Turn to Christ and everything will be all right'; or a loving 'Pray about it.' Such reactions to people's heartaches are too simplistic. But then no one had underlined for us the truth that it is 'those who do not run away from our pains but touch them with compassion [who] bring healing and new strength. The paradox indeed is that the beginning of healing is in the solidarity with the pain.' No one had pointed out to us that 'in our solution-oriented society it is more important than ever to realise that wanting to alleviate pain without sharing it is like wanting to save a child from a burning house without the risk of being hurt'.[2] If we had known these things, I believe we would have behaved differently.

As it was, in our determination to guard the gospel and base our lives on biblical truth, we lost sight of compassion, that Christ-like quality without which much of our evangelism is at best ineffective and at worst crude.

I recall with sorrow that I allowed the good seed of compassion that had been implanted in me as a child to be choked by theological conflict and emotional confusion. In the circumstances I believe this was understandable – but very regrettable.

Immaturity

The third reason why I became a rabbit-hole Christian was that when I went to university I was still in my spiritual infancy. Infants are immature. If they are to grow in confidence and maturity they need, first a womb, then the security of a warm and loving home where guidelines are given and parameters set and explained clearly. The CU was the womb where this infant grew.

The CU's basis of belief and insistence on living biblically gave me the guidelines I needed. And the CU was the home into which I retreated from the challenges of adulthood which I was not ready to face in Christ's name. In CU circles I found the safe place where I was secure enough to discover what a life surrendered to the lordship of Christ meant. Without the fellowship and friendship, the support and the teaching of these likeminded Christians, I might well have wavered in the commitment to Christ I had made while I was still in the sixth form at school. As it was I never turned my back on that life-commitment. And together with the CU friends whose support I cherished, my understanding of certain parts of God's word deepened and grew.

But growth brings change. Babies grow into teenagers. Similarly baby Christians grow into teenage-type Christians. And teenagers rarely accept without question their upbringing and the demands that are made of them.

By the time my final examinations filled my horizon I was becoming a questioning teenager in terms of my spiritual pilgrimage. The weekend before my finals, those examinations which would determine for ever whether or not I emerged from university with a BA degree, the Webb-Peploes again took me into the refuge of their home. I was tense and restless. The year on committee had taken its toll. So had the theological wranglings, long hours working in the library and the constant concern about my mother's health. But again, just being in the Webb-Peploes' home and presence and garden proved to be the therapy I needed. Through the quietness and sensitivity of their concern, the overwound clock of my life learned to tick in time again. Sitting on their lawn soaking up the sun and the stillness, I relaxed into the felt presence of the compassionate Christ. Walking round the garden and the orchard with Mrs Webb-Peploe or the farm with Dr Webb-Peploe, I learned to love so many of God's created things: ripening strawberries and raspberries, clucking hens, grunting pigs and waddling geese, and the shapes and sizes of the trees which towered over the lawn. Once again Mrs Webb-Peploe's serene and prayer-soaked love set the atmosphere where I could experience God's love for myself: the love I knew about in my head but needed so desperately to feel deep inside me. At the end of the weekend I returned refreshed to Southampton to face my final exams.

But this second brief spell at the Webb-Peploes had not only strengthened and encouraged me, it had also caught me off my guard and unnerved me. Their outlook on life seemed so different from ours in the CU. They spent their entire lives seeking to spread the good news that Christ changes lives. They had done this in India and now they were doing it in the New Forest area of Hampshire and beyond. I would listen enthralled as each of them reminisced about the wonderful changes they had seen take place in the lives of some of the people they had met.

A friend recently reminded me of one of the stories Dr Webb-Peploe loved to tell.

Part of his responsibility as a GP was to visit patients in a nearby mental hospital. One of the patients in that hospital was a fellow doctor and Dr Webb-Peploe's heart went out to him in compassion. While praying for this man on one occasion, Dr Webb-Peploe sensed that God was wanting him to share certain verses from the Bible with this man. At first he argued with God, protesting that since this doctor was not a Christian it would be inappropriate to read scripture to him. But the sense of rightness of this course of action deepened, so on his next visit Dr Webb-Peploe chatted to his doctor friend as usual and then asked if he might read the verses to him. The doctor agreed and this is what he heard:

But now, this is what the Lord says . . . he who formed you . . . Fear not, for I have redeemed you; I have summoned you by name; you are mine. When you pass through the waters, I will be with you; and when you pass through the rivers, they will not sweep over you. When you walk through the fire, you will not be

burned; the flames will not set you ablaze. For I am the
Lord, your God, the Holy One of Israel, your
Saviour . . .
Since you are precious and honoured in my sight, and
because I love you. (Isa. 43:1–4)

These words made a profound impact on the sick man
and when Dr Webb-Peploe had left, he asked for a Bible.
After much searching the nurse found a rather battered
Bible which bore an inscription inside the cover, 'ASHLEY
Baptist Church', and the word Ashley was written in
large Gothic lettering. The man was astonished. The
verses he had heard claimed that 'I have summoned you
by name, you are mine'. It so happened that his name
was Ashley.

'How can I enjoy a relationship with Christ?' was the
question Murray Webb-Peploe was asked on his next
visit. And on subsequent visits he was able to see for
himself how God was so touching this man at his point of
need and transforming him that his recovery was being
accelerated. There was real rejoicing on the day he left
hospital fit and well.

In her biography of Dr Webb-Peploe, Katharine
Makower tells another story that the Webb-Peploes
loved to recall. Dr Webb-Peploe had spent three happy
days at Cromer in Norfolk where he helped lead the
annual Beach Mission. On the day he left Cromer he
drove along a deserted road and, as usual, used his
travelling time to pray for various people. To his surprise,
out of the blue he was arrested by an inner voice saying,
'Stop and go back.' He pulled the car in to the side of the
road, switched off the engine and asked God, 'What does
this mean?' The answering thought seemed very strange:
'Go back to Cromer and ask Mrs Bulpitt if you can give
her and her two children a lift to Birmingham.'

Mrs Bulpitt's two children had taken part in the activities organised by the Beach Mission but they had
given no indication that they were in any kind of
need. They had simply said that their father lived in

Birmingham and that they would be joining him when the Beach Mission finished.

Dr Webb-Peploe began to argue with God: 'I can't go and call on a woman I have never met and ask if I can drive her and her two children half across England. It simply isn't done. And anyway I'm late already.' But the impression was so strong that he turned the car round and drove to the hotel where he knew the Bulpitts were staying.

When Mrs Bulpitt came to the foyer, Dr Webb-Peploe explained that he had met her two children at the Beach Mission and then said: 'I am going to North Wales and have to pass through or near Birmingham; may I have the privilege of giving you all a lift home?'

Dr Webb-Peploe recalls:

I don't know who was the more embarrassed, she or I, but she did what any woman would: began to give every possible excuse why she would not accept the offer: 'My husband is not here. We've made arrangements to go by train', and so on. And then she added, 'And anyway, my daughter is not very well this morning.'

I said, 'I am sorry to hear that. Have you had a doctor?'

She replied, 'No, I don't know any doctor here; I'll wait and see how she is.'

I said, 'I happen to be a doctor and my job is mainly the care of children; would you like me to see her?'

She said, 'I would be most relieved if you could.'

Dr Webb-Peploe diagnosed acute appendicitis in its early stages but explained that, since he was just passing through the town, he was obliged to call the local doctor. The local doctor came, examined the patient and disagreed with Dr Webb-Peploe's diagnosis. They were still discussing the prognosis when the mother returned saying that she had been thinking over Dr Webb-Peploe's offer and would be most grateful if he could take the family back to Birmingham as soon as possible. Within twenty minutes everything was packed up and they were *en route* for Birmingham. Every hour Dr Webb-Peploe stopped the car to take his patient's pulse. And every hour he noticed that her pulse rate was quickening. When they were still an hour away from Birmingham the young girl began to turn grey and Dr Webb-Peploe feared that the appendix might rupture before she could be operated on. He stopped the car again, telephoned the hospital from a callbox and arranged for a bed to be ready and for the surgeon and family doctor to be there so that the operation could take place as soon as they arrived.

Dr Webb-Peploe recalls:

They were quite splendid, and she was on the operating table within a short time. The surgeon asked if I would like to assist, and I said, 'Yes, very much.' When he had opened up the abdomen and fished out an appendix on the point of bursting, he looked across at me and said, 'You've driven this child half across England; what's the story?' So I told him what had happened, and he said, 'Well I agree; this is the hand of God.'

By this time the father had turned up at the nursing home. He was a wealthy industrialist, I discovered later. He invited me to their home for the night and, after supper, standing up against the mantelpiece in his drawing room he asked me what had happened. So I told him, and he said, 'Yes, I agree; God is in this.' Then he went on, 'You know, I haven't done much about God – I've been too busy making money, I think – but it's about time I did.'

I said, 'I quite agree.'[3]

That night the industrialist found peace with God. Three weeks later Dr Webb-Peploe returned to Birmingham to stay with the family. The child, Millicent, had made an excellent recovery and was eager to hear the full story from Dr Webb-Peploe's own lips. Great story-teller that he was, he enjoyed giving her a blow-by-blow account of the events of that memorable day, suggesting that it was Jesus who had saved her life. Millicent was so moved that she surrendered her life to God that night, and went on to be used by him to lead a regular Sunday service which was attended by over a hundred children.

Whenever the Webb-Peploes told stories like these, the emphasis was always placed on the sheer goodness of God and the mystery of his wonderful ways. And I would catch a glimpse of the fact that somehow their form of evangelism was in a different league from the kind we were attempting at college. What was their secret?

The penny had not yet dropped that their caring of people was born from the womb of listening prayer and that this was the reason for its effectiveness. Neither had I yet seen that the question is not an either/or: evangelism or caring, but a both/and. And I had not learned to dovetail zeal for souls with a love for people in the winning way H. R. Niebuhr describes: 'When all is said and done the increase of . . . love of God and neighbour remains the purpose and the hope of our preaching of the gospel, of all our church organisation and activity, of all our ministry.'[4]

Instead I was in inner turmoil. Consequently I was glad to be leaving university, the CU and a lifestyle which now seemed out-moded, unsatisfying and unsatisfactory. But such feelings had, of necessity, to be hung on a peg. Exam results appeared on the college notice-board. I had passed. Like most of my friends I found myself caught up in the whirlpool of preparing for the grand finale of these 'salad days': the pomp and circumstance of Graduation day.

4

People Matter More than Meetings

The summer of 1959 was one of the hottest on record. Before my final examinations I had spent day after day sitting in the garden revising. During finals the sun beat on the glass roof of the examination room causing several students to faint from the heat. After finals the heatwave continued and my parents came to Southampton for a holiday before taking their seats in the Guildhall where the graduation ceremony was to take place.

Half way through my second year at Southampton I had fallen in love with a post-graduate student, David Huggett. We celebrated the end of my finals and the submission of his thesis by announcing our engagement. Our first task as an engaged couple was to give my parents a good holiday.

My mother was well the entire week. My father relaxed. And at the end of the week their verdict was that this had been the best holiday of their lives. Graduation day, with the presentation of degrees, the speeches and the buffet lunch in the stately grounds of South Stoneham Hall, was a happy highlight and fitting climax. On that day my parents met David's parents for the first time. The pressures of the past year evaporated in the pure pleasures of the present and though I did not realise it at the time, I had turned a significant spiritual corner.

Others

Though we never put the desire into words, I knew David shared my vision that we should take the Webb-

Peploe's lifestyle as the model on which we would pattern our lives. This lifestyle was summed up for both of
us by the wooden plaque which hung over the mantelpiece in their huge kitchen and on which was engraved a
solitary word: OTHERS. During that first week of our
engagement it was as though our deepening love for one
another overflowed to my parents and we discovered for
ourselves the invisible, intangible rewards which come to
couples who sacrifice self in the interests of others: the
rewards of that inner sense of well-being we call joy.

Back in Roberts Road, with no examinations to cast a
shadow over me and no committee duties to occupy my
time, I was free to think, to evaluate and to choose how to
apportion my days, weeks and summer months. It was
early July and I would not be leaving home again until
October when I would start my post-graduate studies at
Manchester University.

Almost as soon as we arrived back in Roberts Road, my
mother's health deteriorated once more. For the whole of
that summer vacation she continued to suffer in the way
she had done since I was eleven. My father continued to
support her by doing the cooking, the cleaning, the
shopping and the necessary nursing of her. Aunt Rene
continued to come, to listen, encourage and comfort my
mother. And many of the same neighbours continued to
call. Although I had been away from home for three
years, and although my own values and lifestyle had
changed, life in Roberts Road was marked by few significant changes. The faithfulness and solid goodness of the
people who gave my mother so generously of their time,
energy and love made a very deep impression on me.

These people had suffered with my mother in the early
years of her illness and they suffered with her still. They
were unafraid to show solidarity with her pain and my
father's weariness. They ached for my parents because
they put themselves in their shoes and felt where these
shoes rubbed. As they recognised that the ongoing day-
in, day-out nature of their problems brought its own
frustrations and difficulties, they continued to give

much-needed practical help, like shopping. Their support was both warm and genuine. At first their faithfulness stunned me. During my three years at Southampton, we in the CU had talked about love in action and studied what the Bible said about it but none of us had even begun to translate this theory into practice at cost to ourselves. But here, before my very eyes, were men and women who would never have been capable of dissecting love intellectually but who knew what it meant to love at cost to themselves. It was humbling.

And in a way it was frightening. Most of my neighbours were God-fearing but few darkened the doors of any of the churches which lay in close proximity to Roberts Road. Most would have felt out of place in Christian circles. Few would have understood the religious jargon I had learned to use at university. None had an ulterior motive for caring for my mother – like trying to find an opening to speak about God. No. They simply saw her helplessness and did all in their power to rescue our family. And in doing so they were loving us in precisely the same way Jesus might have loved us if he had lived in Roberts Road. So which of my communities was the most Christian? The students who had signed on the dotted line for Christ and spent hours in prayer, Bible study and meetings where the Bible's teaching was expounded, or these working-class men and women without whom my parents' life would have been a misery? Which lifestyle was more authentic: the life I had known in Southampton where we Christians had been so busy attending meetings that there was little time or inclination to befriend anyone who did not suffer from this 'meetingitis'; or the self-sacrificing, caring way of life I was again witnessing in Roberts Road? I am almost ashamed to admit that I found this question impossible to answer; I was confused. And I was riddled with guilt because I could not bring myself to *talk* to my neighbours about Christ.

The Bible's teaching

In one sense, as I look back, I find it hard to believe that I could show such ignorance. I had just graduated in theology. For my finals I had made a detailed study of the fourth gospel and relished it. It seemed such a privilege to pore over the life and teaching of Jesus. The teaching he had given the disciples only hours before his death had moved me very deeply: 'My command is this: Love each other as I have loved you. Greater love has no one than this, that he lay down his life for his friends' (John 15:12–13).

I knew how Jesus had expressed love when he was here on earth. He had done it by showing immense sensitivity to the feelings of others: the family in Cana of Galilee whose wedding wine had run out, the paralytic he visited personally at the pool of Bethesda, the blind man he met near the pool of Siloam, his grief-stricken friends Martha and Mary with whom he stood at the grave of their brother Lazarus, to mention but a few. I knew that he had taken as much care in communicating with despised blatant sinners – like the woman from Samaria whom he met at the well – as with VIPs – leading Jews and Pharisees, like Nicodemus. I always imagined that one of the reasons why he drew people to himself as a magnet draws iron filings was because he went about touching people at their point of need. And I had observed that his love was a transforming love. Because of who he was, what he did and what he said, people's spiritual eyes were opened. They believed.

This happened to the disciples at the wedding in Cana. It happened to Nathanael. It happened to Nicodemus. And it happened to Martha and Mary and hundreds of others. It was as though his life was a signpost which pointed people to his Father.

Yet somehow his final command before he died: 'Love each other like that', had failed to move me. I knew it in my head but it had not percolated into my will nor did it steer my ways.

I knew that, when Jesus gave us this command, he was

repeating a recurring thought from the Old Testament prophets, for instance Amos. The Book of Amos had featured in my theological studies so I was conversant with the colourful language this great teacher uses to spell out that our religiosity is repugnant to God unless our public worship and private devotions are matched with a concern to improve the lot of the poor. Some of the striking similes and warnings used by this prophet are unforgettable – like the insulting way he refers to the women of Israel as 'cows of Bashan', and like this withering warning: 'I hate, I despise your religious feasts; I cannot stand your assemblies . . . Away with the noise of your songs! I will not listen to the music of your harps. But let justice roll on like a river, and righteousness like a never-failing stream' (Amos 5:21,23–24).

Yet I had fallen into the trap of intellectualising the words of scripture; noting them, finding them interesting, even amusing, but not allowing them to affect my life – indeed even dismissing them as irrelevant to my life. For example, singing lusty hymns and choruses was one of the things we had enjoyed about our Christian Union meetings, and in the church I had attended in Southampton. I could not yet accept that our expressions of devotion might, in fact, have been offensive to God since it was so rarely accompanied by the compassion the prophet mentions here.

Similarly I was aware that, like a recurring refrain, the theme of love in action features frequently in the letters of Paul; and that James makes a soul-searing attack on those who *say* they have faith but do nothing about it:

What good is it, my brothers, if a man claims to have faith but has no deeds? Can such faith save him? Suppose a brother or sister is without clothes and daily food. If one of you says to him, 'Go, I wish you well; keep warm and well fed,' but does nothing about his physical needs, what good is it? In the same way, faith by itself, if it is not accompanied by action, is dead . . . You see that a person is justified by what he does and not by faith alone . . . As the body without the spirit is dead, so faith without deeds is dead. (Jas 2:14–17, 24,26)

Share with God's people who are in need. Practise hospitality . . . Rejoice with those who rejoice; mourn with those who mourn. (Rom. 12:13,15)

Carry each other's burdens, and in this way you will fulfil the law of Christ . . . Therefore, as we have opportunity, let us do good to all people. (Gal. 6:2,10)

Somehow it had not occurred to me that this teaching included me. There are several explanations for this self-delusion. One is that it is possible to read God's word, to understand it with our intellect but to fail to pick up with our spiritual antennae the message it is trying to convey. I was reminded of this even as I was writing this chapter. A woman came to see me whose husband now shows no interest in the things of God. 'For years he used to come to church regularly,' she confided. 'How *could* he sit under all that superb teaching and not be changed?' Sadly, it is possible. And it is equally possible for Christians to know a great deal about God without really knowing him just as it is easier to be familiar with Christ's commands than to obey them.

Another reason why this clear scriptural teaching bypassed my behaviour was that it was unfashionable in the 1950s to use words with which we are now familiar, like John Stott's 'friendship evangelism' and 'incarnational mission'. Instead evangelists hammered home their own narrow view of evangelism; that witnessing for Christ means talking about him: to the barber, the grocer, the neighbour or the person standing with us at the bus stop. They underlined over and over again that such overt evangelism should be the priority in every Christian's life.

And a third reason why I suffered this terrible spiritual blindness and deafness was that I, and my fellow Christian undergraduates, were children of our age. As John

Stott explains so helpfully in his fine book, *Issues Facing Christians Today*, although in the nineteenth century, concern for people and evangelical Christianity were like twin sisters living happily together, during the first thirty years of the twentieth century a major shift took place, which the American historian Timothy L. Smith has termed 'The Great Reversal'. For a variety of reasons, evangelical Christians neglected concern for their neighbour, mislaid their conscience and concentrated instead on the primacy of preaching the gospel.[1]

But in the 1960s a wave of the Spirit of God seemed to sweep over England convincing men and women that 'evangelism and compassionate service belong together in the mission of God'.[2] I was unaware at the time that there was a groundswell of social concern among leading evangelicals. What I did know was that I was uneasy in my spirit about the teaching I had received and the lifestyle that appeared to have been modelled for me by my peers and some of the pastors in Southampton.

Biographies

I have often found that when God is trying to etch something on my heart he softens its clay with a Christian book or biography or film. And that is what happened during this vacation.

My parents owned only a handful of books. But every now and again my father would take one of his musty but precious hardbacks from the shelf in the kitchen and thumb through it. One of these treasured books traced the life and ministry of George Müller whose concern for destitute children in the Bristol area of England prompted him to found a series of orphanages there in the first half of the nineteenth century. The reason why my father treasured this book was that he had spent several years in one of these orphanages as a child and while there his imagination had been fired by the faith of the founder of the homes. He loved to relate one of his favourite passages from this book; to tell of one of the many occasions when George Müller discovered that funds had run out.

The homes were run on a shoe-string budget but George Müller had resolved never to purchase anything unless cash was available to complete the transaction. One day to his horror he realised that no money meant no bread for his three hundred orphans. That night, instead of going to bed, he stayed awake to pray. He reminded God that these were *his* orphans; that he had declared himself the Father of the fatherless; that this work was *his* work and that the honour of his name was at stake. He begged God to prove afresh his faithfulness.

Next morning he came down to the refectory to find that the tables were laid as usual but the bread-plates were empty. Nevertheless, watched by three hundred hungry-eyed children, he said grace thanking God for the food they were about to receive. The children were about to sit down to face a row of empty plates when the sound of cart-wheels on the gravel drive drew every eye to the window. This noise heralded the arrival of the local baker who had felt compelled that night to bake an extra batch of loaves and to bring them as a gift to 'Mr Müller's children' before he began his morning rounds. With a flurry of excitement the cart was unloaded, the hungry children were fed, and trust in George Müller's never-failing God soared.

Because the book meant so much to my father, and because I was intrigued by such stories of the miraculous, I dipped into this life of George Müller for myself. And there I discovered that this great man of prayer was speaking to the very problem that was troubling me. He longed to evangelise – 'to win souls for God', as he put it – but recognised that he would never qualify to be an evangelist until his heart burned with compassion for God's lost and hurting people. By rescuing from the streets of Bristol children whose parents had died of consumption, he learned how to care for the whole person – to feed the hungry, clothe the penniless, provide a refuge for the homeless – to incarnate God's love as well as to talk about it.

Another book which influenced me at this time was *The Small Woman* by Alan Burgess. The author tells the story of Gladys Aylward the parlourmaid, who was turned down by missionary societies in England but saved her meagre earnings so that she could pay her own passage to China where she believed God wanted her to work and witness to his love.

The reason why I found this book so engrossing was that from a young age I had had a fascination for the Chinese and their culture. When I was seven years old, my Sunday School teacher had recently returned from China where she had been a missionary, and most Sundays she would tell us stories about the Christians in China she had loved and worked with. This interest in the Chinese had been rekindled in my early teens when I had played a part in a dramatisation of Gladys Aylward's life. It was then that I learned to use chopsticks: it was then that I first handled real silk garments: caps and coats embroidered with wide scrolls in many colours: scarlets, blues, greens and golds; it was then that my admiration for this courageous working-class woman was born. And it was then that I realised how hard her life must have been.

For years after her arrival in China she seemed to have few opportunities to win people for Christ. At times she must have despaired and wondered why God had called her to travel half-way across the world to China; why she had sacrificed so much to do so. Nevertheless she made use of the opportunities she did have – to express to ordinary village people how much she cared for them as fellow human beings. She, too, took in homeless orphans. She visited prisoners in the gaol at Yangcheng, thus earning the respect of the prison governor. And when people were sick it was to Gladys that they would turn.

And though she did not realise it her love and concern for people was speaking more eloquently than any words she ever uttered. Over the years this dynamism of love broke down the barriers between the foreign missionary and none other than the Mandarin of Yangcheng. This leading dignitary had despised the tiny ex-parlourmaid when she first arrived in China. To start with she was a female, which in the eyes of a Chinese meant she was socially and intellectually less than dust. And he considered her presumptuous in coming to his country. A cultured Confucian scholar, he would rebuke her for treating his nation as heathens:

'We have produced great art and great philosophy. The Mandarin speech of China is more beautiful and descriptive than any other in the world. Our poets were singing when Britain was but a rocky outpost on the edge of the known world and America was inhabited solely by red-skinned aborigines. Yet you come to teach us a new faith? I find it very strange.'[3]

Over months and years, news of the missionary's exploits reached the Mandarin and he learned to respect her and even consider her his friend. So much so that one memorable day he said to Gladys, whose Chinese name was Ai-weh-deh:

'I am giving a feast which I would like you to attend . . . I have something to say that I wish you to hear.'

When the Mandarin's feast was held, Gladys, to her surprise, found that although as usual she was the only woman present – that had been her privilege for many years – on this occasion she was sitting next to the Mandarin in the seat of honour at his right hand. This had never happened before. All the important personages of Yangcheng were present: the Governor of the prison; two wealthy merchants, several officials; about a dozen in all. The meal was simple, unlike the sumptuous feasts she had enjoyed in early years, and which had lasted for hours.

Towards its close the Mandarin stood up and made

his speech. He recalled how Ai-weh-deh had first come to Yangcheng; how she had worked for them; what she had done for the poor and the sick and the imprisoned; of the new faith called Christianity which she had brought with her, and which he had discussed with her many times. Gladys was puzzled by his references. But after speaking for some minutes he turned towards her, and said seriously and gravely: 'I would like to embrace your faith, Ai-weh-deh, I would like to become a Christian!'

Around the table rose a murmur of astonishment. Gladys was so astounded that she could hardly speak. The guests nodded and smiled, and she knew that she was expected to reply. She got up and stuttered her surprise, her appreciation and her thanks.[4]

Afterwards Gladys realised that she had made her most influential convert to Christianity since her arrival in China many years before.

An apprenticeship

These examples of vital, practical Christian love in action moved and inspired me just at the time when I was making preparations for the children's camp where I was to be cook and quartermaster for ten days. This camp was organised by the Church Pastoral Aid Society and the aim was to give children from deprived inner-city areas a good holiday away from the polluted air of the town and an opportunity to hear about Jesus. I had been on one such camp before and was looking forward to returning to Fairlight, a village not far from Hastings in Sussex.

In 1959 Fairlight was a tiny hamlet which boasted a church, a small church hall and a string of cottages straddling the road leading from the church to the nearby fire hills – undulating green hills and cliffs which blazed with colour when the yellow gorse was in flower and which ran down into the grey-green sea.

My task was to plan the menus for the camp, order the groceries, mastermind the cooking and give one of the talks to the children in the evening. We cooked in the church hall. The children slept in bunk beds in the same building and the 'officers' slept in tents in a field opposite the church. On Sundays we swelled the congregation at the morning service in the tiny greystone church.

This year the children were girls from the London area. I can see them now, bundles of excitement tumbling out of the coach which brought them to Sussex. They were wide-eyed and chattering noisily as they explored the tents and the adjacent field of cows and I shall never forget their faces as they took the first memorable walk along the cliff path to the beach. Most of them had never seen the sea before. Most of them had never seen a cow before. And none had slept in tents. So the air would ring with the sound of Cockney voices crying out: 'Coo, Miss! Look at that! A real cow!' 'Miss! I didn't know you could smell the sea!'

I loved hearing comments like these. Coming from a concrete jungle myself, I could still remember my first Girl Guide camp: the spaciousness of the countryside, the soothing sound of wood pigeons, the sight of fields studded with golden buttercups, white marigolds, purple and pink vetch and deep blue harebells, the smell of good fertilised soil and sausages sizzling over a wood fire. Now it was my joy to help provide an environment where other children could enjoy similar pleasures. They would pick armfuls of wild flowers and I would find clean jam jars in which they could place these treasures of the hedgerows. The flowers brightened the trestle tables at meal times. I would teach the children the names of the flowers and watch as they caught their first scent of honeysuckle or squeezed milk from the stem of a dandelion for the very first time.

'You can almost watch these children change colour,' I marvelled as I saw roses appear on cheeks that had been pasty when they arrived. The children spent most of the day swimming or playing games or walking on the fire hills or in the country lanes. Consequently their eyes sparkled, their appetites grew, they learned to appreciate wholesome food. And one of the rewards of the camp was to send them home glowing with health and vitality.

But perhaps the greatest reward came in the evenings when we all crowded into the church hall to focus on worshipping and learning about Jesus. The children had had a good day. They were happy and relaxed. They knew they were loved. And they settled down to sing, to listen and to think. Just as many of them contemplated nature with a naturalness that seems to be God's gift to children, so many of these girls contemplated the life and love of Christ with the guilelessness of little people whose capacity to trust has not yet been destroyed. We would try to paint an accurate picture of the God who loves them. We would also explain who Jesus was, why he stripped himself of his glory to come and live among us, why he had to die. And we would explain that God's love has to be received and his kingdom entered. The door opens as we surrender our lives to God.

Whenever one of the leaders spoke in this way a hush would descend on the room as the girls pondered the truths that were being explained. It was the hush I have seen steal over even the most extrovert of tourists when they enter a prayer-soaked church. Laced with awe and reverence as it is, it banishes boisterousness for a while and gives the Holy Spirit of God a unique opportunity to work in the hidden recesses of a person's heart. This was what we saw happening to the girls. The eyes and ears of their souls were opened and their hearts warmed by the love of God.

Because I worked in the kitchen, mine was the privilege of seeing for myself some of the ways in which God was working. The girls knew that after the evening meeting, I would be in the kitchen making cocoa. Some – particularly the shy ones – would come to help me and as we worked together side by side, they would make their quiet requests. They called me 'Squirrel' because I hoarded the camp's food. 'Squirrel! Can I talk to you about Jesus?' 'Squirrel! Will you pray with me?'

When children pray they come straight to the point in a way that sometimes disarms adults, and often as I listened to these young girls thank God for sending Jesus or thank Jesus for dying on Calvary's cross, I would be challenged by their clear and uncomplicated faith. And whenever I heard one of these children hand over to God the reins of her life, I thought I caught a glimpse of the reason why Jesus once said: 'There will be . . . rejoicing in heaven over one sinner who repents' (Luke 15:7). This heavenly joy echoed through my own life and through the entire camp also.

Knowing that these girls were going home with more than rosy cheeks and healthy appetites made the hard work of the camp more than worthwhile. And these camps were hard work. We rose early and went to bed late. Before camp began there were tents to put up, talks to prepare, shopping to be done. During camp we sweated over the kitchen stove for much of the day and spent most of our so-called free time talking to the children about their homes and families and troubles and joys. And when, at the end, the girls piled into the coach again, some of them sobbing at the thought of leaving, others waving and calling out their thank yous, there were floors to be scrubbed, toilets to be cleaned, the site to be cleared and food to be packed up so that Fairlight was tidy for the next contingent of campers who would arrive almost as soon as we had left.

I would not have been able to express the conviction coherently at this stage of my pilgrimage, but these camps were giving me something I desperately needed – an opportunity to see how caring for people and witnessing for Christ overlap and intertwine and feed and affect each other. It would have been possible, I realised, to have given these children a really good holiday without mentioning God but that would have deprived them of the most lasting gift we gave them: peace with God and a purpose in life – to serve him always. Equally it would have been possible to spend so much time talking about God that we deprived them of the exercise and fresh air, the good food and stimulating games and the appreciation of God's wonderful world which they so badly needed and enjoyed so fully. Then they would have been less receptive to receive and respond to God's love when it was explained. In other words I saw the importance of the both/and approach to caring for people. I saw more clearly than ever before that overt evangelism and concern for people are both shoots which sprout from the same root – the good news that Jesus came so that we should enjoy wholeness. I had seen for myself that love in action worked, not only for George Müller and Gladys Aylward, but for ordinary children in ordinary summer camps too. What is more, I felt fulfilled as a person. Whole. It was as though my two loves – love for Jesus and love for people – were coming together so that I felt integrated as a person instead of torn apart.

As I packed my cases once more and travelled to Manchester where I was to train to teach deaf children, I was fired with a new vision. I decided that my last year as a student was going to be different from the previous three. I would remain firmly anchored in Christ by having fellowship with like-minded Christians but I would not allow my week to be so cluttered with meetings that I had no time for people in need. It sounded simple and sensible. But the events of the very first weekend were to warn me that this was going to be more difficult than I had anticipated.

Expectations

The problem was that my reputation had gone before me. I suppose I should have expected this. I had, after all, been the Secretary of the Christian Union at Southampton University. I knew that the old-girl network in such Christian circles works well; that the CU in Manchester would have been told that I was to live in Ellis Lloyd Jones Hall for a year. But I had not expected the welcome I received. The Christians in hall invited me to coffee the day I arrived and it was then that I realised that they were looking to me, the graduate, as a guru figure who would help them organise meetings for the mission to the university which was to take place that academic year. Frightened that I might be sucked back into the whirl of CU meetings from which I had emerged so recently, I panicked inwardly but said nothing.

Meanwhile I was introduced to Margaret. She and I struck up a friendship in the first week of the new term because, like me, she came from Devon. But unlike me, Margaret had not been to university before. She had been teaching primary children for a number of years and had decided to come to Manchester as a mature student to train to teach the deaf. Now, having exchanged her beloved Devonshire countryside for the grim and sooty surroundings of the Old Trafford area of Manchester, she confessed to me that she felt lost, lonely and bewildered.

Margaret was a practising Christian – not the sort to be drawn to Christian Union meetings, but a devout believer none the less. On Sundays she would ask if I would go to church with her. And at first we would troop across town with members of the Christian Union to attend the lively services in the successful 'student church'. But I could tell that these Sunday jaunts and jolly services added to Margaret's feelings of isolation. They were not her scene. So the two of us started to attend a nearby Anglican church. The congregation was small. The vicar was struggling to inject new life into his dispirited flock. No other students were there so he and his wife welcomed Margaret and me warmly. We became a part of the fellowship and recognised that we had something to give as well as enjoying Sunday teas at the vicarage. Margaret blossomed spiritually and emotionally.

But of course this was drawing me away from the 'holy huddle' of the CU. Some of them found it hard to understand how I could worship at a church they considered dead when the church most of them attended hummed with life. Add to this the fact that, frequently on a Saturday evening, I would go to a concert or play or film with Margaret instead of attending the CU meeting and it will be easy to see why certain CU members worried about my spiritual well-being and made it clear that they felt I was losing my cutting edge.

'Perhaps they're right?' The thought worried me. Yet I was becoming increasingly convinced that people matter more than meetings and I could no longer bear the thought of spending hours at prayer meetings and Bible studies when all around me lived people as needy as Margaret. Because she was not the only one. There was Sin Bee, the lovely, lonely, shy Malaysian girl who lived on my corridor. The cold and the grime of Manchester's concrete jungle left her utterly bewildered. She needed friendship. She needed to learn about English customs. She wanted someone to take an interest in the home-life she had left behind. And she and I clicked like long-lost sisters. So I spent time befriending her.

And there was Pat. I was concerned for Pat. It quickly became clear that she hated Manchester and regretted coming on this post-graduate course. Life in the little garret-like bedroom in hall seemed almost unbearable for her. I would go and sit with her sometimes and try to understand her misery, and though I never seemed able to help her I wanted to go on trying. I knew somehow that I could not keep my integrity as a Christian and abandon this girl to her loneliness by rushing to one meeting after another. Even so it came as a complete shock when, at the end of one weekend, the housekeeper in hall told us Pat would not be returning to college. She had slashed her wrists in the bath at her parents' home and left a farewell suicide note. I was stunned for days, unable to come to terms with the fact that we had failed to hear the depths of her pain. And I became ever more convinced that I could no longer go on dissecting love in an intellectual way, I had to go where people are hurting and practise it. This was the law of Christ.

Misunderstandings

Some members of the CU misread my actions. Because I attended comparatively few meetings and because I could contribute little to the mission meetings, they believed I was backsliding and said so. That both hurt and confused me. How could I tell who was right? If they were right, I was being a big disappointment to God and that seemed unpardonable.

I now believe that my well-meaning fellow Christians were misguided. Yet how could they be expected to understand? No leading evangelical was yet expressing what John Stott has since said so clearly:

> Personal evangelism must be friendship evangelism if it is to be true to its name. Without any doubt friendship is the most Christian context within which to share the good news of Jesus. True friendship involves getting close to people. Friends enter into one another's world.
>
> I believe from scripture that in every unbeliever, even in the jolliest extrovert, there are hidden depths of anxiety and pain. Therefore we can only reach them in truth when we are prepared to enter their suffering and to feel their pain.[5]

No one had explained to us that to hide in our safe Christian ghettos is sheer escapism whereas what God wants is engagement:

> 'Escape' means turning our backs on the world in rejection, washing our hands of it (though finding with Pontius Pilate that the responsibility does not come off in the wash) and steeling our hearts against its agonized cries for help. In contrast, 'engagement' means turning our faces towards the world in compassion, getting our hands dirty, sore and worn in its service, and feeling deep within us the stirring of the love of God which cannot be contained.[6]

No one had pointed out that too many Christians are irresponsible escapists who find fellowship with each other more congenial than serving a hurting and hostile world. No one had shown us that to make our occasional evangelistic raids into pagan territory while shying away from incarnating Christ's love in the community cuts little ice.

If I had known what I now know, and if scholars like John Stott had highlighted the fact that, as Christians, we have a twofold ministry, my years in Manchester would surely have been easier, because instinctively I found myself living truths which are now being presented as *biblical* truth:

If the Christian mission is to be modelled on Christ's mission, it will surely involve for us, as it did for him, an entering into other people's worlds. In evangelism it will mean entering their thought world, and the world of their tragedy and lostness, in order to share Christ with them where they are. In social activity it will mean a willingness to renounce the comfort and security of our own cultural background in order to give ourselves in service to people of another culture, whose needs we may never before have known or experienced. Incarnational mission, whether evangelistic or social or both, necessitates a costly identification with people in their actual situations. Jesus of Nazareth was moved with compassion by the sight of needy human beings, whether sick or bereaved, hungry, harassed or helpless; should not his people's compassion be aroused by the same sights?[7]

But this was 1960. The movement of God's convicting Spirit was still largely hidden. It was seven years later that some leading Anglican evangelicals were to repent in public of their tendency to escape from rather than engage in the pain of the world of which we are a part.[8]

Meanwhile I left Manchester University with a qualification to teach deaf children. But before I took up my first teaching post there was a wedding to look forward to. I married David Huggett on July 16th 1960 and, at our request, Dr Murray Webb-Peploe preached at the wedding service and took the word OTHERS as his theme. With some wedding-present money we bought a dinner service – brown and blue Denby ware. Just like the Webb-Peploes'. For us it was an outward sign of an inner resolve that, like them, we would express our faith with a love which rolled up its sleeves and served others. The die was cast. For us, people must matter more than things or meetings.

5

Learning to Listen

A few months before our wedding, my father and mother-in-law moved to Bournemouth and asked whether David and I would like to buy the house that was built for them when they married and in which they had lived ever since.

The Dormers, Pine Walk, Carshalton Beeches, Surrey, as the name suggests, was a spacious detached four-bedroomed suburban house with pretty dormer windows. Its sylvan setting, Pine Walk, with its avenue of pine and larch trees separating one side of the road from the other was both peaceful and pleasing. This rural tranquil atmosphere was further enhanced by the hills and woods which lay within a few minutes' walking distance of our front door, yet we were in London's commuter belt. I used to write to my mother each week and try to capture on paper my new surroundings. One day I tried to describe the garden for her, so set myself the task of counting the trees. Seventy-two larch and pine trees towered over the house in the back garden. Thirty-two more graced the front garden. It was a wonderful home.

David and I spent the summer settling in and putting our own stamp on the house and garden. Homemaking quickly became a hobby. We enjoyed the creativity of unpacking our wedding presents and finding homes for them, decorating the loggia until it was too dark to see, planting vegetables and floribunda roses and doctoring the rockery my mother-in-law had made and which had been her particular pride and joy.

All too soon September dawned, and with it the start of the school term and the beginning of my teaching career. Nutfield Priory School for the Deaf had once been a manor house but was now tastefully converted into a residential school for severely deaf children. To my delight I discovered that my classroom in the wing looked out over the rolling hills of Surrey and beyond to Sussex, Kent and Middlesex. The view changed with the seasons and never ceased to take my breath away. And my work with these profoundly deaf secondary school children proved far more fulfilling even than my wildest dreams.

I had first dreamed of becoming a teacher of the deaf when, as a Brownie, I had befriended girls from the Deaf School in Exeter. 'You'll grow out of it,' my mother warned. But I never did. On the contrary, the desire increased when, as a Girl Guide, I again spent a great deal of time with girls from the Deaf School. And in my final year at Southampton I was overjoyed when my application to train under Professor Ewing at Manchester University was accepted.

To teach deaf children is to tune into pain and frustration. This was a lesson I was to learn in my very first term of teaching. Michael underlined it for me.

Michael was one of the eleven pupils in my class. He was not quite twelve years old but was big for his age and could have passed for fourteen quite easily. Michael was as rude as he was rough and he used his strength to bully and threaten the girls in my class, frequently disrupting entire lessons. At the end of the term when I wrote Michael's report, I expressed concern about his aggressive behaviour. Consequently the headmaster called me to his office to explain the problem. He was embarrassed by what I had written because Michael's father was the school's gardener and his mother worked in the kitchens. Anxious not to lose two valuable workers, Mr Blount suggested that I should talk to them about Michael. I did. And in doing so I learned that Michael's parents too were worried about him.

Nutfield Priory had an excellent reputation and

Michael's parents had been determined that their son should complete his education there. To make this possible, his father had resigned from his post in Kew Gardens and assumed the more menial role of school gardener. This had meant a move for all of them and they had watched Michael's insecurity increase when faced with a new home, a new school and new teachers who were struggling to understand his speech. Their sacrifice seemed to have misfired. Had they done the right thing in moving? This was the question they asked themselves continually.

My heart bled for them and after this conversation I tried to put myself in Michael's shoes: growing fast, missing his former home and former friends, feeling utterly bewildered by his new environment, yet because his speech was so undeveloped having no one with whom he could share his frustration; indeed having no one with whom he could communicate freely about anything. Even when he tried to communicate with us, very often even the most experienced members of staff would fail to understand what he was trying so hard to say.

'How would you feel if you were hemmed in by these limitations?' I asked myself. And in answer to that question I sensed that, in Michael's shoes, I would have been angry and frustrated too. 'No wonder he sometimes behaves like a caged animal,' I said to myself.

Thinking the situation through in this way caused my attitude to change. It softened. And as I softened towards him, slowly Michael changed. By the end of the second term we would occasionally see him smile. And by the third term he would co-operate with me and even come to ask my advice about his work. We were beginning to understand and respect each other and when he came to me on his own for speech lessons he would work really hard.

Even so I hurt when I thought of Michael and his parents. Theirs would be an uphill task if he was one day to hold his own in a competitive world of hearing people who make little time to stop to try to understand the world of the deaf.

I hurt too for the sixth-formers I taught. The relationship between a teacher of the deaf and sixth-form pupils is more friend-to-friend than teacher-to-pupil and I valued the closeness that developed between some of the girls and myself. These girls would be leaving school soon and part of our task was to equip them to face the world outside the sanctuary of Nutfield Priory. They learned certain skills like shorthand and typing so that they were qualified to take up employment, but if they were to be employable we knew it was vital that they should learn to communicate with the hearing people they would be meeting – in the office or canteen or other place of work.

For this reason Mr Blount had arranged for his sixth-formers to attend evening classes in the nearby town of Reigate. On Monday evenings therefore I would take a handful of girls there. We learned basket-work, quilting and dressmaking, and the girls discovered how to converse with the women of Reigate who had joined the class to develop their skills. When the girls failed to make themselves understood or were unable to lip read the women, I would act as interpreter. And again I would try to put myself inside the skin of these teenagers; to try to discern the feelings that might well up inside them. And I realised just how rejecting some of them would find the world outside the haven of Nutfield Priory when the time to leave eventually came.

From time to time David and I would invite these sixth-formers to our home for Sunday tea. They loved coming. And we enjoyed providing them with an environment so different from boarding school, where they could relax and enjoy the peace and the beauty of our lovely home.

The bereaved, the lonely, the perplexed

By the time I was five months pregnant it became clear that I could no longer cope with the long daily journey across country to Nutfield Priory nor continue to teach games and PE as I had been doing. The time had come to leave. I had been there for less than two years but my sadness at leaving the school almost overwhelmed me. I had enjoyed being a working wife. And the few house-wives I knew in the Pine Walk area seemed to spend most of their time at coffee mornings and talking about nap-pies. To exchange the fulfilling life and work of Nutfield Priory for that seemed to me quite unbearable.

By then David and I were worshipping at St Patrick's Church in Wallington and had struck up a firm friendship with Arthur Drowley, the Curate-in-charge, and his wife Doreen. Most Sundays after the evening service we would go round to their home for a sandwich supper. It was to Doreen that I expressed my ambiva-lence about being a full-time housewife. I still found it difficult to voice my innermost feelings but somehow, while we worked together in the kitchen cutting up tomatoes or grating cheese, it seemed easier to ventilate the fears and frustrations that were bottled up inside me.

Doreen understood. It was she who helped me to discover that when God closes a door he opens a win-dow. The door to teaching deaf children full-time was closed for the time being but that did not mean that I was to be condemned to a life of idleness or uselessness. 'Would you come to our young wives' group and talk about your work with deaf children?' Doreen asked.

Another of my dreads was women's groups. I feared that there, too, frustrated women would have nothing to discuss except nappies and the latest recipes. But I warmed to the idea of talking about my work. 'I could show some slides of Nutfield Priory,' I enthused. And I spent several days sorting out slides and preparing a talk which would give these women an insight into the world of the deaf, the joy of being able to teach these children to speak and the way I had seen God at work in the lives of some of the children I had taught.

That meeting was a turning point for me. The women were warm and welcoming. They seemed to appreciate

the way I had opened up a whole new world to them.
And I saw that my prejudices had been misplaced. These
were intelligent women whose love for God matched,
and in some cases outstripped, my own. I began to attend
the group regularly, found it stimulating and was soon to
be asked by Doreen to help her to run it. And in saying
yes to that, a whole new dimension of ministry opened
up for me.

People in need began to come to our home to seek
counsel and refuge, and because I was no longer at school
all day I was able to give that most precious commodity:
time. There was Pat who, like me, was pregnant and
finding it difficult to adjust to being 'just a housewife'.
There was John, a member of the youth group at church,
who was lonely and mixed up about his relationship with
the girl he was going out with; and after my baby arrived
there was Connie, the mother of five children whose
husband had died tragically in a drowning accident.

I wished I knew how to help Connie. Doreen seemed
to have just the right touch to gain her confidence and
encourage her to talk. I seemed able to do no more than
offer her a restful environment away from her own home
– and my baby to play with, which seemed therapeutic
for her now that her own children were well past the baby
stage. I failed to realise at the time how important this
was for her. But Henri Nouwen has expressed it well:

When do we receive real comfort and consolation? Is it
when someone teaches us how to think or act? Is it
when we receive advice about where to go or what to
do? Is it when we hear words of reassurance and hope?
Sometimes, perhaps. But what really counts is that in
moments of pain and suffering someone stays with us.
More important than any particular action or word or
advice is the simple presence of someone who cares.
When someone says to us in the midst of a crisis, 'I do
not know what to say or what to do, but I want you to
realize that I am with you, that I will not leave you
alone,' we have a friend through whom we can find

consolation and comfort . . . Simply being with someone is difficult because it asks of us that we share in the
other's vulnerability, enter with him or her into the
experience of weakness and powerlessness, become
part of uncertainty, and give up control and self-
determination. And still, whenever this happens, new
strength and new hope is being born.[1]

It was twelve years later, after many moves and much
change, that I was to discover truths like these.

Our second child was on the way when, although
David and I were both content in Carshalton Beeches and
fulfilled in our many roles at 'St Pat's', a strange restlessness disturbed us. I have since met other Christians who,
when God is trying to effect a radical change in their lives,
experience a similar sensation. It seems to be one of the
many ways the Holy Spirit uses to speak to us.

David had reached a crossroads in his career. He was
now faced with the choice of climbing the professional
ladder, which would mean spending more and more
time on his subject – aeronautics and space technology –
and less and less time with people. Or he must resign
his lectureship at London University and concentrate
instead on full-time Christian work.

Before we had committed ourselves to discovering
what God's will for our future was, David was invited to
attend a conference in Sweden. I stayed at home to look
after our son. While we were apart God seemed to speak
to both of us very clearly, challenging us to offer
ourselves for full-time Christian service. One Sunday
evening, shortly after David's return, we shared this
hunch with Arthur and Doreen. Arthur's response con-
firmed that God had indeed spoken. He looked overjoyed and simply said: 'I've been praying for this!' and he
encouraged David to push the doors to see whether they
would open so that he could train for the Anglican
ministry.

A year later the Dormers, Pine Walk had been sold, our
little family had been uprooted, we had torn ourselves

away from the fellowship of St Pat's and we were being transplanted in Bristol where David was to train.

His training included an opportunity to join with the medical students in Bristol in their study of psychiatry, and the added opportunity of working with patients in the nearby homeopathic hospital. Sadly no such training was then available to the wives of ordinands. But in Bristol and then in Parkstone and Cambridge, where David served his curacies, I found that, as a clergy wife, I seemed to attract people with problems. Wherever we lived people in pain would come to our home in the hope of finding some kind of help and support.

In Bristol there was the young mother who was distressed for her son because she needed a hernia operation which would require both hospitalisation and a lengthy period of convalescence. Her little boy Jonathan was the same age as my son Kevin, so Jonathan would come each day and he and Kevin would play happily together, relieving Jonathan's parents of anxiety.

In Parkstone David and I ran the youth group together, and because we lived in a terraced house in the heart of the parish, youngsters would pop in on their way home from school to discuss their problems with us: spiritual problems as well as boy-girl relationship problems.

In Cambridge, because we worked alongside a vicar who was a bachelor, again we were the ones who handled the boy-girl relationship heartaches and the marriage problems.

By the time we moved to Nottingham so many people were presenting me with perplexing problems for which I could find no take-away answers, that I enrolled for the counselling course at St John's Theological College, just three miles from my home.[2] It seemed natural to enrol for this course for two reasons. One, because David and I had already established close links with St John's College. Two, because Anne Long, the lecturer in pastoral counselling, was someone I had learned to admire and respect.

Anne had arrived in Nottingham a few weeks after David and me. We first met at the college at the beginning of the autumn term of 1973. David and I had been invited to speak at the pre-term conference with which the academic year began in those days. I was to speak on the Saturday afternoon and Anne was to introduce me.

'What would you like me to say by way of introduction?' she asked me. I don't remember precisely how I responded to that question. What I do remember is that I confided in Anne that I was feeling strangely nervous and that I supposed it was because this was the first time I had spoken in public since I had been shaken up by a car crash I had been involved in earlier in the year.

What I also remember is the way Anne handled that introduction. She used the opportunity to thank the students and staff of the College for the warmth of the welcome they had given her. The genuineness of her thanks was clearly endearing her to everyone. She then made an enormous impression on me because of the sensitivity with which she introduced me, explained that this was my first public appearance since April and suggested that they should all pray for me.

I still remember that prayer. Not the words. But the hush which descended on the uninspiring lecture room as Anne prayed.

Was it the authoritative but gentle way in which she prayed that drew me to her? Or was it simply that it was obvious when she prayed that she knew herself to be in the presence of the living God? Was it the attractive way she dressed that impressed me? Or was it the quiet wisdom and warmth which gave birth to the desire to spend time with Anne?

I don't know. What I do know is that after that initial encounter, we would meet from time to time and I would ask her about the counselling course which she was organising for the students of the College. The more I learned about the course, the more I longed for the kind of training Anne was giving.

I was surprised and delighted when permission was granted for me to become a student again. The Tuesday afternoon sessions at St John's quickly became the highlight of my week.

The value of listening

One of the first lessons Anne underlined was that the need for caring people in today's churches is urgent. All of us cry out for help at some time or another. At such times there are a variety of ways in which we can be helped. One vitally important method is the ministry of listening. If someone will draw alongside us, recognise that simply to listen is not a waste of time, nor is it less helpful than offering advice or Bible verses, they can provide us with untold support by encouraging us to share our innermost feelings of anxiety or fear or frustration or anger. I have since heard Myra Chave-Jones, former Director of Care and Counsel, put this succinctly and helpfully:

> What the person [in pain] wants is that, in our listening, we show the ability to stay with her in her pain. There is no need to flounder and panic and think we have to say something. Sometimes it is enough to stay alongside someone silently; to weep with those who weep.[3]

I would sit in the lecture room thinking of the trail of people who were currently coming to me for help as well as those who had consulted me in the past. Anne's insights seemed invaluable. Inexperienced though I was, I had detected for myself that the cry to be heard is universal. Whether one lives in the terraced streets of the inner city, like Roberts Road, or among the wealthy upper-crust residents of Pine Walk, whether one talks to people in the seaside town of Parkstone or to the successful dons of Cambridge, the cry can be heard: *'Please* will somebody stop what they're doing and listen to me?'

Of course hurting people rarely come straight out with their request in this way. Usually their cry for help is more subtle or camouflaged than that. Perhaps that was why Anne emphasised that listening to others is an art form which has to be learned. If we are truly to help others its theory and ground rules must be grasped and practised until they become a part of life. She likened this learning to discovering how to drive a car. At first the work of changing gear requires one's full powers of concentration. But eventually it becomes second nature. For the experienced driver changing gear comes naturally.

I knew I wanted to master this art form. The seam of compassion that had been ingrained in me in Roberts Road had not worn thin. I wanted to find appropriate ways of expressing this learned warmth of personality because I was aware that hurting people drew me towards themselves even when I felt powerless to help them.

What listening communicates

Paul Tournier, the much loved Swiss doctor and prolific writer, once made the claim that when we so listen to a person that he has felt understood, we help him to live and to face even the most difficult of situations without being false to himself. We give him confidence.

Anne fed us with similar insights:

> If you listen to me, I feel valued, you give me your time, acceptance – something I may never have had – and a relationship with another human being – something I may have problems with. You share the burden of my grief, my loneliness, my frustration, my indecision, my guilt. I've been alone with it so far. You let me think my thoughts aloud and sometimes, that way, I find answers – or at least discover where to look for them.[4]

While I was drinking in this kind of teaching I would think back to the people who had listened to me over the years: to the Webb-Peploes and Arthur and Doreen Drowley in particular. Anne was right. When they had listened to my fears and dreads without criticising me, it was as though I glowed inside because I felt that I really mattered even to such 'important' people. Because they expressed their love in this unselfish but costly way they enabled me to discharge my emotions constructively. This was so cathartic that, in purging me of many prejudices and irrational fears, it helped me to re-negotiate life on a new set of terms. And in instilling confidence in me they were modelling to me the never-failing love of the God who listens. I like the way Norman Wakefield highlights this:

> Listening says, 'I want to understand you. I want to know you.' It is one of the most basic ways to convey a sense of respect, to treat another person with dignity. Through this act we affirm to another person that God is willing to listen, that He eagerly waits for His troubled child to come to Him and discover the compassion and deep concern of His loving Father.
>
> Unquestionably, the listening I have been speaking about is a powerful form of ministry. Such listening embodies something of the nature of God Himself. It makes available to the Holy Spirit a channel through which to communicate love and a helpful, appropriate response.[5]

The listeners

And, as Anne had reminded us right at the beginning, this powerful ministry is not the prerogative of the professional, for anyone can learn to listen. Many others would agree with her.

Michael Jacobs, Director of Pastoral Care and Counselling for the Dioceses of Derby, Lincoln and Southwell, for example, suggests that: 'We have as a society effectively deskilled the ordinary man or woman in those tasks which are part of common life.' He goes on to point out that there are many occasions when the ordinary skills at the fingertips of most men and women are quite sufficient to help a person in need. 'What is frequently missing is the confidence to apply them.'[6]

Myra Chave-Jones, an experienced psychotherapist,

implies something similar in her valuable primer, *The Gift of Helping*. John Stott sums up her viewpoint in his foreword to the book: 'There are many situations of need in which ordinary Christians can learn how to love and serve people with sensitivity.'[7]

Gary Collins, Professor of Psychology at Trinity Evangelical Divinity School, Illinois, shows that most people in need still turn, not to a professional, but to a friend for help. He claims that 'if these peer counselors . . . can recognise their limitations, they can with very little training make a significant impact on the mental health of people around them. This is real people helping.'[8]

And Roger Hurding, another experienced counsellor, general practitioner and psychotherapist, seems to agree, showing that 'the Psalms, Proverbs, Ecclesiastes, the Gospels and Epistles are full of instructions for believers on the life-long business of helping one another towards maturity.'[9] He also suggests something which Anne and Myra Chave-Jones both emphasise: that though, through God, we can all be enabled to help one another, he does seem to equip certain people with a special ministry of helping and counselling. But he adds an important rider: most of us feel quite unequal to this task.

Paul Tillich suggests that we must lay these feelings of inadequacy on one side for, 'The first duty of love is to listen.'

All this and so much more was précised for me in some words written by George Eliot, which I first found stuck over the sink in Anne's kitchen:

Oh the comfort, the inexpressible comfort of feeling safe with a person; having neither to weigh thoughts nor measure words but to pour them all out, just as it is, chaff and grain together, knowing that a faithful hand will take and sift them, keep what is worth keeping, and then, with the breath of kindness blow the rest away.

Ground rules of listening

I was so persuaded of the 'inexpressible comfort' of
'just listening' that I lapped up the guidelines to good
listening that we were given.

These helped us understand that a person communicates on a whole variety of wavelengths simultaneously.
We must therefore listen, not only to the words and
sentences a person selects, but also to the non-verbal
signals which are being transmitted: the tone of that
person's voice, its inflection and the speed with which he
speaks – the rush of words at one point in the conversation, the slow and hesitant speech at another, the long
pauses in other places and the broken, incomplete
sentences. We must listen too to the way in which a
person expresses himself – whether his phraseology is
coherent or muddled. His facial expression, bodily movements, hand gestures and dress also give vital clues to
the way a person is feeling. A depressed person, for
example, will often lack the energy to take trouble over the
way they dress or do their hair. Their voice will sometimes sound flat, even monotonous. They might yawn
frequently as though even to string a few words together
takes an effort. They might twiddle their thumbs lazily
and endlessly as though their hands were giving expression to their aimlessness.

Good listeners therefore watch as well as listen. They
seek to hear the message which is being conveyed
through the words. They also make a mental note of the
hidden messages which authenticate and embellish the
spoken word: 'Di's voice was quiet and she spoke calmly,
but her eyes looked full of pain, her face was pale and her
shoulders drooped as though her problems weighed
heavily on her.'

Michael Jacobs highlights the value of listening to these
non-verbal messages:

Non-verbal communication is the very first communication we receive from a person . . . asking for
help. Before that person opens his or her mouth, he or

she will be showing through non-verbal signs how they feel, perhaps about the interview which is about to take place, or about their general situation. The listener, who now also needs to become the person who watches, can see this basic mood at the point of meeting a person in a waiting room, opening the front door for them if they come to the house, or even when greeted at the person's own front door. Non-verbal clues continue to be observable as people walk into the room, the way in which the person (who is to become the speaker) crosses the room, sits down in the chair, and the position in which he or she remains seated. This is, of course, only the first use of non-verbal communication, but may be very important to the start of an interview, especially if a person looks anxious.[10]

I began to put this ABC of listening into practice. At that time a man crippled with arthritis was coming to me for help. I would watch him limp from the doorstep into the lounge, lower himself gingerly into our soft settee and then wince with pain as he edged himself to the front of the seat where he perched for greater comfort. This man would talk to me about his worries, and as he did so he would mutilate my spider plant which sat on the table next to the settee or take a paper tissue from his pocket and tug at it nervously, tearing it to shreds. As I watched him I realised just how accurately his body was picking up and expressing his emotional stress. The message of those hands, the movements of his pain-racked body and the sorrow which seemed to fill his eyes gave me far more insight into his situation than the few words he managed to stammer out. It was this 'body language' which helped me to empathise with him. And empathy is another ingredient of good listening.

Empathy is not the same as sympathy. Sympathy listens to a person's pain and makes this kind of response: 'Oh! Poor you!' Or if a woman describes the seemingly unreasonable behaviour of her mother-in-law, sympathy says: 'I know just how you feel. My mother-in-

law's a bitch too.' Such sympathetic responses often
sound superior or patronising and are unhelpful. They
can even be intrusive.

Empathy, on the other hand, seeks, not to feel the
same as the person in pain, but rather to see the world
through that person's eyes without becoming swamped
by the other person's troubles or pain. It is the discipline I
began to learn when I was teaching at Nutfield Priory and
tried to put myself into my pupils' skin so that I could
imagine life as they were actually experiencing it. Most of
us do this automatically when we watch a film or read a
well written novel. We identify with the hero or heroine.
We enter into their dread or fear or hope or excitement or
joy. In one sense we 'become' that person for a while.

But true empathy, I discovered, comes in two stages.
To return to the example of the woman complaining
about her mother-in-law's unreasonable behaviour,
empathy asks itself: 'How might I feel if my mother-in-
law behaved like that?' It then moves on to ask itself
another question: 'How is this woman feeling in the wake
of her mother-in-law's behaviour?' In other words,
empathy tries to identify with the emotions troubling
another person and feeling into the situation with them.
Rather than assuming that the message has been accurately received, empathy goes on to clarify that the
message has been understood correctly.

Clarify

David Augsburger, a family therapist in California, has
shown how vital this art of clarification is. The word a
person uses to express a certain emotion may or may not
convey to the listener the precise emotion the person is
feeling. The reason for this, to borrow his colourful
language, is that:

the word is not the meaning just as the wrapper is not
the chocolate; the word is not the object it names just
as the photo is not the person; the word is not the

experience expressed just as my story is only a small part of that moment in history:[11]

600,000
words
are
available
in the English
language.
Of these,
an educated adult uses
2,000.
And the most used
500
have according to
standard dictionaries
14,000
different definitions.
Each common word
must be used to cover
a wide range of 'meanings'.
This pitifully small number of symbols
must describe the infinite richness
of your and my experiences.
(Some words have 100 or more different meanings.)[12]

Empathy therefore must make sure it understands such simple words as 'bad'. When my arthritic friend used to use this word: 'I've been bad this week', sometimes he meant that he was in physical pain. At other times he meant that he felt guilty because he had been drinking heavily. And sometimes he was simply trying to tell me that he was disillusioned with his materialistic lifestyle. I had to learn to check that I really understood what he was trying so hard to tell me by asking simple questions: 'Do you mean . . . ?' or 'Are you saying?' or by paraphrasing: 'So you're feeling really fed up with the pain in your knees to-day?'

This was the way I learned to pick up the bass line, as

Michael Jacobs calls it, or 'to pick up the vibes', to quote
Myra Chave-Jones.

Other helpful hints

My list of ground rules was growing. But there were
other principles to grasp: 'Don't be afraid of silences.
Worried people often think slowly and need long pauses.
Learn to understand silence as much as speech,' Anne
told us. 'If a person hesitates or stops talking, ask yourself: Is this a sullen silence or a reflective one; a shocked
silence or a thoughtful one? Is the person embarrassed or
simply searching for words to describe what is on their
heart?' And listen to the language of tears, Anne further
advised. Like silence, tears can convey all kinds of
messages: joy, pain, sorrow, frustration and even anger.
The wise listener does not assume that they know what
the tears are saying. Our eyes and ears can help us to
differentiate between hysterical, attention-seeking
crying and sobs which come from deep within a person.
Even so, sometimes I still find it necessary to ask, gently
and sensitively, 'What are those tears trying to say?'

When people came to me for help I would try to put
into practice these lessons I was learning. I became
particularly interested in people's eyes. Someone has
said that eyes are the mirror of the soul. They reflect the
emotional secrets we try to hide. I detected such pain and
emptiness, anger and sorrow in people's eyes that it
sometimes became painful to 'listen' to them. Often I
could tell whether the verbal thanks someone was voicing
was genuine by the change that had taken place in their
eyes. Often it was as though heavy veils had been lifted
allowing light and sparkle to shine once more through
those bodily windows.

Frequently, in these early days, by the time the person
had left me I would find that I was exhausted. I had failed
to understand what I now know: that listening to words
and emotions and vibes and subtle emphases, trying to
remember what has been shared and identifying with the

person concerned, takes all one's powers of concentration and a great deal of emotional energy. It was proving a costly form of loving for which I still seemed ill-equipped.

But it was producing rich rewards. People in pain were beginning to say things like: 'Thanks so much for listening.' 'It's so good to have someone to talk to.' 'You've really put your finger on the way it feels.' 'I feel much better now that we've talked.' 'You've been a great help.' On many occasions I had not 'done' anything. I had 'just listened'. I quickly came to the conclusion that 'just listening' was indeed an effective way of helping others no matter whether the person was suffering from a virus or cancer, depression or bereavement, guilt or anger or that common disease of the spirit, loneliness.

I was no nearer understanding *how* it helped. But then, I understand little of what goes on under the bonnet of my car, but I still enjoy using it. I was content to live with the mystery: hearing seems to be one of the ways God brings a person into a measure of healing. Eager student that I was, I determined to learn everything I could about the theory of listening and, I was soon to discover, there were many more lessons to learn.

6

The Listening Heart

The foundations were laid. We had learned that good listening requires our full attention; that if we are to listen well, this listening must be three-dimensional: we must tune in to the words a person selects, the language of the eyes, the face, the body and the tears, and we must also learn the art of translating 'vibes' accurately.

The course at St John's College now built on these foundations. Having learned how to listen with accuracy and empathy, we next learned how to respond – and how not to respond – to the person we were trying to help.

The first golden rule seemed to be obvious: *Don't interrupt*. I find it extremely irritating if someone interrupts me when I am trying my best to voice something important. Some people, I realised, were compulsive talkers who seem unable to listen without interrupting every few minutes. But I did not consider myself to be one of these. Nevertheless when I began to compare what I actually did with the rules for good listening I was learning, I was shocked to discover how frequently I caught myself butting in when someone was struggling to express painful emotions.

I think of an occasion when a seemingly-successful businessman told me he had lost his job. He was trying hard to express the emotions that vied for attention in his mind: the hurt and anger, the frustration and fear, the humiliation and hopelessness which tormented him. I wanted to understand. I wanted to show that I cared. But even though my motivation was high I found myself punctuating some of the pregnant pauses with questions to help him along. And when I reflected on that particular encounter I was forced to admit that most of those questions were unnecessary. Instead of helping him to pour out his innermost feelings they intruded on the thoughtful silences which were an integral part of his story-telling.

I felt ashamed. I knew in my head that good listeners have a good reason for any question they ask; that they do not ask questions out of idle curiosity but only out of the desire to promote the growth of the one they are listening to, but on that occasion I had not translated this helpful theory into practice. I knew too that the questions the listener asks should be open, that is, the kind that draw out more information about a given subject: 'Can you tell me more about that?' or 'How did that feel?' but this time many of the questions I had asked had invited a monosyllabic reply. 'Did that make you feel angry?'

I learned to confess this lack of love for that is how I view such neglect of the rules of good listening. I learned to repent and to receive the forgiveness God delights to give. Even so, despite years of practice, I still find myself interrupting inappropriately from time to time and still catch myself encouraging a conversation to explore an unnecessary cul-de-sac by the questions I ask. But I take comfort from John Powell when he writes:

Most of us, when we are in the listener's role, feel compelled to be speakers. We feel a compulsive inner urgency to interrupt others as soon as they start to reveal themselves. We feel a strange obligation to advise them, and to support our advice with a few chapters from our autobiographies. We jump in at the first pause, and go on nonstop unless we are exhausted and the other person is near despair. Regrettably, I have done this to others. I have also had this done to me. I have experienced the sadness of not being heard because someone had not cared enough to listen to my sharing and to learn who I really am.[1]

That 'strange obligation to advise' which John Powell mentions was highlighted as one of the snares we should avoid. 'Don't offer advice,' writes Myra Chave-Jones:

> Most people do not want it and will not use it. It is unhelpful to say, 'If I were you I would . . .' or 'I think you ought to . . .' because you are not me, and your view of what I ought to do is yours . . . The only real value of good advice is that it makes the person giving it feel better. (Of course, advice which relates to factual knowledge – for example, which course of study to follow for a particular career – is a different matter.)[2]

Again I was somewhat shocked to discover just how difficult I found it to avoid the trap of becoming a problem solver for others. Sometimes it seemed so obvious what course of action a perplexed person should take that I wanted to tell them so – even take them by the hand and lead them along the pathway which seemed to me to be so right. At such times the theory I was learning at St John's seemed hard to translate into practice. But of course to act like that would be to manipulate people, and so Anne Long's reminder was a vital one: 'Avoid premature solutions offered before the heart of the matter has been reached. Sometimes your own anxieties will press for a speedy answer'.

I learned that basic principle twelve years ago and have been trying to honour it ever since. But even as I write, I am trying to help a couple in crisis and once again I have caught myself playing my old tricks: waking up with 'the perfect solution' so clearly in my mind that I have wanted to telephone them to tell them I have found *the* way forward. Again I take comfort from John Powell's disarmingly honest – and very American – confession:

> I sometimes have to work at stifling my old urge to turn into a computer printer spitting out all kinds of interpretations and advice. I have personally been working on the technique of the well-placed question. It goes something like this: 'Gee, I don't know what you

should do. What do you think? In your judgement, what are the possibilities?' Sometimes a suggestion can be successfully floated into the conversation by way of a question. 'Say, did you ever think of going back to school and getting a degree?'[3]

And I came to recognise the importance of John Powell's observation that 'in the role of the listener we should offer only suggestions and never directions'.[4] He goes on to explain that the reason for this is that if adults are to behave as adults and not overgrown children they must assume personal responsibility for their behaviour and their lives. They must therefore be allowed to have their own thoughts and to make their own choices. The listener who insists on telling another what they should or should not do runs the risk of hindering a person's growth: 'The one sure way not to grow up is to hitchhike on the mind and will of someone else.'[5]

More 'don'ts'

I had no desire to invite hitchhikers to take a ride on my advice or my prayer. Nevertheless I found that certain people did become overdependent on me. This proved disastrous for them and for me. It was disastrous for them because, instead of thinking things through for themselves and taking responsibility for the decisions they made, these people would consult me as though I were an oracle and even reach the point where they believed that my prayers were more effective than theirs. Consequently they failed to grow. And it was disastrous for me because, though at first their confidence in me seemed like a compliment and boosted my ego, my false pride quickly turned to fear as I realised that such people were piling Messianic expectations on me which I could not hope to meet. I am not omniscient. I do not have the answers to everyone's problems. Whenever I tried to behave as though I was omnicompetent, my energy was sapped and my family suffered.

Eventually I saw that I was breaking yet another

golden rule of listening: *Don't encourage dependency*. I am still learning the difficult art of coming alongside a person and offering my love and my listening as a crutch but never as an armchair into which they settle comfortably but unhelpfully. Sometimes I seem to get it right, at other times I still get it wrong. It helps, I find, to set boundaries: making it clear to a person when they may telephone and when such a call would be intrusive; when to come to talk about their problems and when I need space. Such boundaries protect me and are reassuring to the person in need. They know that if I say I am happy for them to telephone or to call, I mean what I say.

Gary Collins's book *How to Be a People Helper*[6] helped me to set clear goals when I was trying to help a person through a sticky patch. He uses Jesus' encounter with the disciples on the road to Emmaus to illustrate how best to go about such goal-setting.

First he explains how, in Luke 24:14,15, we watch Jesus draw alongside the travellers who, from the way they turn the events of the past three nightmarish days over and over in their minds, still seem to be suffering from shock. Jesus takes the initiative and the trouble to establish a rapport with them so that they trust him.

Having built up a relationship, Jesus goes on to explore with them the nature of their problem. Why were they so discouraged? Why were they so stunned? He seems to have listened attentively as they poured out their perplexing tale, giving them ample opportunity to ventilate their frustrations, doubts and disappointments, and having penetrated to the heart of the problem and understood it Jesus decides on a course of action.

With a skilful use of questions and suggestions, Jesus sorts out the confusion by challenging their thinking and encouraging them to think differently about the string of curious events which has precipitated their crisis of faith.

But far from keeping himself detached or aloof, he comes close to his fellow-travellers and joins them for a meal. This fraternising was not an invitation to become dependent on him, however. On the contrary, we read that, quite literally, Jesus vanishes from their sight. This disappearing act seems to have spurred them into action and, on their own initiative, the travellers head back for Jerusalem where they become encouragers of others.

Gary Collins concludes from this that effective listening should include five steps:

1. Building a relationship.
2. Exploring the problem(s).
3. Deciding on a course of action.
4. Stimulating action.
5. Encouraging the person to apply what he has learned by launching out on his own.

At first Jesus' rather ruthless method of confronting his fellow travellers took me by surprise. Don't judge, the teachers of listening warned. But here was Jesus saying, 'How foolish you are, and how slow of heart to believe all that the prophets have spoken!' (Luke 24:25). Wasn't that being judgemental?

'No,' I decided. He had built his relationship with these men. He had tuned in accurately to their confusion. And he had decided that one course of action was to help them to think straight. In order to do this, it was essential for him to point out the discrepancies which lay between their feelings, biblical truth and the situation as it really was. I like to imagine that when Jesus said 'How foolish you are, and how slow to believe', there was a loving twinkle in his eye. Certainly it is unlikely that his challenge was harsh. Rather, he came over so convincingly that he won their hearts, renewed their minds and brought light into their darkness so that within a short while the direction of their life had completely changed. Instead of being caught up in a web of confusion they had been cut gloriously free to spread the good news: 'Christ is risen!'

Similarly I learned that careful and caring listening to a person's pain or confusion gave me permission to challenge discrepancies and distortions of the truth which I detected. The way I usually do this is to ask a question like: 'I wonder if this makes sense to you . . .' and I go on to try to show that though I understand and empathise with the real and powerful feelings which are bothering the person, these feelings may not add up to a correct analysis of the situation.

For example, I think of a girl I once tried to help who said she was suffering from depression. She wept as she told me that the reason, she thought, was that her engagement had broken up. As I explored the situation further, she confessed that she had slept with this young man even though she had known this to be wrong. She was now left with an overwhelming sense of guilt which she had confessed to God many times but nothing had happened. 'I suppose I'm too bad to be touched by God's forgiveness,' she confided.

After I had shown her that I understood the sense of hopelessness which was weighing her down and, while attempting to show her, through touch and the look on my face and in my eyes, and the tone of my voice, that I really cared what happened to her, I simply said: 'I wonder if it makes sense to you that though you *feel* as though you are a kind of spiritual leper, God's word makes it quite clear that the kind of sin you are confessing can be forgiven?'

She looked into my eyes for an instant and quickly looked away again. But that brief glance had been enough. In her eyes I had detected a glimmer of hope. She remained silent for several minutes while this hope struggled to the surface. Eventually she looked at me again and said, 'Yes. I know you're right. What do I do to receive it?' Now that her perspective was clear, my task was comparatively easy. I stood by and watched her guilt being melted by the God who loves to forgive.

In the early days of learning to listen, I would some- times feel soiled after a person had been describing their sexual sins. 'I sometimes feel as though a dust-bin has been tipped all over me,' I commented to Anne Long on one occasion. But at the same time I found that, when I really listened in the way I was being taught, it was rarely difficult to care for the people who were telling me about their misdemeanours. One reason was that, as I tried to put myself in their skin and view life from their perspective, I could understand what had prompted them to act in the way they had. That was not to say that I was condoning the sin. It is to say that I was recognising how vital it is at one and the same time to offer acceptance to the sinner without ever condoning the sin which they were confessing.

Some aims

'To offer acceptance.' This was what Jesus had offered me on that day, as a teenager, when I surrendered as much as I knew of myself to as much as I knew of him. This was what the Webb-Peploes had offered me when, as an undergraduate, I had collapsed in their home. And this was what Doreen Drowley had offered me when, as a pregnant mum, I was struggling to come to terms with my seeming lack of status now that my career as a teacher was being interrupted. On these occasions I had been on the receiving end of listening love. I had experienced its transforming power. I had seen for myself that Abraham Schmitt's observation is so accurate: 'To listen totally means that one takes another's whole life into one's being and cares for it.'[7] Now I wanted to pass on this kind of love to others. Twelve years later I am still learning how to do it.

One way, as Myra Chave-Jones stresses so helpfully, is to recognise that to listen to someone is to receive a gift. 'If you give a gift to someone, and they rip the paper off, take a cursory glance and then go off and do something else, it doesn't look as though they have really valued the gift.'[8] But if, on the other hand, you take the wrapped gift, remove the paper with care, turn the gift over and over in your hand, admire it and thank them for it, the giver glows inside and feels valued.

I find it helpful to think of listening like that: receiving a gift; recognising that by listening to someone's story or pain or problem or crisis I am bringing to them a measure of healing because I am communicating that vital message which we all need to hear over and over again: 'You really matter.'

There is a method of listening which at first seemed to me both curious and artificial but which I discovered quickly communicates acceptance and understanding love to the person in need. This method is sometimes called reflective listening.

When a person listens reflectively, they take careful note of the words a person selects and concentrates hard on the content of the verbal gift which is being offered. Then at appropriate moments in the conversation, they repeat back to the person with the problem a summarised version of what has been said.

Let me explain what I mean. Someone suffering from bereavement might arrive at church looking ashen, their eyes might swim with tears and, after the service, they might pour out their anguish that this pain and these tears just refuse to go away; that the sting of being separated from the father who died a few months earlier seems to grow worse rather than better; that time certainly isn't the healer it is claimed to be; that they are angry with God because he seems to have disappeared just when their need for him was desperate. They are even becoming hard and cynical when they hear Christian things talked about.

The listener takes in the 'body language', the words and the vibes, and summarises the situation by saying to the grief-stricken person in the pew: 'You seem to be surprised that it's taking so long to recover and that you still need to cry a lot? And you're angry and cynical because the God who is said to be such a wonderful healer seems to be doing nothing about the pain in you that hurts just as much now as when your father died?'

Although the listener has done nothing more than receive the bereaved person's verbal gift and begun to unwrap it gently and sensitively, a look of relief will probably pass over the face of the bereaved person. They have been understood. They therefore feel valued. And although this conversation can do nothing to bring back the longed-for father, yet this simple act of listening has given them the courage to go on living and trusting.

Real rapport is established between the person helping and the one being helped when this kind of listening is applied. It then becomes easy and natural to thank the person for giving us the privilege of being the one to hear and handle their innermost thoughts and feelings. John Powell reminds us that it is risky and frightening to put our most sensitive confidences in the hands of another, to examine our failures or to reveal our vulnerability. 'Consequently, we should practise the habit of thanking others for their self-disclosure and for their trust in us.'[9]

This suggestion seemed strange to me at first. But I remember the overwhelming sense of privilege and gratitude which swept over me when, in the early days of taking courage in both hands and putting this theory into practice, I said to someone: 'You know there are many people who would have counted it a privilege to listen to you in the way you have allowed me to do today. So thank you for your trust – for entrusting yourself to *me*.' This genuine expression of thanks took the person completely by surprise. But I could see that at the same time he felt valued because of what I had said.

Of course it would be useless to say something like that if we felt that the person we are helping was being a burden or a nuisance. People are quick to pick up pretence. If truly we are to communicate care, the warm regard which assures a person that they are of unquestionable value, and non-possessive love we must communicate not only with our lips but with our eyes, our hugs, our smiles and our gestures as well. It is this total response that the person in pain will register.

'Non-possessive love.' As I served my apprenticeship in listening I was surprised to discover how emotionally close two people can become when one is sharing confidences and the other is attempting to listen in the

attentive, caring way I have described. Such intimacy
need not be inappropriate or wrong. It can be healing.
But I was to discover the painful truth that it is not my
love which heals but God's. Indeed if all I offer to a
person is the paucity of my human warmth and acceptance, the person might feel supported, affirmed and
valued, but the transformation we are both looking for
will not take place. What is needed is not simply that I
should feel for and with a person in pain nor that I should
be able to express this concern. What I must always
remember to do is so to open myself to the love of God
that I simply become the embodiment of his love to that
person. Agnes Sanford underlined this for me in her
book *Sealed Orders*:

> 'Love heals', people say. I do not find that necessarily
> so. God's love heals, yes. But our own love, if too
> emotional, may even stand in the way of that great
> flow of God's love which is an energy rather than an
> emotion . . . I learned to put Christ between me and
> the person for whom I was praying, to send my love to
> Christ and let him do with it what he would. Thus
> people felt from me or through me, power rather than
> affection.[10]

Shortly after I had read this resolve of Agnes Sanford's God seemed to highlight its importance for me. I
was listening to a friend who was trying to help me to
understand how black life felt for her. Suddenly words
dried up, she buried her head in her hands and began to
sob – just quietly, but from deep inside herself. She was
someone for whom I cared deeply and in order to assure
her of that love, I went to her and gently placed my arm
around her. Instantly, I felt her body freeze. She stopped
crying, put on a plastic smile and changed the subject.
But her eyes were still filled with pain and the terrible
truth dawned on me that I had done the wrong thing. She
had needed to cry. This was the only language capable of
giving expression to the darkness inside her. And in

offering her touch at that moment, she had felt smothered. I had hindered the healing process and not helped it. Whereas if I had placed Jesus between her and me I would have discerned that she needed space to cry and that Jesus would have done the necessary holding.

After this unfortunate encounter I asked God to give me a greater sensitivity to the needs of others so that I would know when such touch was appropriate and necessary and when it should be withheld.

My warm personality intruded in another way too. I was discovering that when I love, I love deeply, and most of us are tempted to cling to the things and people we love. Yet to hang on to a person when the time has come for them to leave is to strangle love.

True love demands that the person be set free when the time is ripe. But I was slow to learn the art of holding such people on an open palm. I was slow to learn that, in pouring out love to others, I must expect nothing from them in return. I was slow too to learn that vital lesson, that when I listen to a person in need I listen for the sake of their well-being, not because I have a need for close-ness with others; my real and legitimate needs for friendship and intimacy must be met through the mutuality of supportive friendships – in my relationship with my husband, in the fellowship of Christ's people and through the support of a soul-friend who will listen to me in this caring attentive way.

Dangers

Just as I learned the hard way not to neglect friendships, so I learned the hard way the very real danger of neglect-ing physical health, sleep and exercise. 'Honour your body, mind, spirit and emotions,' Anne used to warn us. This kind of involvement with people in need sounds glamorous. But it is hard work. It will cost not less than everything. Therefore discover what, for you, is input. To emphasise this piece of teaching, one afternoon Anne scrawled this equation across the entire width of the blackboard:

$$\text{OUTPUT} = \text{INPUT} = \text{OUTPUT} = \text{INPUT} = \text{OUTPUT}$$

We understood what she meant. If we are giving ourselves to people in this demanding way, we must also receive into ourselves the necessary resources so that we do not burn out in the way I did as a student when I was trying to support my mother, attend to my studies and hold down a full-time job. In other words we must know how to relax, where to go for spiritual and emotional refreshment and how to set definite boundaries which limit our availability to people in need. We must know how to live balanced lives.

Although I understood the wisdom of this teaching, when I first started to erect such boundaries twinges of guilt would trouble me. What right had I to relax when so many people were longing for the kind of help I have described but who knew of nowhere to find it?

I was still struggling to find the courage to put this principle into practice when I heard a tape-recorded talk in which Francis MacNutt, whose book on healing had recently been published, confesses to facing a similar problem. He told us how embarrassed he felt on one occasion when he was speaking on healing at a residential conference. He was expected not only to give a series of talks but to minister late into the night to sick and needy people. And he realised that he was being drained of vital energy.

One of his hobbies was tennis. He had only to play a quick game and he would relax because he would focus away from people's needs and on to the healthy competitive nature of the game. So he decided to spend part of each afternoon on the tennis courts. But how could he possibly bring himself to walk right past a row of people in wheelchairs, who would all like prayer, when he was dressed in shorts, carrying a tennis racquet and obviously looking forward to some exercise. He found he could not do it. Instead he discovered the back door of the conference centre and sneaked out without anyone seeing him.

I identified with his dilemma, admired his limited courage and tried to learn from it, especially when I noticed that Jesus set a similar example.

In Mark 1 we read of a certain Sabbath when Jesus had taught in the synagogue in Capernaum, delivered a man of an evil spirit, healed Peter's mother-in-law, and at sundown had ministered to crowds of needy people. Before sunrise he retreated to a solitary place to be with his Father, but on returning to Capernaum the disciples alerted him to a new set of demands: 'Everyone is looking for you!' Whereupon Jesus replied: 'Let us go somewhere else' (Mark 1:37,38). And although we are told that the 'somewhere else' was nearby villages where he would preach again, we also know that the walk to those villages would have given Jesus the space and exercise he needed to replenish his own resources.

I took great comfort from Jesus' example, from his command to the seventy-two after their exhausting mission, 'Come apart and rest', and from Francis MacNutt's humble testimony. And I determined to discover how I could best relax, rest and have my spiritual batteries recharged.

I quickly discovered the therapy of the countryside. I love to tramp the hills of Derbyshire and I would try to go there each week to be recreated. Sometimes I would walk on my own, drink in the grandeur of the moors or the stillness of the bluebell woods or the extravaganza of rhododendron gardens or the comfortableness of holly-hocks growing close to dry-stone cottage walls. At other times I would walk with my husband – the only person with whom I feel really free to be me – to shuffle through piles of fallen leaves just like I did when I was a child, to run with the wind in winter or squeal with delight at the surprises of spring, the first snowdrops, premature cat-kins, newborn lambs. Concerts, the ballet, a good play also help me to unwind.

And creativity, I discovered, is a form of therapy. I gain immense satisfaction from making my own clothes, weeding a rockery or flower bed, planting hyacinths, preparing a special meal for friends, or spring-cleaning a room. When I am trying to help people whose pain is clearly not going to evaporate overnight, I recognise that I also need to spend time creating lovely things which bring quick returns. Without these, my life lacks balance and I become a dreary, depressed and depressing person.

I discovered too the inestimable value of retreating to a quiet place to be alone with God.

Listening to God

A little phrase Anne used in the course of her teaching had made a deep impression on me because I sensed its importance as soon as she said it: 'We need to listen with one ear to the person who is talking and we need to have the other big ear tuned in to God.'

After I heard this, whenever I knew someone was coming to see me or before I visited a sick or bereaved person, I would try to spend time in my prayer room confessing to God that I knew my own wisdom and insight were insufficient to meet this person's needs and therefore asking him if there was anything he wanted to tell me or to show me which would help me to bring relief or comfort or healing to the person concerned. Then I would spend time being still, waiting and listening.

Sometimes, as I have explained in *Listening to God*,[11] I seemed to have a clear sense of the appropriate course of action. It was as though God had spoken with the same still, small but authoritative voice with which he spoke to Elijah and Samuel. I think, for example, of the occasions when I asked God what I could do to help the arthritic man mentioned earlier in this chapter. Over a period of months I sensed that God was saying: 'I want to heal him of his arthritis.'

At first I was startled by these words; frightened that I was making them up. Our church had not yet started to hold healing services and though we believed that God could heal (he is God, after all) I am not sure that many of us really believed he would.

Yet the voice seemed to insist that he wanted to heal Alistair. I talked to my husband about it. When David Watson came to our home I mentioned it to him, and I also asked for Jean Darnall's advice. Everyone seemed to be of the opinion that this was indeed the voice of God. So I discussed it with Alistair. To my surprise he agreed to receive the laying on of hands and prayer for healing.

I was grateful that Jean Darnall happened to be in Nottingham at the time and gave me the privilege of praying with her. She was experienced in these things. I was a novice. And Alistair had surrendered his life to Christ only twelve hours earlier. Even so, as we prayed it became clear that something dramatic was happening to Alistair's body. When we finished praying he stood up, and as he walked around our lounge an impish grin spread from ear to ear. Next he came over to the settee where Jean and I sat watching him and knelt on the floor in front of us. Alistair kneeling? His knees had been stiff as sticks for years. Now he could bend them without pain.

That whisper I had heard: 'I want to heal him,' had been God's voice. And I was glad I had been given the grace not simply to hear but to take the risk and obey.

On another occasion, while I was waiting on God in preparation for a counselling session with a couple whose marriage was going through a sticky patch, I simply heard one word: 'mother'. I had no idea what it meant. But as I chatted to this couple, it quickly became evident that the man resented his mother because she had smothered him not only when he was a child but as a teenager too. He had always allowed his mother to dominate him, even though he hated himself for it. But now, if his wife began to behave in a way which reminded him of his mother, he reacted angrily and lashed out at his wife in the way he would have liked to have thumped his mother. Again the divine diagnosis had given me a clue. It was clear how I could help this particular couple in crisis.

Sometimes I would sense what *God* was wanting to do. There was the time when I was listening to a person pour out white-hot anger about her husband, the church, her colleagues and God, for example. I was finding it difficult to be on the receiving end of all this venom and when we prayed together I could find no words. Instead, into the silence came a picture of a hedgehog being held in the curve of a big hand. I sensed that the prickly creature was this woman, that the hand was God's and he was trying to tell me that, despite her anger, he loved her and understood her anguish. There was no need for me to describe this picture to the person concerned. It was sufficient that God had shown me how to pray for her.

But these times of solitude served another purpose too. To share someone else's burden can be like carrying a heavy rucksack: a strain. I would sometimes come to God over-burdened, exhausted and over-identifying with a complaint once made by Michel Quoist:

> Lord, why did you tell me to love all men, my brothers? . . .
> They are bending under heavy loads; loads of injustice, of resentment and hate, of suffering and sin . . .
> They drag the world behind them, with everything rusted, twisted, or badly adjusted.
> Lord, they hurt me! . . .
> They are consuming me! . . .
> What about my job?
>   my family?
>   my peace?
>   my liberty?
>   and me?[12]

At such times I would catch myself worrying about what was going to happen to the person I was trying to help. Like an overwound spring, my mind would cease to function efficiently and I would feel spiritually drained and dry.

In *Listening to God* I have explained that I was learning the value of spending an hour in my prayer room each morning, taking time out to go away for a Quiet Day regularly and making a retreat two or three times a year. I was also exploring the gift of contemplation which I sensed God was giving me; learning that the first phase is relaxation. 'Relax. Let the pressures roll off you. Put your burdens down,' the voice of God seemed to say. And I would picture Jesus standing in front of me with his big strong arms outspread, ready to receive to himself the burdens which were proving too heavy for me to carry. And I would let go of them and the other pressures and anxieties which were paralysing me and, while relaxing, I would become aware of the presence of the living God and open myself up to him completely.

Contemplation is about putting ourselves in the hands of the God who loves us, experiencing that love, basking in its radiance and warmth; being overwhelmed by its power, responding to it; being transformed by its tenderness, strengthened by the giver's compassion; being met in our emptiness by the fullness of God, being found in our lostness by the Shepherd who cares; being refreshed by his never-failing well-springs, being refilled by his life-giving Spirit; discovering by experience the truth of his promises: 'I will come to you', 'My strength is made perfect in your weakness.'

The more I gave, not only to my husband, my children and my friends but to people in need as well, the more I panted for these times of solitude with God. Catharine de Hueck Doherty's observation seemed particularly relevant:

If we are to witness to Christ in today's market places, where there are constant demands on our whole person, we need silence. If we are to be always available, not only physically, but by empathy, sympathy, friendship, understanding and boundless *caritas*, we need silence. To be able to give joyous, unflagging hospitality, not only of house and food, but of mind, heart, body and soul, we need silence.[13]

In the silence and solitude of my prayer room I would sometimes lie prostrate at the foot of the cross which hung on my wall and admit to God: 'All I have to offer you is my emptiness. Please fill me.' And very often the tenderness of his presence and love would creep over me and the words of this hymn would take on new meaning:

O the deep, deep love of Jesus!
vast, unmeasured, boundless, free;
Rolling as a mighty ocean
In its fullness over me.
Underneath me, all around me,
Is the current of Thy love;
Leading onward, leading homeward,
To Thy glorious rest above.
    (Samuel Trevor Francis 1834–1925)

Praying for a heart that listens

Just as listening to people is not so much a technique as an attitude, so listening to God is an attitude of heart every would-be people helper needs to cultivate. Solomon summed the situation up right at the beginning of his reign when he prayed: 'Give me, O Lord, a heart that listens.'

That is an amazing prayer in the light of the invitation God had given him: to ask for whatever he wanted. This verse (1 Kgs. 3:9) has been variously translated: an attentive heart, an intelligent heart, a heart full of judgement, a heart full of understanding, a wise heart, a discerning heart. The prayer seems to include all these shades of meaning and many more besides for Solomon was not simply asking for the gift of wisdom which would have boosted his own ego and therefore been a personal enrichment and gain. What he did was to ask for 'that openness of heart which is a preparation for the reception of wisdom'; a soul which listened out for every appeal and whisper from God, which was constantly on the watch for every breath of the Spirit and which so opened itself to people that it offered them 'an interior welcome at a deep level' and a silence so impregnated with love that it tuned in accurately to the groans of sufferers.[14]

That was the kind of prayer that was being born in my own heart. It is the prayer that everyone who would be effective in helping hurting people needs to pray. And we can take courage from the fact that God so obviously delighted in this prayer when it fell from Solomon's lips. But even as I have recalled these early lessons in learning for the sake of writing this chapter and the last, I recognise that it is much easier to know that the heart that listens can be of greater value to the poor and the sick than food or comfort and it is much easier to write about the theory of good listening than to translate that theory into practice. I still break the most basic rules. And so I take comfort from Roger Hurding's observation:

> The Spirit-filled, fruit-bearing Christian is likely to be endowed with a genuineness that arises from goodness and faithfulness, a non-possessive warmth that is fostered by kindness, gentleness and self-control, and an accurate empathy sustained by patience, all under-girded by peace and joy, and motivated by love.[15]

I take heart too from the awareness that God uses as an instrument of healing even our imperfect listening. I was reminded of this fact while I was writing this book.

A girl broke down and wept after a church service where I had been speaking. Another woman and I listened to her story and I was somewhat appalled and critical to hear and see my companion break most of the ground rules of good listening before launching into a long emotional prayer for the person in pain. But at the end of the prayer the girl beamed with joy: 'God has really touched me,' she testified and as she left us her face was wreathed in smiles.

This divine overruling does not excuse us from paying careful attention to the discipline and art form of good listening. Nor must we assume naively that, since God is the one at work, what we do matters little. If we are truly concerned about people and truly concerned to be channels through whom he can work, we will do all in our power to go on and on improving our listening skills so that God's work may be perfected in us.

That this may become more and more true in me, I continue to pray, with Mother Teresa of Calcutta:

Dear Jesus, help me to spread your fragrance everywhere I go. Flood my soul with your spirit and life. Penetrate and possess my whole being so utterly that my life may only be a radiance of yours. Shine through me, and so be in me, that every soul I come in contact with may feel your presence. Let them look up and see no longer me but only Jesus. Stay with me, and then I shall begin to shine as you shine; so to shine as to be a light to others; the light O Jesus, will be all from you, none of it will be mine; it will be you shining on others through me. Let me praise you in the way you love best by shining on those around me. Let me preach you, not by words only, but by the catching force of example, the evident fullness of the love my heart bears to you.[16]

7

Listening to the Bereaved

Listening to others is much harder than it sounds. That was the conclusion I reached soon after I began the counselling course at St John's College. That conviction has grown with the years. Indeed listening to others is so complex that I sometimes think we need four ears, not just two – one to listen to the words a person speaks, another to pick up that person's feelings, a third to tune in to God and a fourth inner ear to hear what is going on inside ourselves.

To listen to ourselves. At first it came as a surprise to me to realise that if we are to listen to others accurately we must know how to listen to ourselves.

Myra Chave-Jones[1] explains one reason why this is so important. 'If we're not in touch with ourselves, we shan't be in touch with the people out there.' In underlining that listening is like receiving a gift from someone she challenges would-be listeners to examine the way in which they receive the delicate offerings of a person's innermost thoughts and feelings:

Are you really eager to receive them? Do you handle them with care as you would a valuable present? Or are you just waiting for a pause in the conversation so that you can say something? What kind of people do you find it most difficult to identify with? Why? What makes it hard for you to receive their gift? Do you have any particular fears or phobias: of death, for example, or of cancer? Or are there any bees in your bonnet which might affect the way you listen: 'I must press everyone I meet to make a decision for Jesus.' Or are there things you find it hard to hear from others? Such self-knowledge is vital if we are to be effective in our helping of others.

I discovered the truth of this claim when I made my earliest adventures into self-awareness. I discovered, for example, that I am a warm person who needs to give love and to receive it. This is both a strength and a weakness. The strength is obvious because this love includes the compassion I mentioned at the beginning of this book which is the prerequisite of good people-helping. But the weakness is more subtle. Warm loving people can smother others or cling to them or be possessive and jealous. And warm people are inclined to hug or put an arm around others when what the other person needs is space. This is something I have to be careful of so that I do not invade another person's privacy nor offer protective love when the person would grow faster if I stood back and allowed them time to grow without my support.

I also discovered that, because of the mistakes I made personally when learning to listen to God, I had developed an ingrained suspicion of anyone who claims 'The Lord has told me to do this'. If a young person came to me and said, 'The Lord has told me to marry so and so,' I would feel my tummy muscles tighten, my eyes harden and words of caution rushing to my lips. Often I would catch myself being far more anxious to warn such people against the dangers of self-deceit than to listen to their joy or their pain. I realised too that I had an intolerance of garrulous people who talk at me rather than to me. When such people started telling me their story I would switch off, hear the seemingly-endless stream of words, but fail to tune in to the insecurities which the multiplicity of words were camouflaging. It surprised me to discover that with such people I would feel not compassion, but impatience. My own impatience would then hurtle me on to a guilt trip. John Powell shows how such 'hidden agendas' block the path to good listening:

Pain has a way of magnetizing our attention to ourselves . . . Almost continually we experience some feelings of inadequacy, inferiority, anxiety, and guilt. If we let these feelings attract all our attention, we will have little presence to offer others. We will have a neon sign on our foreheads, flashing: 'Not Available'.[2]

Another reason why self-awareness is important is that, when a person is being helped through a crisis, it is easy for them to imagine that their helpers might be critical of them or even despairing of them. 'You must be tired of hearing all my troubles,' one might say. 'You must think I'm terribly boring,' another might suggest. 'I must be a terrible disappointment to you – I mean, your prayers haven't been answered, have they?' a third person might whisper, projecting their own worries on to the person seeking to help.

It is safer to face such fears than to conceal them. But if we are to encourage others to be as honest, open and vulnerable as this, we must be prepared to be equally open about our own feelings so that our response is genuine: 'Well, actually, it may surprise you to hear that I don't find you or your problems boring. Do you?' Or 'I want you to know that *you* are not a disappointment to me. I'm disappointed for you. But *you* certainly haven't disappointed me. Are you disappointed with yourself?'

When it came to responding to situations like this, I encountered a problem – a gross lack of self-awareness. Often I was not sufficiently in touch with my thoughts and feelings to be able to respond with the genuineness, spontaneity and sensitivity which is required. So I had to learn.

Much of that learning was painful. Among other things it involved confronting some soul-searching questions. Why did I want to listen to people? Was it because I enjoyed having people confide their troubles in me? If so, why? Was it because this boosted my morale; made me feel important? Was it because I was curious about the troubles others face? Was it because I needed to be needed? Or was I, perhaps, feeding on these people emotionally – using people in need as a substitute for the mutuality of friendship?

I also worked hard to understand myself better and, in order to do this, would liken the various parts of myself to the segments of an orange. 'When you cut the orange in half, what do you find?' I would say to myself as I tramped the hills of Derbyshire, spent a quiet day at the convent or beavered away at my desk.

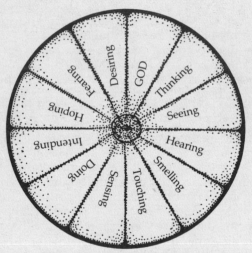

The segments of my orange

What is going on in your mind? What are you thinking about?

What is going on in your emotions? What are you feeling?

What is going on in your senses? What can you see? What can you hear? What can you smell? What can you feel? What kind of vibes are you picking up?

What is going on in your body? What are you doing with it?

What are your intentions?
What are your hopes?
What are your fears?
What are your desires?
Where are you in your relationship to God?

Listening to pain

Learning to listen to myself in this way became an
adventure alongside the other adventures of listening to
God and to people. But there were times when listening
to myself became almost more painful than I could cope
with.

I first became aware of this when the subject we were
studying at St John's was bereavement.

Right at the beginning of the seminar we were invited
to break up into little groups of three and to talk to the
others in our group about a bereavement we had experienced. The word bereavement was used in its widest
sense to mean loss through death; or the loss some
people feel when they move from a familiar area to a new
one; or the losses incurred by redundancy or when a
close friend has married and the relationship with them
has had to change gear; or a broken engagement. Even as
we shuffled our chairs around the lecture room I detected
a nervous fluttering in my stomach – as though a
thousand butterflies had been let loose inside me. I
noticed too a tightening in my throat. Panic gave rise to
fear and I was conscious that tears were already pricking
my eyes. When my turn came to speak, I described the
events leading up to my mother's death.

Mother's death

As so often happens, even though my mother had been
ill for so many years the end came suddenly. There had
been several 'false alarms' when one of my relatives had
phoned our Parkstone home to warn me that my mother

might not live much longer. But she had always rallied and resumed her semi-invalid life once more.

So one Sunday night when my sister-in-law telephoned to say that my mother was in hospital again, I saw no need to drop everything and drive to Exeter immediately. I would come in the morning, I promised.

On Monday I drove to Exeter as fast as I could and arrived at the hospital to find my mother already in a coma. I sat by her bed and held her hand, talked to her and prayed with her. But she did not stir. I felt helpless.

The hospital staff warned me that she could linger in this state for days so I drove to Roberts Road to be with my father. We spent most of that day and evening at my mother's bedside, leaving her only to go to my brother's home to eat and to return home to sleep. Early on Tuesday morning we returned. Having been at the bedside for several hours, my father and I decided to return to Roberts Road for an hour or so and to return to the hospital ward that evening. My father kissed my mother tenderly and spoke to her as naturally as though she were fully conscious. 'Cheerio Win! I'll come and see you again later.'

I too kissed her, but though I had been told that a person in a coma can hear the things that are said to them, I now found it impossible to speak. Suddenly I was tongue-tied, not knowing what to say to a mother who was visibly slipping away from us. But I admired my father's lack of inhibition and hoped my mother could hear and feel the warmth and the genuineness of this man who had loved her for so many years and at such great cost to himself.

We had scarcely unlocked the bottle-green door when there was a knock on it. It was Mr Cartwright, the new neighbour in number 38 who was a great friend of my father. Since there was no phone in my parents' home my father had left this man's number at the hospital. Now the request had come. Would my father please telephone.

My father rushed into number 28. A few minutes later

he returned looking shocked. All colour had drained from his cheeks and, turning a ghostly white, he simply said: 'She's gone. The Sister said she died about a quarter of an hour after we left.'

I was speechless. While my father slumped into 'his' chair – the one by the wireless where he prayed in the evenings – and put his head in his hands and sobbed, I went into the front room. Dazed.

There on the floor lay a rolled-up carpet which my parents had chosen together a few days before my mother had been admitted to hospital. She would never enjoy it now. I gazed out of the window at the scarlet telephone box across the road. Soon I would need to spend a long time in that box informing relatives and friends. 'Mum died this afternoon.' I wanted them all to know but I did not want to be the one to tell them. It sounded so final. And I was not sure that I believed it. Truths like that are hard to drink in. Yet deep down I knew it was true and in the privacy of that room, where for so many years I had slaved away at my homework, I now gave vent to my feelings in the only way I knew how – with a few stifled sobs.

Grief work

It seemed as though I had only just begun to tell the students this story when Anne called us back so that she could begin her lecture on bereavement.

In telling my story I had not cried. But the exercise had served its purpose. It had brought to the surface the emotions I had felt at the time of my mother's death and now I listened, fascinated, while Anne explained to us what usually happens to a person when a loved one dies or when they are bereaved for some other reason.

There is a recognisable pattern of grief, she explained – stages the bereaved person goes through while they struggle to come to terms with what has happened. The first reaction is shock.

I could identify with that. The feeling of disbelief

stayed with me for days after my mother's death. In fact I walked around like someone suffering from concussion. My brain seemed to be paralysed. It refused to function. I felt like a zombie.

This was embarrassing because it meant that I found it almost impossible to make decisions. The day after my mother died I drove my father to the hospital to collect her few belongings. These were neatly piled up on a table. We simply had to check them, then sign for them.

'Do you want to keep her wedding ring?' they asked my father. 'Or shall we leave it on her finger?'

My father looked startled. 'What do you think?' he asked, turning to me. A wave of disgust swept over me preventing me from finding an answer. What did it matter about a ring? It wasn't a ring which either of us wanted at that moment. We wanted the owner of the ring to rise from the dead – at least to say goodbye to us. My father made his own decision. He asked for the ring.

On the way home it was my father who broke the silence. 'I suppose we ought to go shopping. There's nothing for dinner.'

I parked the car. Together we wandered around a supermarket. But it was as though we were in a dream – or perhaps living a nightmare.

'What would you like for your dinner?' I asked. My father replied that he had lost his appetite. I understood. I did not feel like eating anything either. Neither did I feel that I could summon the energy to decide which food-stuffs to buy from the bewildering selection facing me in the supermarket. That indecisiveness worried me. I was not normally like this. What was happening to me? Was I going mad?

After wandering round the maze of shelves for nearly half an hour we decided to buy a packet of sliced ham. 'There's some pickle in the cupboard,' my father recalled. That lunch-time we ate mechanically and because we knew it was the sensible thing to do. But the meal might have been plastic. The ham, pickle and mashed potatoes were tasteless. Bland.

Yes. Anne was correct when she said that the bereaved person may experience numbness, disorganisation, bewilderment, deep sighing and restlessness. That had certainly been my experience and my father's. It was as though we were viewing life from the double-glazed window of a high tower office block watching the world go by yet not feeling a part of that world – not even wanting to be a part of it.

Emptiness, pining and regrets

The second stage of grief is marked by a persistent longing for the lost one, psychologists warn. There is a feeling of emptiness. The bereaved person may pine for the loved one; they may well weep or attempt to search for the one they have lost.

When I read claims like these I would have more flashbacks to the days following my mother's death. On the evening of her death, my father and I reached for the St Bruno tobacco tin which still sat in the sideboard and still contained the old photographs I had so enjoyed scrutinising as a child. Now my father sorted them out, selecting the ones in which my mother featured. There was a picture of her before she had married my father. There was a picture of them on their wedding day. There was a picture of her with Ray wearing his navy uniform.

More recent photographs were then found in the sideboard drawer. A picture of my mother with Ray's baby daughter, her first grandchild. A picture of her with John, my other brother. Some lovely shots of her with my father on that memorable holiday near Southampton at the time of my graduation. And one of her outside Salisbury Cathedral with my husband on his Ordination day. She looked so petite against my six-foot-tall, well-built husband.

We spent hours too trying to decide what to write as an obituary for the *Express and Echo*, Exeter's evening newspaper. While we toyed with various phrases, she still seemed to be a part of us. And that was what we wanted.

The books on bereavement which I read as part of my training emphasised that the bereaved person will often cherish mementoes of the loved one in an attempt to keep their memory alive. It is a natural, normal reaction. And so is the idealisation of the loved one. I smiled as I recalled the phrases my father insisted on using for my mother's obituary. 'Beloved wife'; 'loving mother of all her children'; 'forty-three years of happily married life'. Of course all of these things were true. But there was another side. We had sometimes felt irritated and frustrated by my mother's refusal to give in. But all memory of that was banished with her death.

During this phase of grieving my father also wanted to see her lying in her coffin. My heart stood still with fear when he announced this was what he wanted and asked whether I wanted to go too.

If I had been brutally honest I would have said no, that was not what I wanted. But by this time Ray had emigrated to Australia. John was suffering from kidney failure, too ill to help, so that left me to accompany him.

'Isn't she lovely!' my father exclaimed when he saw her body. But after that we said nothing. Instead we just gazed, trying to drink in the mystery and, in the silence, said the goodbyes of the heart which we had not been able to say in the hospital. In seeing her lying there in the coffin, it was as though we had found her and that was what we both wanted and needed at that moment.

All the books explained that bereaved people are often oppressed by guilt and feelings of self-reproach. This also rang true in my own experience. In the hours following my mother's death, on the rare occasions when my mind would engage, I would chastise myself: 'If only you'd left Parkstone earlier, you might have arrived at the hospital before she went into a coma.' 'If only you hadn't left the hospital that afternoon you would have been with her at the moment when she went into the presence of Jesus.'

'If only . . .' 'if only . . .' This was a phrase my father used frequently too. 'If only they'd told us that she was about to die we needn't have come home.' It is a phrase which comes quickly to the lips of the grief-stricken person. It expresses one of the phases of grief.

Practical, emotional and spiritual help

At the beginning of the session on bereavement Anne had invited us to recall those who had helped us at a time when we were bereaved. Now she invited us to share our findings.

The exercise made me profoundly grateful to those who had not abandoned my father and me to the desolation of bereavement but who had come to give us practical, emotional and spiritual support.

My sister-in-law was one. While my mother was in hospital and on those traumatic days after her death, Anne cooked a meal for my father and me every evening. That saved us the effort of shopping and cooking and clearing up. I was grateful for that. Both my father and I seemed to be dogged with tiredness. Preparing meals when neither of us had an appetite would have been one burden too many. There were so many things to remember as it was: collecting the death certificate and finding the place to collect it from, visiting the undertaker, selecting hymns for the funeral, choosing a coffin, writing to friends and relatives, ordering wreaths. Yes. That practical help carried us through those days when we seemed to be working on automatic.

The Roberts Road community played their part too. Once the news had sunk in, 'Win is dead,' my father went into the front room and drew the curtains. Then he went to his bedroom and did the same before opening a drawer and taking out a black tie and a black arm band which he proceeded to wear whenever he went out of the house.

These were his ways of announcing to the neighbours that my mother had died. There was no need to say anything. That would have been too painful for everyone. Those who saw the signs interpreted the code. The bush telegraph did the rest.

From the time the curtains were drawn until several days after the funeral, the customary hush enshrouded Roberts Road. People whispered when they passed our house. If neighbours saw me on my own they would ask how my father had taken it. But if they saw him with me they would simply say, 'Hello, Mr Duguid' or 'Hello, Sid', with a tenderness that communicated. They understood. They cared. But they did not want to intrude.

This solidarity with our pain helped. Other people, like the ones shopping in the supermarket we had visited, carried on with the rush and tumble of their normal everyday life. But not our neighbours. They stopped as best they could and identified with our grief by sharing it. This helped to silence within me the protest I had wanted to make on that shopping expedition: 'My mother has just died. How *can* you carry on living as though nothing had happened?'

We were grateful to the Roberts Road community. We were grateful too that some people plucked up the courage to visit us.

Aunt Rene came with her husband and listened while my father related the events of the final hours of my mother's life. Aunt Sally and Aunt Lize, two of my favourite great aunts, came and listened while we went over the story again. Mr Bolt the butcher called even though he had sold his business and now lived fifteen miles away and had to travel in by bus. And Mr Cartwright came from number 28 and just sat with my father and never seemed to mind if he wept.

These listeners comforted us more than they knew. My father and I, like most bereaved people, just longed to talk about my mother. When we were on our own we talked about her most of the time. When compassionate people came to our home and allowed us to talk about our loss, allowing us to cry if the tears flowed, they were God's instruments of healing to us, though they probably never realised it.

Simon Stephens has put the situation well:

To be a compassionate listener, then, is the role of relatives and friends in this particular crisis situation. They must forget self and encourage the bereaved to talk at length and in detail about their loss. There will be tears and long silences. They will hear the life history of the deceased person and the intimate details of his or her death bed over and over again. The compassionate listener need say very little, for his interested presence at the side of the mourner is far more important than anything that he can say. Just to be there and listening to what the mourner has to say is a major contribution to that person's social re-habilitation. It is no easy task! Sometimes it is very painful and distressing.[3]

Others who paid us shorter visits were appreciated quite as much as those who stayed longer. Mr Kettlewell, who used to be headmaster of the School for the Deaf but was now retired, came to offer his sincere sympathy. Our family doctor came. And the vicar came and helped us to plan the funeral.

The funeral! I sometimes wondered how we would get through that service. It all felt so public. But again people ministered God's healing to our heartbreak, not by anything they said but simply by their presence.

When my father and I were disgorged from the funeral car at the top of the stony church drive, we were ushered to our place behind the waiting coffin. The sight of that elm box with its brass handles was like a slap in the face. The last time we had stood together on that spot was on my wedding day when my father was so proud to have me on his arm; dressed in all my wedding finery. Now we were dressed sombrely and together we were giving my mother away. We could no longer deny the harsh reality. Mum was dead. For a few agonising minutes the anaesthetic of grief wore off. Our wounds were exposed. And we stumbled, weeping, behind that flower-studded box into the church. But once we reached the church porch everything changed. 'Look at all those people,' my father whispered. I looked – and gasped. The church was packed. The presence of those people who had taken the trouble to take time off work to come to say goodbye to my mother strengthened us more than anything else could have done in that moment.

I saw my godfather who had given me the Raleigh bicycle when I won my scholarship to grammar school. I noticed Mrs Furseman who had been a waitress with my mother at Tinlay's Cafe. And I spotted several neighbours: Mr and Mrs Tolman, Mr and Mrs Bolt, and Fred Vosper who lived at 32 Roberts Road, to mention a few.

The strength that flowed into me as I stared at them, emptily but gratefully, took me by surprise. I did not know in those days what I now know; that the word comfort means to strengthen. What I did know was that these people who were not saying or doing anything except by being there were giving me untold comfort.

And so were the words of scripture. As we processed up the aisle, those words of Jesus which the vicar was reading aloud tumbled round my bruised heart and soothed the pain: 'Jesus said: "I am the resurrection and the life. He who believes in me will live, even though he dies; and whoever lives and believes in me will never die"' (John 11:25–26).

'It's not your mother in that box,' these words seemed to say. 'That's only her earthly remains. She lives on.'

I knew that to be true and again I was strengthened – so much so that I could sing the hymns with conviction and confidence. God's presence and love seemed very real. And had not my father and I read together on the night my mother died those wonderful promises penned by the Psalmist:

> He who dwells in the shelter of the Most High
>   will rest in the shadow of the Almighty . . .
> He will cover you with his feathers,
>   and under his wings you will find refuge.
>   (Ps. 91:1,4)

Even so I was grateful for others who incarnated God's love for my father and me.

My eighty-year-old Uncle Bob did this in the funeral car as we travelled to the crematorium. He spent the entire journey quizzing me about my relationship with God.

'I was watching you during the service,' he said. 'You seemed to believe everything you were hearing and seeing. I wish I could find such assurance of God's love.

'It's strange,' he went on. 'I've been playing the double bass in Handel's *Messiah* every year for as long as I care to remember. I've listened to all those wonderful words. But I still lack the trust in God which seems to be your mainstay.'

In reply I was able to testify to the fact that I was experiencing the divine overshadowing the Psalmist describes and that it was under the wings of God that I found my security in times of testing and trauma. He listened. And giving voice to God's faithfulness increased that sense in me of the peace of God which defies understanding and circumstances and pervades even in the middle of the storm.

Letters and ongoing love

Uncle Bob and the other relatives crowded into number 24 after the funeral. Though I had dreaded this part of the post-funeral proceedings, I found that this too helped. There was only one topic of conversation – my mother. And that continued to be healing.

We all read and re-read the letters which had come trickling in when news of my mother's death had percolated round the city. The appreciation of my mother's pluck, my father's faithfulness, the assurance of people's prayers and their support of us as a family, humbled and helped us. My father had already read these countless times. He was to drink in the consolation they brought very often.

We all admired the bouquet of flowers which someone

had delivered for my father and me on the morning of the funeral. 'These are not for the cemetery,' they had said as they thrust them into my arms, 'they are for the ones who are left behind.'

And we all looked at the photographs which my father had stuck in the red leather-bound album he had bought with some money Aunt Sally had given him 'to buy something for yourself to remind you of Win'.

That gathering was rather like a party. A farewell party, it is true. But a most satisfactory and satisfying one none the less.

Then came the slump.

Uncle Bob and his wife left, promising to write to me. Aunt Rene and her husband left, promising to come to see my father soon. David went to fetch our two children who had been looked after for the afternoon by the curate's wife. And my father and I were left with a haze of memories and impressions and a long lonely evening with only the coal fire for comfort.

I shall never forget the relief I felt when Mr Cartwright called that evening. We needed to talk to someone about the wonderful day we had just had. And he came and listened. He would have known nothing of the principles of good listening Anne was teaching us in the St John's course. It did not matter. It was enough that he cared enough to come, to stay, to listen until it was obvious that those pangs of loneliness had been alleviated, at least for that evening. But of course they were to return – especially for my father.

I stayed with him for several days, but David and our two children had returned to Dorset and we all knew that the day would have to come when I would leave my father to work through the remainder of his grieving alone. That day arrived. As I stepped over the brass doorstep to walk to my Dormobile, the pain of the impending separation seemed almost too much to bear.

'Thanks for all you've done, Joycie!' my father managed to mutter through his tears.

'I'll write,' I blurted out, brushing my own tears from

my cheeks and kissing him goodbye before climbing into the driver's seat, starting the engine and driving down Roberts Road, past the butcher's, the grocer's, the dairy, the post office and the stationers and turning right into Holloway Street.

'For me, life will rush on as usual,' I mused. 'I have a home to run, a husband and two children to look after, a young wives' group to lead, and a youth group to care for. But dad! He has no one. Nothing. Time will drag.'

Time did drag. During this period my father kept a diary which shows how the few things he did were closely intertwined with the memory of my mother. These entries are typical of many others:

Tuesday	Stayed in.
Wednesday	A fairly quiet morning.
Thursday	Went to see old Mrs Arcott (a lady he and my mother had known forty years earlier).
Friday	Stayed in.
Saturday	Stayed in.
Sunday	Church service.

From time to time he would emerge from this lethargy and enjoy spurts of hyper-activity:

Monday	New carpet laid. Grocery cupboard cleared out.
Tuesday	Shopping and visiting.
Wednesday	Helped Mr Cartwright this evening. Paid funeral expenses.
Thursday	Went for long walk today. Did some shopping in Tinlay's (the cafe where my mother had been a waitress).
Friday	Cleaned right through the house. Did some shopping.
Saturday	Spending the weekend with Reg Bolt at Topsham.

But this outgoing phase would quickly pass to give way to another period of apathy when he would experience that down-drag of bereavement when the loss feels so all-embracing that it seems impossible to get going again in any meaningful way.

A whole variety of people continued to help. The vicar called regularly and encouraged my father to join the Monday meeting for men. My sister-in-law and the Cartwrights continued to invite him for meals regularly. People brought him home-made cakes. And all of this eased this pain for which there are no pain killers – the pain of bereavement.

Colin Murray Parkes underlines the value of such practical care:

> The funeral often precedes the peak of the pangs of grief, which tends to be reached during the second week of bereavement. The 'bold face' put on for the funeral can then no longer be maintained and there is a need for some close relative or friend to take over many of the accustomed roles and responsibilities of the bereaved person, thereby setting him or her free to grieve. The person who is most valued at this time is not the one who expresses the most sympathy but the person who 'sticks around', quietly gets on with day-to-day household tasks and makes few demands upon the bereaved.[4]

Meanwhile, for me, life *did* go on much as usual. At times I could even forget that my mother had died so recently and I would imagine that I was recovering from my bereavement quickly, until something happened to jolt me into the painful realisation that the pangs of grief are not easily silenced.

My mother died in January. That March, as Mother's day approached, I went as usual to buy her a card. I had the carefully chosen card in my hand and was about to pay for it when I realised what I was doing.

I put the card back in the rack, and sobbed all the way home. 'I haven't got a mother.' The realisation still stung.

A similar thing happened at Christmas. I went into a

shoe shop to buy my mother some slippers for a present, when again the realisation dawned that she would not be needing slippers this year.

But this time I did not sob. I smiled. It was a sign to me that, after eleven months of grieving, I really was recovering. The final phase of grieving, I was to learn at St John's, comes when we are ready to re-negotiate life on a new set of terms. It was not that I loved my mother any less. It simply meant that I was ready to say the necessary goodbye and to live life without her.

My father too seemed to be gaining a new identity. The tone of his letters was changing. He had become verger of the Baptist Church where he worshipped each week and obviously took a pride in polishing the pews and bringing a shine to the silver. He no longer seemed preoccupied with memories of my mother nor did he idealise her any longer. Instead he began to express concern about my brother's failing health. And shortly after the anniversary of my mother's death, he wrote to say he would like to see me because he had something to discuss with me.

When I arrived at number 24, he broke the news that he had met a wonderful widow at church. How would I feel if he married again? They were both lonely and each found in the other the companion they so much needed.

Later that year David preached at my father's wedding at South Street Baptist Church. We rejoiced with him in this new start in life. Since my father was to move to his wife's home, David and I offered to clear number 24 of its furniture. As we loaded into the van the wardrobe and chest of drawers that I had tried so hard to polish when I was still a child, the sideboard which had housed the photographs that had given me so much pleasure, and the carpet my father had laid after my mother died, I realised that this was the end of a chapter. But as we closed the front door of number 24 for the last time and I took a last look at the street which had been home for so many years, it did not occur to me that this painful year had marked a turning point in my life for another reason;

that because of it I was to become one of God's wounded healers.

But as I listened to the teaching on bereavement Anne was giving the students at St John's, I knew that, just as others had reached out to me when I was in need, so I wanted to reach out to those who were struggling to find their way through the maze of feelings which confuse most people when they suffer the loss of someone or something they love. Even so, I was aware, as I listened to Anne, that though healing had come to touch and soothe the wounds inflicted by the loss of my mother; and although the reactions my father and I had experienced in the aftermath of her death were perfectly natural and normal, deep inside me there lurked pangs of bereavement that had never been touched. It was when Anne began to describe what can happen to a person who does not grieve when a loved one dies that those butterflies started fluttering in my stomach again and I began to panic.

Listening to Past Pain

Psychiatrists warn us that one of the most severe strains we ever have to face is the loss of a loved one through death. Even when that person's death is to be expected, because, like my mother, they have been ill for many years, those who are left behind often suffer an acute sense of shock when the news reaches them that their loved one has died. But when one we love dies suddenly so that we have had no time to prepare for it, the shock is greater, the grief may last longer, more long-term damage may be done, and an anxiety state may be precipitated.

And my brother John died suddenly.

Soon after my father remarried, my husband and I moved to Cambridge where David was to serve his second curacy. We had been there just over a year when, one Monday evening, my sister-in-law Anne telephoned with the news: 'John died this afternoon.'

The sense of shock was so great that words seemed to freeze in my throat. 'Oh! No!' was all I could manage by way of reaction at first. After Anne had assured me that she and the children were being well supported by neighbours, I put the phone down. I was in David's study at the time but before I could go to share the news with him I had to cling to his grey, steel desk. Dazed, devastated as I was, everything in the room seemed to be swimming round me as I tried to drink in the news.

John dead? How could he be? He was only thirty-four years old. He had two young children – just a few years older than my own son and daughter. He had so much to live for: a good job, a comfortable home, the youth group at church. And when they had come to stay a few weeks earlier he had looked so fit – better than he had looked for a year or more. Oh yes. There was that kidney trouble that had been troubling him. But the kidney machine had been dealing with that. The doctor had told him that the prognosis was good – very good. He cannot have died. There must be some mistake.

But there was no mistake. John had died. And a few days later David and I drove to Exeter for his funeral.

Even when I entered John's home I refused to believe he was gone. I looked for him. And as we sat in his lounge waiting for the car to fetch family and friends for the funeral, I felt irritated. What were we all doing there? Why were all these people talking about my brother as though he had ceased to exist?

And everything hurt. John failed to appear. That hurt. Anne seemed to be well in control. That hurt. She read several letters she had received that morning, including one from the Grandmaster of the lodge where my brother had been a freemason. That sent a sharp pain right through me.

The funeral car arrived. I was relieved. I needed to escape from the claustrophobia of that house. The driver was an old friend of John's. They had played the bugles together in the Roberts Road Boys' Brigade. He and I talked about old times all the way to the church. Our reminiscing seemed to make John real again. I needed that. He simply could not be dead.

In contrast to my mother's funeral, going through the motions at John's was like living a nightmare. The church was strange. I recognised few people. David, my husband, walked with Anne. My father was with his new wife. I was alone. Desolate. Even those words of scripture which had seemed so comforting at my mother's funeral: 'I am the resurrection and the life . . .' brought no peace. They seemed to bounce off the cold stone walls of the unfamiliar church, echo round the barn-like building and mock. And a terrible and turbulent darkness seemed to whirl round me with hurricane force and ferocity. Even when the funeral was over the storm refused to subside, and though we drove to John's home I could not face going back into that house where every room and piece of furniture, every picture and cushion reminded me of my tall handsome, fair-haired, impeccably-dressed brother, who would normally be there teasing me and calling me by my pet name 'Joycie', but who had departed this life suddenly and unexpectedly without giving anyone an opportunity to say goodbye. Sobbing on my father's shoulder I begged him to give my apologies to my relatives. And David and I drove home.

The darkness continued to engulf me for the entire journey. David and I scarcely said a word. I could not bring myself to share this inner emptiness even with my husband. Instead I pushed the horrible heaviness of John's tragic death deep inside me and, locking the cellar door, I behaved as though death had not revisited our family. I filled the days that followed with frenetic activity.

A series of losses

At first this proved difficult because, in Cambridge, the expectation of me, the curate's wife, was quite different from the expectations which had been placed upon me in the Parkstone parish. In our first curacy I was expected to be the proverbial 'unpaid curate'. And I loved it. But not so in Cambridge. The vicar we worked with was a bachelor who had had a string of bachelor curates. The parish was not used to a clergy wife and instead of depending on one, several members of the church performed more than, adequately the tasks traditionally assigned to the wife of the vicar or his assistant.

In the absence of fixed roles within the fellowship, I looked outside for an outlet for my gifts and found myself a part-time job teaching speech to two pre-school deaf children. I loved these little girls and had great fun helping them to voice their very first words. But within the church I found no immediate natural niche. Perhaps this was one reason why I refused to confront my grief. I do not know. What I do know is that if I had understood then that bereavement means loss – any kind of loss – I hope I would have reacted differently. I now realise that people grieve, not only because a love tie has been severed through death, but they may well grieve in the wake of any other loss: the loss of a limb through surgery or accident, the loss of a job through redundancy or retirement, the loss of treasured possessions, freedom, status or home, the loss of a loved one through a broken engagement or divorce or a move. And the loss of 'what might have been' is a form of bereavement that childless couples recovering from a miscarriage, and some single people who would love to marry, suffer continually.

Gary Collins puts this powerfully:

> Grief is an important, normal response to the loss of any significant object or person. It is an experience of deprivation and anxiety which can show itself physically, emotionally, cognitively, socially and spiritually. Any loss can bring about grief: divorce, retirement from one's job, amputations, death of a pet or plant, departure of a child to college or of a pastor to some other church, moving from a friendly neighbourhood, selling one's car, losing a home or valued object, loss of a contest or athletic game, health failures, and even the loss of confidence or enthusiasm. Doubts, the loss of one's faith, the waning of one's spiritual vitality, or the inability to find meaning in life can all produce a sadness and emptiness which indicate grief. Indeed, whenever a part of life is removed there is grief.[1]

If I had known that, I would have recognised that I had already suffered a whole series of losses. I had lost my mother through death, my cosy Parkstone home and supportive, sensitive friends through the move, my status as the 'unpaid curate', my partnership in the ministry to which David and I believed ourselves to be called jointly, and now my brother. What is more I had exchanged my beloved Purbeck hills for the flatness of Cambridge (a small loss compared with the others but real none the less) and I had slipped a disc playing badminton, so had lost the therapy of releasing tension through energetic competitive sport.

But I could cook. So I baked cakes for the weekly student teas in the vicarage, entertained people for lunch several times a week and served coffee to countless students and young professionals when they shoe-horned themselves into our lounge after church on Sunday evenings.

These young adults were members of the church's twenties group. We called it Focus.

During the summer months in Cambridge, students from overseas throng the streets, and that summer, together with members of Focus, I organised a friend-ship campaign for these students. In this way my relationships with members of Focus deepened. I also started a Bible study in our home for young wives, and preparing for and leading this consumed several hours a week.

I neither grieved for John nor thought about him. And the only way I could cope with the loss of all I held dear in Parkstone was to distance the precious people and places from my mind. For me, the three years there had been such happy ones that I could no longer bear to recall them. The contrast between the past and the present was too painful.

I did not realise at the time that I was on an emotional collision course. Neither did I realise that to bury the memory of loved ones in this way consumes a great deal of energy and is psychologically harmful; that when we lose someone we love we need to give expression to that love; that one way to do this is to weep or mourn; and that to deny ourselves this therapy is to increase the sense of stress.

This busying of myself, this keeping all signs of sad-ness safely under lock and key, were not deliberate attempts to avoid the painful process of grieving. It was just the way it happened. I knew no other method of coping. People in the church also misinterpreted the signals and read, not signs of sickness, but rather evidence of Christian courage. They applauded this hyper-activity, not recognising that it camouflaged a dangerous vacuum of emotions.

Grief going wrong

Perhaps it is not surprising that, nine months after John's death, I caught flu. This was followed by a severe attack of post-viral depression. David was alarmed and decided that we needed a good holiday. With his customary verve and flair he planned the holiday of a lifetime: a trip to Greece which would include a week in the lovely village of Lindos on the island of Rhodes.

The sun and the sea, time to be quiet with God and together as a family all contributed to the healing process. I regained strength quickly. Even my back improved. As I raced my son along the beach on our last day in Greece, I called out to my husband, 'My back really is better.'

A few hours later I was lying on a trestle table in a crude 'operating theatre' in a primitive hospital in the south of Yugoslavia. While we were driving from Skopje to the Yugoslav-Austrian border, our Dormobile was forced off the road. As it overturned it bounced down a fourteen foot embankment, and my spine was damaged, I sustained head injuries, and we lost most of our possessions.

Instead of spending Easter in Cambridge, as planned, I spent it crowned with bandages in this hospital in the south of Yugoslavia.

'Dear friends, do not be surprised at the painful trial you are suffering, as though something strange were happening to you. But rejoice that you participate in the sufferings of Christ' (1 Pet. 4:12–13). Those were the words on which I had been meditating in Lindos. I had commented on them in a letter to a friend.

David had rescued my Bible from the car, so, propped up in the iron hospital bed, I read these verses from 1 Peter again. I noticed that in the margin near chapter 4 verse 12 I had scribbled: 'these trials will make you partners with Christ in His suffering and afterwards you will have the wonderful joy of sharing his glory'. And against chapter 5 verse 10 I had written this paraphrase: 'After you have suffered a little while, our God, who is full of kindness through Christ, will give you his eternal glory. He personally will come and pick you up and set you firmly in place and make you stronger than ever.'

I marvelled at the way God had seemingly prepared me for yet more losses, but when I returned home it was a different story.

The last straw

Our car was a total wreck – written off. Our cases were ruined. So David packed as many of our belongings as he could salvage into cardboard boxes and, as bedraggled as a refugee family, we travelled across Europe by train. The pain in my back frightened me and I lay on the seat of the train and the ferry for as much of the forty-eight hour journey as I possibly could, hoping I was not causing irreparable damage to my spine.

A friend from church met us in London and drove us to Cambridge. By the time I reached my bedroom I was trembling with shock and fatigue. This friend and David undressed me, put me to bed, made me a drink, and somewhat revived I started to read the letters which had piled up in our absence.

One was post-marked Nottingham. I knew no one in Nottingham in those days and had never visited the city. I was puzzled. But I smiled when I discovered that a girl who had been going out with a member of the Focus group had written to tell me they had decided to get engaged. She ended her letter with a sympathetic sentence which perplexed me: 'I was so very sorry, Joyce, to hear about your father. On top of everything else that must seem like the last straw.'

'Whatever does she mean?' I asked David when he came into the room. He blanched, his jaw dropped open, and clearly he did not know what to say.

'I wasn't going to tell you yet,' he admitted. 'But now I suppose you'll have to know. While you were in hospital your father collapsed at the wheel of his car and died. There was no way anyone here could contact us. But we've missed the funeral, I'm afraid. It was last week. I hid all the letters post-marked Exeter but it didn't occur to me that anyone in Nottingham would know about it. Would you like to see the other letters?'

While David fetched the letters from my family, a few tears found their way to the corner of my eyes. Not many. This sudden severance from my father felt like an amputation performed without anaesthetic. It left me so shocked that after the initial slice of the knife I could feel nothing. This trial seemed too big for me to bear. With a heave I pushed it into the cellar where my unresolved grief for my brother still lay. Stunned, I shared with no one the pain that had pierced my heart when David broke the news. Instead I forced my mind to concentrate on the many signs of God's faithfulness.

That was easy. People at church were wonderful. A student lent us her car for an indefinite period. A businessman gave us an interest-free loan. The women from the Bible study group visited me regularly. My Christian friends commended me for my 'bravery'; 'She's wonderful,' they used to say. 'After all she's been through, she's still smiling.' They were right. I was still smiling. But they could not be expected to know that the smile camouflaged the classic signs of grief going wrong.

In touch with grief

None of us knew that to deny the reality of the death of a loved one, as I was doing, is not bravery but one sign of an abnormal grief reaction. None of us knew that when a person lives in the kind of daze I was in or acts in the kind of wooden, mechanical way I was doing, that these are further signs that things are going drastically wrong. None of us realised that when there is no body to see or bury, the bereaved person can suffer a pathological instead of a normal grief reaction. And none of us was aware that if the grief work we observed in Chapter 7 is postponed or delayed at the time when the loss occurred, then the bereaved person may find that, months or even years later, they will be forced to work through an exaggerated form of the various stages of grief; that until this happens they will not be able to make the necessary adjustments to life without the loved person or thing.

Healing past pain

Four years passed before I learned these facts. It was then that I was introduced to the careful studies of grief reactions made by the Harvard professor, Erich Lindemann. He classified abnormal grief reactions in the following way:

1. A person might be over-active, show no sign of loss and even deny in their subconscious that the loss has occurred.
2. He might acquire symptoms similar to those of the last illness of the deceased. These might be prolonged resulting in the sufferer being labelled an hysteric or a hypochondriac.
3. He might develop a recognised psychosomatic condition: ulcerative colitis, rheumatoid arthritis or asthma.
4. His relationship with his friends and relatives might alter. Sometimes the bereaved person gives up all social contact and lives the life of a recluse.
5. He might go about in a continuous daze, behaving in a formal or mechanical way and avoiding all emotional expression.
6. Anger against specific persons might be spewed out

time and time again – the doctor who is accused of neglect, the social worker against whom he threatens to take action.

7. He might lack initiative or drive. The bereaved finds it extremely difficult to make decisions or to complete any course of action without the help of relatives or friends.

8. He might nose-dive into severe depression with insomnia, feelings of unworthiness, great tension, bitter self-reproach and a need for punishment.

With the wisdom of hindsight, I now see that I was manifesting many of these signs of a-typical grief. Though I was physically frail for months, my mind became as hyper-active as ever. Within weeks of the accident David was offered a living in Nottingham. We accepted. The rectory we were to move into had been empty for several months. Every room needed redecorating. I sat in the garden that summer planning colour-schemes, where various pieces of furniture would go in the new home and preparing generally for the move. It never occurred to me that I was about to face yet another mini-bereavement as I left in Cambridge people who had become very special. Neither did I face up to the loss of my father to whom I had drawn so close when my mother died. In fact thoughts of my father were banished from my mind until four years later when Anne asked us to talk about bereavement. Then I panicked.

Inner healing

The reason for the panic became clear when Anne Long turned our thoughts to the subject of healing. Drawing on the teaching of Francis MacNutt, whose ministry was attracting the interest of many Christians at that time, she explained that there are three basic kinds of sickness, each requiring a different kind of touch in prayer:

1. The sickness of our spirit which we have brought upon ourselves because of our personal sin.

2. The emotional sickness and problems which have arisen through no fault of our own but which have been inflicted on us by circumstances or other people.
3. The physical sickness in our bodies caused by disease, accident or heredity.

She homed in on the second category and helped us to see that the roots of the emotional problems troubling some people are long; that they originate, not from anything the person did, but from things which have happened to them. Such people, she suggested, may benefit from the ministry of inner healing, and she quoted Francis MacNutt to substantiate this claim:

The basic idea of inner healing is simply this: that Jesus, who is the same yesterday, today, and forever, can take the memories of our past and:
1. Heal them from the wounds that still remain and affect our present life.
2. Fill with his love all these places in us that have been empty for so long.[2]

Likening our lives to a house, Anne explained how inner healing works. She gave each of us a picture of a house whose walls were caving in and looking precarious and whose floor area was severely limited because dry rot had left gaping holes through which the occupier might fall headlong at any moment. Under the living room lay a cellar which was not empty but which hid certain stow-aways. These stowaways were rather like forceful little people or rebellious children who, though they had been imprisoned, could make their presence felt at the most inappropriate times and in the most inappropriate places. She went on to explain how they had come to live in the cellar area in the first place.

When a child's basic needs are not met, he is filled with fear. The pain is so severe that, in order to survive emotionally, he splits himself from his innermost feelings. Because children are resilient he continues to live and even appears to have forgotten what has happened. But a fundamental part of himself has in fact been pushed away – down into the cellar. The subsequent hurts he experiences as a child, a teenager or an adult force him to fall through the holes in the living room floor and down into the cellar where he is besieged again by all those troubled 'children'. When the storm is over, he pulls himself up to the living room area again and continues to live as though the cellar did not exist. But because of the gaps in the floorboards, the living area is severely restricted.

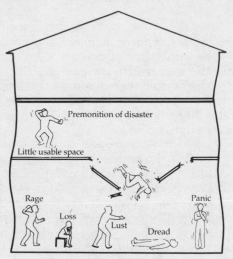

The need for inner healing

The good news which Francis MacNutt, Agnes Sanford, Frank Lake and others were discovering is that these little people need not remain hidden, hurting or needing to hi-jack their owners. On the contrary, they can be brought under the healing and controlling power of Christ. Where this was happening in people's lives, the owner of the house, the troubled person, was unlocking the cellar door, deliberately descending the cellar stairs in the company of Christ, meeting these rioting prisoners, and reliving with them the time and the place when the split had been made. The result was that, for many of these people, the pain disappeared, the person's past and present were so integrated that the cellar area became a peaceful rather than a tempestuous place, the psychological floorboards were mended and consequently the adult could enjoy the spaciousness of the entire living room – or, to translate that into theological language, the spaciousness of salvation, which really means wholeness.

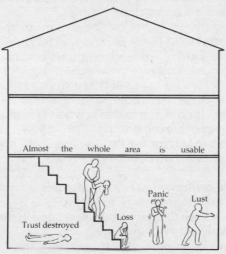

Going into the cellar with Jesus

These simple pictures[3] made a powerful impact on me for three reasons. First, because at this time I was living in a rectory with a huge cellar area under the lounge. This was approached by a substantial staircase. Part of it was used as storage space and part of it for church meetings. When we arrived, David saw its potential. We carpeted and furnished the biggest room, transforming it from a cold and clinical hall into a church lounge; the other room was converted eventually into an airy office. I could see that something similar could happen in people's lives if emotional cellars were worked over by God.

Secondly, while the counselling course was still going on, a friend invited David and me to see a play about the life of John Wesley. In this play the great Methodist preacher visited a notorious prison. While he was there even the vilest criminals, the murderers, prostitutes and hardened thieves, responded to the love of Christ. Again I could see that if revival could break out in an English prison in the nineteenth century, God could similarly touch and transform the imprisoned emotions which disturb the stability of many people.

And thirdly, as I studied the picture of the tumble-down house, my eyes focused on that forlorn little figure 'loss'. In the light of Anne's lectures on bereavement and the background reading on the subject which I had been doing, I was forced to admit that a creature like that was crying in the cellar of my life. It was this little person who had stirred when Anne first asked us to recall a personal experience of bereavement. It was this little creature who began to reach out for the healing touch of Christ when I read Francis MacNutt's book for myself:

The idea behind inner healing is simply that we can ask Jesus Christ to walk back to the time we were hurt and to free us from the effects of that wound in the present. This involves two things then:

1. *Bringing to light* the things that have hurt us. Usually this is best done with another person; even the talking out of the problem is in itself a healing process.

2. *Praying the Lord to heal the binding effects of the hurtful incidents of the past.* Some of these hurts go way back into the past; others are quite recent.[4]

Asking for help

'Bringing to light the things that have hurt us.' 'With another person.' These were the two points which registered in my mind. Even so I am not sure that I would have acted on them unless God had given me a definite nudge.

C. S. Lewis calls pain God's megaphone through which he speaks to a hard of hearing world. That April, while I was in bed recovering from flu, I realised that I was not only physically weak from the virus, I was also emotionally bruised; that inside the cellar of *my* life lay a part of my personality which had never recovered from the shock and searing pain caused by the series of losses of people and places and prestige I had loved. I was a mere novice in the school of listening to God at the time. Even so, now that I was faced with the reality of my situation, I asked God to show me what to do.

As though in response to that prayer, the story of the Good Samaritan came vividly alive for me. As I lay in bed I tried to imagine what it must have been like to be the man travelling from Jerusalem to Jericho and to be mugged and left lying on the road. I even imagined that *I* was that man; that I had been left bruised, bleeding, abandoned. I watched while two potential helpers hurried by and realised how often I had rushed off to church meetings or Christian Union events rather than stopping to help such a battered person. I became weary and despondent, as this victim of violence in Jesus' story must surely have become. When I heard the sound of the donkey's hoofs I scarcely dared hope that this traveller would stop so much as to look at my wounds. But he did. The sound of his voice was gentle and kind. The feel of his hands on my wounds was sensitive and healing. The taste of his refreshment revived my drooping spirits and the support of his arms restored my dwindling hope.

'I'm sending a Good Samaritan to you,' God seemed to whisper.

The Good Samaritan came in the form of Anne Long. On one of the occasions when she was having lunch with

David and me, the conversation revolved around the story of our car crash in Yugoslavia and the sad saga of my father's death. 'How long did it take you to recover from that lot, Joyce?' Anne asked. My reply was spontaneous but took me by surprise: 'I don't think I ever have.'

The subject was not pursued over the meal. It would not have been the right occasion. But it was an important first step for me. I was not the sort of person who found it easy to talk about myself in those days. I had never revealed to anyone, not even myself, just how much I had been affected by the deaths and mini-deaths I had encountered. But now I had made a beginning. It was only one sentence, it is true. But it was a start. And I had noticed Anne's reaction. She had not registered alarm or disapproval. On the contrary, her accepting, warm response, 'I'm not surprised,' gave me the confidence to phone her at a later date; to ask whether she would be God's Good Samaritan and attend my festering emotional wounds. And she agreed.

Going with Jesus into the cellar

As I drove to Anne's flat I wondered just how I would begin to explain what was troubling me. But I need not have worried. With the skill of someone experienced in listening to God and listening to others, Anne took the initiative. We both love nature. While we drank the coffee she had made we admired the view from her flat: the restful green of the fields surrounding St John's College, the huge oak tree that seemed to exude strength, the flower beds outside her window which were ablaze with colour.

Then, gently, Anne suggested that we offer our time together to God. I was grateful for this prayerful beginning because I knew that, skilful and experienced though Anne was, healing would come, not from her but from the Wonderful Counsellor, Jesus; that if I was to unlock the cellar door with Anne, I would need God's help.

As Anne prayed, the room seemed to be filled with a sense of the presence of God. This gave me the courage to respond to her invitation to take my time to tell her what had prompted me to make the request for help.

At first I struggled to find words to tell her about the anger and panic I had experienced during her first seminar on bereavement. In return, she invited me to tell her more of the story David and I had précised when she came for lunch.

She seemed really interested. And she seemed to care. After the story had tumbled out, Anne asked me a simple but profound question:

'Joyce, have you ever been able to say goodbye to your father?'

The question terrified me. 'Said goodbye? But surely, that means admitting that he's dead,' I thought to myself. 'Well, no. I don't suppose I have,' I admitted.

Anne then explained that it seemed that I had not begun the work of grieving for my father; that the needle of my life was stuck in the groove of denying that he had died. This was not an accusation – just an observation. She went on to explain that in such situations it is important that the work of re-grieving should be done; that a person must admit their loss, face up to its implications and work towards the time when they can wave goodbye to the thing or the person they have been forced to relinquish. The Christian does not have to do this alone. In fact this is where the ministry of inner healing fits in. We can unlock the cellar door, go with Jesus down the staircase and ask him to touch and talk to the bereft and grief-stricken person. Would I like her to be with me while this happened? I wanted to think through the implications of this carefully so we agreed to place a piece of prayer sticking-plaster over the wounds which I had opened up and to meet again when I was ready.

As I drove home that lunch-time it was as though a huge and heavy burden had been lifted from me. In one sense nothing had changed. In another sense everything had changed. Anne had heard my anguish and accepted it as a part of me. She had seen that my capable, coping mask camouflaged a mass of unresolved pain. But she had not rejected me. On the contrary, she had taken my story and me seriously and already the cellar area of my life seemed less formidable.

The Holy Spirit

I have described in *Listening to God* how, shortly after our arrival in Nottingham, the God of surprises took me by surprise by giving me an encounter with himself which transformed my prayer life. This encounter pushed me into making a study of the person and work of the Holy Spirit. The very first reference to him captured my imagination. Before the foundation of the world, we see him brooding over chaos and bringing beauty from it; hovering over emptiness and darkness and creating that many-splendoured thing we call light. His work, it seems, is to replace cacophony with harmony, to bring about integration where there has been fragmentation, and in the words of Isaiah, to give gladness in exchange for mourning.

Somehow I knew that he could do that for me. And I wanted it. So I told Anne that I felt ready to talk again.

Anne suggested that when we next met, she should have another person with her. Two people would be more able than one to discern what was going on in the cellar of my life. Two people would be more effective than one in bringing God's healing to me.

I recognised the value of this suggestion at the time and still do. When someone is being helped in the way Anne was helping me, it is easy to become over-dependent on that person. If the person is also a friend, as Anne was, there is the double danger that the relationship might become over-intense. But an unhealthy dependency and intensity are less likely to become problems when two people are involved in the helping process.

Another reason why two people or even a team of three might be brought in to listen to a person in pain is that to identify with troubled people can be very draining. When more than one helper is involved, while one may take the initiative in the listening and responding and praying process, the others can be tuning in to the person's need and to the still, small voice of God whose wisdom, discernment and knowledge is needed in such circumstances.

The three of us met. There was no need to tell the story all over again. That had been done. Our task this time was to push open the cellar door and go with Jesus to meet the little lost person who lived in the dungeon.

Anne prayed that this would happen and asked that the Holy Spirit would baptise my imagination and bring me in touch with my true feelings. The sense of anticipation in me was high as I imagined myself unlocking the cellar door and walking down that staircase with Jesus. But when we encountered the bereaved person in the cellar, even though Jesus was there, I felt paralysed with pain.

I relived that nightmarish evening when I first learned that my father had died. I felt again that pain which, like a knuckle-duster wound, had left me reeling and stinging all over. Once again, I wanted to escape. But Anne gently and sensitively encouraged me to face it.

I did. I took on board the fact that the father who had rung me the night before I had left for Greece, who had just installed his first-ever telephone so that he and I could more easily keep in touch, had suffered a massive heart attack and had gone without being able to say goodbye. He was dead.

Dead. That word lay on my heart like a lump of lead. It was crushing me, pinning me down.

'Joyce. Is there anything you would like to say to your father or to God?' Anne invited after we had been silent for a while. Suddenly I became conscious of energy filling my body. There was nothing I wanted to say to my father. There was something I wanted to cry out to God. I was angry with him. 'Why did you let him die while I was away? Why couldn't I see him just once more? Why didn't you let me say goodbye?'

The energy generated by that anger seemed to shift the heavy boulder. The anger turned to anguish. I had not thought about my father for four years yet I loved him. That love came surging back.

'Is there anything you want to say to him now?' Anne asked quietly. At last the tears of years came. I don't know how long I wept. What I do know is that I hid my face and sobbed and it was such a relief to cry in that way.

When, eventually, I looked up, Anne was still there, kneeling beside me, watching, caring. Her helper was praying.

Anne smiled – just a sensitive, loving smile. 'Those tears were long overdue,' she said.

I closed my eyes, glad to rest. A few minutes later Anne's voice broke in on the stillness. 'Joyce. I'm wondering whether you're ready now to say goodbye to your father.'

'Goodbye?' It sounded so final. Yet, when I faced the question I realised that I *was* ready. 'How do I do it?' I asked.

'Do it in whatever way seems right to you,' Anne whispered.

I closed my eyes again. This time I pictured my father as I had last seen him at John's funeral: ruddy with health, full of understanding, supportive, protective love, fulfilled in his role as verger of his beloved Baptist Church, anchored in God and closer to me than he had ever been now that we were weathering this second loss together. I imagined myself driving away from him, leaning out of the window and waving goodbye.

Goodbye to the father who had taught me to pray, to the father who had made endless sacrifices so that I could go to university, to the father who had loved my mother right through to her bitter end and who was now reunited with her in heaven.

The heaviness lifted. Peace flowed into me. I felt whole.

That weekend I walked on my own in the hills of Derbyshire. It was spring. A thrush was sitting on the branch of a tree in the fields where I love to wander. It was singing full throttle, enjoying the sunshine quite as much as I was. The sound of this song arrested my footsteps. I had not been conscious of hearing a bird sing like that since my father died. 'Dad would love to hear you,' I called out to the speckle-breasted fellow. 'He loved songs like that.'

And with that reminder joy and energy, peace and renewed love for my father seemed to flow into me. Suddenly the world seemed so beautiful again that I wanted to embrace it. As I skipped through the fields and over the stile that leads to my home, my heart was light. Suddenly I was happy.

A few days later I was shopping in the fish market in Nottingham. I was about to pay for the prawns I had purchased when I looked up and, for a split second, thought it was my father who was serving me. The ruddy complexion, bright brown eyes and wavy auburn hair of the man behind the counter were so like him.

I paid for the prawns, put them in my basket and smiled. It was a sign to me that real and effective healing had taken place. The heaviness of a-typical grief had been replaced with the searching and finding which are part and parcel of normal grief work. In admitting that my father had died, I had re-found my love for him. This was uniting us now and giving me the courage to renegotiate my life on a new set of terms – without my father's earthly presence but suddenly acutely aware of the many happy hours we had spent together. Gradually I was discovering that saying goodbye to a loved one who has died is not the same as forgetting them or ceasing to think of them. It is simply the way of owning the loss, integrating it, accepting its restrictions and limitations and saying 'yes' to life without the one who has died. This process is painful – but possible.

Helping others

I have no idea why God allowed me to suffer one loss after another in the way I have described. What I do know is that through the help which I received from him and from others, I became one of God's wounded healers.

Shortly after I had said my goodbyes to my father, a member of our own congregation was bereaved. Aware now of the grieving process, I found it a privilege to stay alongside her, to hear her pain, to receive her anger, to assure her that she was not going mad, but that the tangle of emotions which threatened to strangle her were perfectly normal.

At the same time the husband of another friend lay in bed dying of cancer. When I went to visit her one day, I found her hanging her washing on the line. We had not met for some years but she ran into my arms, hid her face and sobbed. I understood. Neither of us spoke. There were no words. It was enough just to be, to let her cry, and to cry with her.

'To cry with her.' A few weeks earlier, while I was still denying the reality of my father's death, I would not have been able to do that. My own hidden grief would have absorbed me. The neon light of non-availability would have flashed from my forehead. But now I counted it a privilege to stay alongside her, comforting her in the same sort of way that I myself had been comforted.

As I learned to stay alongside the bereaved in this way, I discovered that there were certain ways which always seemed to help and certain things which always seemed to hurt.

Listening always helps. As one friend of mine has put it: 'Listening and not trying to judge or pray.' Or if we are not near enough to visit, letters can bring comfort. Because anniversaries – birthdays, Christmas, the anniversary of the death, wedding anniversaries, and so on – can resurrect the sting of bereavement, it helps if we give extra support at such times. Bereavement can last for months, even years, and the person needs to be supported all the way through until they are ready to wave the final farewell.

It is therefore unhelpful to say 'Pull yourself together' or to offer platitudes like 'It'll all work out' or 'Time will heal'. And the inability to listen to the tears and the fears will be as cruel as turning a knife in a gaping wound.

The bereaved person needs to be cherished, they may need company at night for a while, they will appreciate being invited to social functions as long as it is understood that, at the last minute, they might not be able to cope after all.

And although such caring is costly, it brings its own rewards. When the bereaved person does eventually start to re-negotiate life on a new set of terms, we can be assured that the time spent with them has been time well spent. I was glad of the opportunity to give to others what I had received for myself. But what I failed to recognise at the time was the fact that I was still more wounded than whole; that if my heart's desire was truly to draw alongside those entrusted with suffering I would need to open myself further to the healing touch of Christ, because certain emotional hurts, like rebellious children, were still stirring up trouble deep down in the cellar of my life.

9

Making Peace with the Past

Several things pin-pointed the fact that there was a pressing need for me to pay further attention to the little people in the cellar of my life. The first was my relationship with David's secretary. But as I traced the manner in which she had been appointed the curious twist in this relationship baffled me.

Because the work in the church was growing, David and I agreed that his need for secretarial help was urgent. We prayed that God would bring across our path someone with secretarial skills who could relieve him of some of the administrative pressures. Within weeks a young vivacious American girl joined the church. While I was talking to her at a fellowship meeting one Monday evening I discovered that she was a qualified secretary and that she was job-hunting. I liked her. When I went home I told David about her. She and her husband came for dinner and we discussed the possibility of her working alongside David in the parish. A few weeks later she took on the thankless task of setting up the church office.

Church office? We had no premises for such an office and so I suggested that our dining room should be used by the secretary during the day and by our family in the evening. This room was conveniently situated near David's study and it seemed an ideal arrangement – until the secretary started work.

She had been working with us for only a few weeks when I began to behave in an irrational and unreasonable way. Instead of viewing her presence as an answer to prayer, I resented it. Instead of liking her and welcoming the help she gave in answering the telephone and the doorbell, I felt irritated by her presence, which now seemed more an intrusion than a help. And worse, when she and David worked together in his study I found myself hurting inside in rather the same way as I imagine a person who has been stabbed in the chest must feel.

At first I assumed this was the jealousy any wife might feel if her husband is working closely alongside an attractive impressionable young woman. So I gave myself a firm ticking off, confessed my 'sin' to God and expected the situation to change. It did change. It grew worse. And worse. And worse.

It was not that I did not trust David's moral integrity. I did. I knew he was trustworthy. But that belief did nothing to temper the irrationality of the panic which seemed to sweep over me whenever he and the secretary were alone together.

I could not understand myself. I had never felt this way before. It was as though I was consumed by emotions too powerful for me to control. I confessed them, tried to repent of them, asked God to cleanse me of them, but still they refused to budge. Outwardly I was projecting the capable, coping image most clergy wives manage most of the time. Inwardly I was despising myself because the situation seemed so hypocritical and because this conflict was threatening the health and happiness of our home.

This went on for months before my study of the ministry of inner healing, or the healing of the memories as it is sometimes called, brought me hope and also persuaded me to take action.

Several books dealing with the subject of healing past hurts were finding their way from America on to the shelves of Christian bookshops in England at this time. I read them all.

These books reminded me of four facts. First, that time does not necessarily heal memories of past incidents which have been so painful that an individual has had to repress rather than tolerate them. Second, that these memories, though buried deep within the human psyche, can sting quite as effectively twenty or more years after the initial event as they did when they were pushed down into the subconscious. Third, that these memories, though seemingly dormant, possess the power to affect our concepts, our emotions, our behaviour, our view of God, our view of ourselves and our relationships. And fourth, that the ministry of inner healing might benefit those who, though they have confessed and repented, find themselves incapable of making amendments to their behaviour; that there are others who might well be helped through this prayer ministry: those who have become aware that they are held down in any way by ancient hurts from the past or the memory of them; those so held in the grip of unreasonable or irrational fears, anxieties or beliefs that they seem handicapped; incapable of behaving in a normal, loving, Christ-like way. And those who were once excited by the concept of the freedom they could enjoy in Christ but for whom this promise now seemed nothing more than a mirage.

The book which influenced me most was that of the Jesuit Francis MacNutt. His claims made a deep impression on me – in particular the suggestion that the kind of irrational behaviour which I was displaying might spring, not primarily from a person's innate sinfulness but rather from the vulnerability which arises from a hurt inflicted on the person in the dim and distant past:

> Somewhere between our sins and our physical ailments lies that part of our lives where we find many of our real failings as human beings – our emotional weaknesses and problems . . .[1]
>
> Some of these hurts go way back into the past; others are quite recent. Our experience coincides with the findings of psychologists: that many of the deepest hurts go way back to the time when we were most vulnerable and least able to defend ourselves. There is a good deal of evidence that some hurts go back even

before birth while the child was still being carried in the mother's womb. Just as John the Baptist leapt in Elizabeth's womb when she heard Mary's greeting, so every child seems sensitive to its mother's moods. If the mother does not really want the child or is suffering from anxiety or fear, the infant seems somehow to pick up the feelings of the mother and to respond to them . . . These earliest memories up to the time we are two or three years old seem to be the most important in setting the patterns of our future behavior – long before we are free to make our own personal decisions.

If a person has always felt unlovable or has always been restless or fearful, the need for inner healing probably goes all the way back to the very earliest years of life.[2]

The hope in me gave rise to a prayer that Jesus, the Wonderful Counsellor, would shine his searchlight into the cellar of my life and expose anything there which was stunting my growth. 'Lord, if there is anything from my past which is invading the present and spoiling my walk with you and my relationship with David, please show me,' I whispered one night as I went to bed. As though in answer to that prayer, I woke up next morning with three distinct childhood memories playing on the video of my mind.

Childhood hurts

The three childhood memories seemed to be a variation on one theme. Rejection. Or more accurately, perceived rejection. The most painful one was of myself lying in my child-size bed in the corner of my parents' bedroom in Roberts Road. I was burying my head under the blankets while they made love, tears were stinging my eyes but I was fighting them lest I should let out the sobs of loneliness I wanted to cry. I scarcely dared breathe because my mind was telling me that I should not be there. I was intruding. So I lay like a whimpering puppy, too frightened to let out its yelp. And I felt desolate.

With this picture came the reminder that, when I was little, my father had worked in the bakery at nights and had slept during the day. This meant that at night time there was a spare place in the double bed beside my mother and that is where I slept. But the day came when, for health reasons, my father had to give up his job as a master-baker and then there was a crisis. Where was I to sleep? A child-size bed was bought for me and at first I enjoyed having my own corner of the room. But gradually I missed the warmth and comfort of my mother's presence in bed and wanted to go back to the old arrangement. This of course was neither possible nor appropriate. But I felt isolated in my small dark, make-shift corner.

These feelings of isolation intensified if I was still awake when my parents came to bed. On such occasions my mother would talk to me until I was drowsy and drifting off to sleep. Except when she and my father planned to make love. Then she would pretend to have a headache, tell me she could not talk tonight, that she was rolling over to go to sleep. A few minutes later I would hear them whispering and kissing and fondling one another and I would feel confused, unwanted, unhappy, abandoned. Pushed out.

Each of the books I had read suggested that when painful memories like this were brought to the light of consciousness, the event should be recalled as vividly as possible and relived. The person reconnected with that pain should then seek to discern what Jesus had been wanting to do or to say to them when the original event was taking place. As his presence was revealed, healing would come to the hurt, love would be poured into the loveless places, the effects of the hurtful past could be so bound that its stranglehold would be broken and the sting would be removed. Consequently the past would lose its ability to affect the behaviour of the adult adversely in the present.

I wanted this freedom but did not want to betray or appear to be blaming my parents. So instead of seeking the help of someone skilled to counsel, I used my own prayer time to ask God to touch this painful memory and so to heal it that my behaviour might be transformed.

In my imagination I returned to the bedroom in Roberts Road and as I lay in the bed in my corner, I could feel the blankets and hear the muffled sounds coming from my parents' bed. I was hurting now just as I had hurt as I lay in that room listening to sounds I should have been protected from. And I cried to God to reach down and rescue me. As I prayed in this way, I plucked up courage to peep out of the blankets and I saw that a screen was now dividing my bed from my parents'. The screen, I noticed, was decorated with angels whose wings stretched almost to the ceiling and touched, giving me the privacy I needed. As I examined the screen those angels seemed to come alive, forming a partition which separated my corner from the rest of the room. And with their presence came the reassuring promise: 'He shall give his angels charge over you to protect you in all your ways.'

I gazed in wonder at the screen. It was enchanting. And as I gazed, that corner of the bedroom lost its terror. It was as though the sting had indeed been removed from this particular memory. I was at peace.

In one sense nothing had changed. The fact remained that I had had to share a bedroom with my parents. The fact remained that I had not been able to cope with feeling on the fringe of their relationship when they were expressing their love for one another. The fact remained that I had interpreted this as rejection of me. Nothing can change those facts. They happened. Yet in another sense everything had changed because the aura that surrounded the memory had changed. Instead of feeling isolated, too frightened even to whimper, I felt bathed in the warmth and light of the love of God communicated to me through these messengers of his – the angels.

I was so convinced that this lay at the root of my irrational behaviour that I expected that once this memory had been touched by God I would change overnight and become warm and outgoing and loving to David's secretary. But, alas, I was to discover that the healing of the memories is not a short cut to maturity or a formula for finding instant freedom. No. It can be a vital and significant start. But it is only a start to a process which may take months or even years to complete. God, after all, is not in a hurry. He is looking for perfection, not quick results.

I did not realise this at the time and since I was unwise enough to seek God's healing touch on my own, no one was there to explain to me that what had happened was that I now understood why my behaviour was so bizarre. I also understood why my jealousy was accompanied by such panic and I felt better inside when I thought about my childhood, but before my behaviour was likely to change there was more work to be done.

Distressed, I went back to God and asked him to touch me again, to set me free from this terrible handicap. As though in answer to this prayer, I participated in a meditation with some students on the counselling course at St John's College.

'I'd like you to imagine that you're lying in bed,' Anne Long invited one afternoon, 'and you are holding a mirror over your head. Look into it and see what you can see.'

At this stage of the meditation I saw myself, not as an adult lying in the bed at the rectory, but as a child lying in the bed in Roberts Road, hedged in by my angels. I could see the mirror over my head but as I looked into it, it became the face of God and I seemed to hear him say over and over again: 'I love you.'

This place which had once been filled with terror had become a place where I was cocooned in love. God's love. And again I sensed that healing was taking place, in the sense – to borrow a phrase from St John of the Cross – that God was pouring love in where love was not.

My love for God deepened as my heart overflowed with gratitude. But still my behaviour did not change. It was as though I was fixed now in a pattern of behaviour which was childish in the sense that I was reacting to the situation in the rectory as though I were a petulant, hurting child and though I could make the connection with past pain and though I had seen God in it all, I could not relate this first phase of inner healing to the irrationality of my thinking and my behaving.

But God, as always, was wonderfully patient. When, on another occasion, I asked him to shed light on the situation, he pieced another part of the jigsaw into place. This time, as I lay in the bed surrounded by my now-familiar angelic companions and still cocooned in the felt love of God, Jesus himself seemed to come to me. He knelt by my bed, held my hand and explained to me that what was happening on the other side of the partition – my parents' love-making – was natural and healthy; that they were not rejecting me but rather expressing love to one another in a rightful God-ordained way. Because he was so tender and sensitive in his explanation of these truths, I could both understand and accept what he was saying. And my mind was renewed.

This time my behaviour did change. But in a way I had not expected.

Until this time, I would squirm if a courting couple came to settle themselves on the benches I could see from the kitchen window of the rectory or if a couple started to make love in a film or play I was watching. One sunny summer lunch-time, however, while I was washing up and a couple were kissing and cuddling on the bench by the rose bushes in the pedestrian precinct below my home, I registered a complete absence of the normal pain and discomfort. 'God *has* been at work,' I marvelled. 'I've never been able to do that before.'

But my gratitude was laced with disappointment. The jealousy problem continued to plague me. And I felt cheated. I had done everything the books described. I had asked the Holy Spirit to show me where the trouble stemmed from. I had invited Jesus to heal the hurts of the past and set me free from their crippling effects. I had experienced his presence in the place of childhood pain, but still I was locked into immature ways of behaving and this was still spoiling my relationship with David, his secretary and God.

A year passed. The secretary left. I knew that I had hurt her. And my emotions were mixed. There was relief that, at last, home could once more be home. But I was riddled with guilt too. And of course the problem did not go away. Other colleagues came to support David in the work and I discovered that the panic of feeling pushed out and rejected flared up, not only when David was working with women, it reared its ugly head when he worked closely with men also because the chief problem was the fear that I was being squeezed out of his life and his love.

The tap root

I was unaware when I embarked on this quest for whole-ness that God delights to hand us one piece of the jigsaw at a time. When that one is in place, he provides the next. Another missing piece was to come in the course of the lectures on counselling which I was still enjoying at St John's.

The second term was designed to help us to under-stand the complex and fascinating ways in which the personality develops. To illustrate one of her lectures on child development, Anne Long used a model created by Christian psychiatrist Frank Lake, which illustrates the importance to the baby of the mother-child relationship particularly during the first nine months of life.[3]

The diagram shows that, just as in the womb the baby is dependent on its mother for physical and emotional sustenance, so after it has been born, the child is help-lessly dependent on its mother for the sense of well-being which comes first through unconditional accept-ance and second through various kinds of sustenance. Acceptance, according to Frank Lake, is transmitted most effectively through 'the umbilical cord of sight'. He

The Dynamic Cycle: *showing the nature of the unspoiled relationship between mother and child*

As the mother gives the baby sustenance on every level, physical and emotional, the child's sense of well-being expands

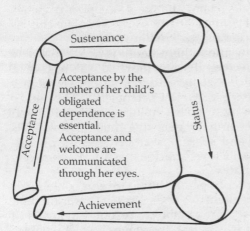

Sustenance

Acceptance

Status

Achievement

Acceptance by the mother of her child's obligated dependence is essential. Acceptance and welcome are communicated through her eyes.

The child now enjoys a sense of warmth and belongingness. Life with mother feels so spacious, yet secure, that the child wants to learn how to love others in the way it has been loved.

The child is now ready for the demands of learning: identification with hurt creatures, patience with other children, gentleness in actions.

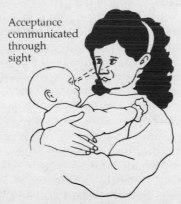

Acceptance communicated through sight

The importance to the child of loving looks

claims that access to the sight of mother is access to life, to knowledge of who I am; to belonging. 'The Infant's Being lives in the light of her countenance. To be shut out is slow death. The way in . . . is opened up by Mother's return; the look in her eyes and the sound of her voice.' Other psychiatrists claim that this acceptance comes through physical contact – particularly when the child is under stress or is confused: 'Holding protects.'

Sustenance, on the other hand, is fed physically through the inflow of milk when the child is at the breast, but equally emotional sustenance flows from the mother to the infant 'on every level of personality'. The child's emptiness is met by mother's fullness, satisfaction and joy. Through relating to her, the child discovers its worth, meaning and sense of well-being as the abundance of her life and love, graciousness and generosity overflows to the baby.

This kind of accepting, sustaining love not only gives birth to trust – the ability to open oneself to warmth and love – it gives rise to the ability to respond to love and it fills the child with the creative energy which enables it to feel, though not necessarily to voice, that joyful confidence: 'I am me. And it's good to be me.'

When such rightful self-confidence surges through a child, that child is strongly motivated to take the initiative in learning the skills which are part of the adventure of life and also to open its arms and heart to others: father, grandparents, aunts, uncles, playmates. It is as though the child has travelled through a tunnel of love. Fed and stimulated by the mother's accepting, sustaining love, the child has discovered the delights of being a person in its own right. It therefore emerges from the tunnel bursting with vitality and spontaneity; filled with a sense of personal well-being, quite capable of taking the initiative.

But where this unconditional love has been withheld for some reason, the trust patterns which have been established in the womb are broken, hope dies, a feeling of worthlessness steals over the infant and he lacks that *joie de vivre* which characterises his more fortunate peers.

Such infants will not necessarily grow up lacking in
initiative. What they might do as adults is to move round
the cycle in the wrong direction – trying to gain acceptance and status through the things that they achieve
rather than because of the people they have become.

As I drank in the implications of this particular model, I
felt raw inside. It was as though someone had torn the
skin from my flesh and left parts of me grazed, exposed
and stinging. This pain refused to be pushed below the
surface again. But conscious that praying about past pain
on my own had not produced the desired fruit on the
earlier occasion, I plucked up the courage this time to ask
Anne Long to pray over these grazed feelings with me.

Combining good listening with prayer

Again, as I drove to Anne's flat, I wondered how I would
begin. But I need not have worried. Anne was an experienced and gifted listener who was well practised in the
twin arts of listening to God and listening to others.
When I arrived I tuned in to the prayerfulness which
pervaded her flat and knew that she would already have
committed this session with me to God. I also knew Anne
well enough to know that she would offer me her full
concentration, try to understand why I was feeling sore,
and, as best she could, be the bridge on which God and I
could meet. I knew too that she would not hurry me. She
had set aside a chunk of her morning to minister to me.

I did my best to describe the inner turmoil that was
tormenting me; the fear that my parents loved me, not for
who I was but for what I could do. I told her, too, that
when she had used that little phrase 'broken trust patterns' to describe what happens when a baby is deprived
of the mother-love it craves, it was as though someone
had pierced my heart with a dagger. When I tried to
translate the pain into words it sounded pathetic and
childish but I could tell that Anne understood – that she
was not condemning me for being stupid or melodram-
atic – so I went on to try to explore with her why I was
reacting in this way to the diagram she had used.

'I feel uncomfortable talking like this,' I confessed. 'It sounds as though I am criticising my parents and I don't want to do that because I know that they loved me. It's just that, at times, I didn't *feel* loved.'

Anne assured me that she could listen to the details of my story without pointing the finger at my parents. She also pointed out that although children are very quick to pick up messages, they are not so good at interpreting them accurately. Sometimes, therefore, they perceive a hurt like rejection even though the people caring for them had no intention of turning their back on them. Reassured, I told her what was troubling me.

At the beginning of our time together we had asked God to give us wisdom and knowledge and the necessary discernment to make this a healing time. And as we talked, two things my mother had told me more than once as she reminisced about my birth flashed into my mind. They seemed irrelevant, but I voiced them none the less. The first was that I had arrived earlier than expected – so early that she had not even bought a pram for me and had had to borrow one from Mrs Bennett, who lived at the top of Roberts Road and whose son Laurence was born several weeks after me. The second was that it had been a difficult labour and for five days after my birth she had gone blind.

Blind! That word hurt. I thought again of that picture of the mother and the baby enjoying eye contact. No wonder a stab of pain had gone right through me when I saw that. This life-giving look from my mother was a necessity which had been denied me in those earliest hours and days of my life. That pain had been buried all these years but now, like an inflatable ball in water, it refused to be held down any longer; instead, it insisted on bobbing around on the surface of my life so that it could be dealt with.

Anne's acceptance of me and her ability to tune in to the desolation I was experiencing made it safe to share. Indeed it was a relief just to ventilate these feelings. But both Anne and I were aware that, in a situation like this, 'just listening' is not enough. That would simply bring to the foreground of my consciousness and in sharp focus the pain of the past but do nothing to help me to cope with the reality of its crippling presence. This was an occasion when listening paved the way for a more direct touch from God. And so Anne suggested that we should pray.

Prayer for inner healing

As far as I remember, Anne simply prayed that God, who is the Lord of the past as well as the present, would reach back in time to touch and to heal these wounds which had been inflicted on me. Then we waited to see what God would do.

While we were waiting, silently, it was as though I 'became' a baby again. What I mean by this is that I was imagining myself lying all alone in a field on the edge of a wood. I neither struggled nor cried. I just lay there – utterly helpless. But as I lay there alone, empty, helpless, vulnerable, I detected footsteps and later became aware of a presence. It was Jesus. He was emerging from the wood and coming to the field where I lay. When he arrived he bent over me lovingly. With one strong but tender finger I felt him stroke the downy hair on my head. That touch was comforting. He placed his finger in my tiny fist and I clutched it in the way babies delight to do. I liked that. Then my eyes focused on his face. I saw the smile which lighted it as he gazed at me. 'Gazed at me!' Yes. Through his eyes he was loving me in a way in which my mother had been unable to do for no fault of her own. He was bringing me into a new dimension of life.

Warmth, strength, hope, even joy flooded into me as Jesus poured his fullness into my emptiness, as he met my helplessness with his sensitive strength and as he exchanged my desolation for the consolation of his felt presence.

The scene changed. The wood was replaced by a brightly lit room. I was still lying down, a helpless,

vulnerable baby. But this time I was surrounded by
noise, hyper-activity and panic. None of the attention
was centred on me. On the contrary, it was as though I
had been abandoned. I was all alone. Frightened. But
passive. Alone? No. Here again I sensed that loving,
healing presence. Jesus.

I was able to describe little of this to Anne. All I could
say by way of explanation was that, whereas I had
arrived at her flat hurting all over as though I had been
rolled in a bed of stinging nettles, now I seemed to be
bathed in peace. Anne was sensitive to the wordlessness
of what was happening to me. When she saw that God
had answered our prayer and touched me she slipped
away, leaving me to luxuriate in his presence.

I do not remember how long I stayed in Anne's flat just
drinking in God's love. What I do remember is that a few
days later I stumbled on a passage of scripture which I
had never consciously encountered before but which
seemed to describe graphically the miracle that had
happened to me. It was embedded in Ezekiel:

On the day you were born your cord was not cut, nor
were you washed with water to make you clean, nor
were you . . . wrapped in cloths. No-one looked on
you with pity or had compassion enough to do any of
these things for you. Rather, you were thrown out into
the open field, for on the day you were born you were
despised. Then I passed by and saw you kicking about
in your blood, and as you lay there in your blood I said
to you, 'Live!' I made you grow like a plant of the field.
You grew up and developed and became the most
beautiful of jewels. Your breasts were formed and your
hair grew, you who were naked and bare. Later I
passed by, and when I looked at you and saw that you
were old enough for love, I spread the corner of my
garment over you and covered your nakedness. I gave
you my solemn oath and entered into a covenant with
you, declares the Sovereign Lord, and you became
mine. (Ezek. 16:4–8)

Although this passage was originally intended to paint a thumb-nail picture of God's faithfulness to Israel, I could see that, in so many ways, it described his unfailing love to me also. It seemed as though he was telling me that, because my mother went blind at my birth, all the attention had been centred on her and not me; that I had been denied the holding and the cherishing a newborn infant needs. But he, God, had not abandoned me. On the contrary, he had come to me then just as he had come to me when, as a teenager, I had surrendered myself to him.

This moved me very deeply. In speaking to me of the love of God it touched the pain of rejection right at its root.

The next stage

Anne and I met on a subsequent occasion to seek to learn from what I had experienced. It was then that I described to her the pain I had relived in my parents' bedroom. And together we drew the parallels from these two memories. On both occasions I had *felt* frightened, abandoned and pushed out of my rightful place. No one had actually elbowed me out but it felt to me as though they had. On both occasions I had not protested but, on the contrary, had remained quiet and still. On both occasions I had felt unloved. Neglected. And the message which I had absorbed was: 'I'm an intruder. I must keep out of the way or lie very quiet and still. I must not be a nuisance.'

Psychiatrists have a term for the passive kind of reaction I relived. Defensive detachment. Dr Bowlby, in his study of child development, explains that in such situations there is a recognisable pattern of behaviour. A distressed infant will protest in some way – maybe with frantic crying. If the mother or some other significant figure fails to appear, the crying will subside as the child becomes passive and withdrawn. Those caring for him believe that he has calmed down; that he no longer needs attention. But the reverse is true. By this time the child has crossed the threshold of his own tolerance to pain and, in an attempt to survive, he detaches himself from the situation and the people. His silence is not peaceful. It is pregnant with stress and heavy with loss.

Something of this stress reaction contributed, I believe, to the irrational but seemingly real equations I formulated at an early age. And because I believed them I learned to live within their restrictive framework. Even though I was supposed to be an adult, whenever a new member of staff joined our team I would enquire anxiously whether they could cope with a husband-wife partnership 'at the top'. If I sensed that they were finding this difficult, I would panic, withdraw and seek escape rather than run the risk of being proved to be a hindrance to David and his work; rather than run the risk of being pushed out yet again. But whereas, as a child, I would lie passive and refuse to make any response, now that I was an adult I was responding to this new situation with anger. It was this smouldering anger which confused David because I would accuse him of not wanting me beside him in the work and he would look bewildered. He believed, as I do, that we were called by God to minister together. He wanted me alongside him. The last thing he wanted was to exclude me. But when he tried to reassure me of that fact, even after God had touched the memories and restored a vestige of peace, I dared not believe him.

My immature behaviour hurt many of our colleagues. And it distressed me. But through it I discovered what the books at that time had not highlighted: that to seek a touch from God for the emotions can simply be self-indulgent unless we are prepared to follow this up with four more steps. These do not necessarily come in any strict sequence but they are all vital.

One is to forgive. When a person discovers that life has dealt them with a seemingly incomplete pack of cards and that consequently they seem to have been conditioned to play a very inadequate game, they can become consumed with bitterness and resentment.

The resentment against my parents, which I identified

as I relived the scene in their bedroom, took me by surprise. 'Why couldn't they have moved?' I complained to God. 'Yes. I know they were poor; that they couldn't afford to buy a house but my godfather who owned 24 Roberts Road had offered them two other bigger properties. We even went to see them and I'd been so excited at the thought of having a room of my own.' As I made this complaint I recalled how my godfather had taken us personally to both of these houses; how he had tried to persuade my parents to move, saying, with a knowing look in his eye: 'It's not good for you to have Joyce in your room any more.' No wonder I felt a nuisance, an intruder. 'Lord, it was so humiliating to have to be there,' I said with some self-pity.

But they had chosen not to move. And the day came when I had to let go of my anger and bitterness and resentment. To forgive. When I did this, feelings of sorrow that they had not been able to see the situation from my perspective persisted but at the same time I realised that they had never intended to scar me in the way they had done. They loved me. 'Father, forgive them. They didn't know what they were doing,' I prayed.

Some hard work

But even this was not enough. I had hurt people with my childish behaviour. Now the time had come to repent. To repent does not simply mean to feel remorse or even sorrow. It does not even mean righting the wrongs of the past. Indeed some wrongs can never be put right. Repentance remains bare and barren until it has effected a change in our behaviour. God had touched my emotions so that I could recall these past hurts without pain. He had also touched my perception so that I saw clearly where I had drawn an inaccurate conclusion from events which had caused me pain. Now I was faced with the task of changing my beliefs and changing my behaviour. This would mean re-learning how to relate to people. It would involve me in taking risks. It would entail a whole new way of thinking about myself and situations. And it demanded that I forsake childish things, to use the language of St Paul; that I learn to live as an adult.

This was easier said than done. The way it eventually became possible for me to achieve my goal was to confront my thoughts and beliefs. To return to the picture of the house, this time I visited not the cellar, where rebellious emotions had lain hidden for so long, but the loft where irrational thoughts and erroneous beliefs ruled the roost: the belief, for example, that I would never change; that the situation was hopeless.

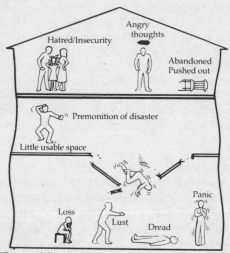

The need for the second stage of inner healing

I was to discover that just as there is a staircase down into the cellar making that area of one's life controllable, so by the grace of God there is a ladder leading to the loft of our lives. Over a period I learned to climb into that loft, and to put to the little people living there some pertinent questions:

Do you want to change?

How do you feel about the way you are behaving?

How would you advise someone else to behave in the kind of situations which cause you to panic?

Are you prepared to co-operate with God in taking full responsibility for bringing about the necessary changes?

I was able to say a resounding yes to the first question. I did want to change. And my response to the second was equally firm and honest. I admitted that I felt ashamed of the childishness which had dogged me for too long.

The third question brought some much-needed objectivity into the situation because I was highly-motivated to change by this time and to such a person I knew that I would put questions like this:

Is there any evidence to support your fears or are they manifestations of the old irrationality creeping back?

What is the rationale for the way your mind is working?

Are you mistaking feelings and perception for hard facts?

Could there be another way of viewing the situation?

If you're not sure whether your interpretation is accurate, could you ask a trusted friend how they view the situation and learn to take them at their word?

Are you thinking biblically?

Little by little, I learned to apply questions like these to myself. They helped. Most often, when I was tempted to react in the old childish way, it was because I was reacting immaturely rather than responsibly. And I found that by applying my mind to what I was doing, now that the hurts of the past had been touched by God, I could learn to live differently. But it took time and I needed a great deal of support from my husband to help me make the necessary changes in thinking and behaving. The most liberating moment of this whole healing process came when I said my 'I will' to God in response to the question: Are you prepared to co-operate with God in bringing about the necessary changes? After that it was with a sense of excitement that I set myself realistic short-term goals and learned to take the risks involved in reaching them.

These steps towards wholeness were far from pain-free. I soon discovered that, just as my old back injury, although healed to all intents and purposes, can still cause trouble if I ask too much of it or if I am overtired, so these memories which have been touched in the way I have described, are an Achilles' heel in the sense that I am still capable of misinterpreting situations where I feel pushed out. But God's work of transformation continues. I am still changing. Still growing up. And I am so enjoying the experience that I am glad I mounted the ladder that leads to the loft.

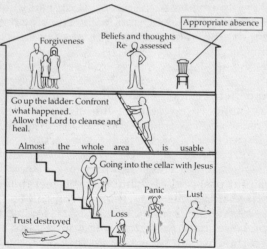

Inner healing after the second stage

Ministering to others

John and Paula Sandford, in their book *The Transformation of the Inner Man*, make this memorable claim: 'Out of the ashes of what we have been and have done has grown the ministry we are . . . Transformation celebrates that the lizard which rode our back is the very thing which will become the noble steed to carry us to victory in the battle for others.'[4]

This has been true to my experience.

Just as God touched and transformed my perception and my behaviour and gave me a taste of that greater wholeness which he always intended his creatures to enjoy, so I have had the privilege of staying alongside others who have been struggling to be set free from the hurts of the past. I have watched some of them enter into the freedom and the abundance of life that there is in Christ. Some seem to have been released from the crippling bondage to past hurts in a remarkable way. Others have relaxed as God has removed the sting from painful memories of the past. And I have wept and laughed with those who have taken courage in both hands and forgiven the people who inflicted such heinous wounds on them when they were weak and vulnerable. Indeed to take the power and love of the crucified, risen, ascended, returning Lord Jesus to a person's pain and watch while he handles it is one of the greatest joys of my counselling ministry. But over the years, alongside this joy has grown an increasing concern about its misuse. Some have seen inner healing as a panacea for all woes. It is not. Some believe that everyone should undergo such spiritual surgery. This is far from the truth. Some believe that inner healing only involves reconnecting the person with the painful past and enabling them to feel the healing touch of Jesus. It does not. Others go on and on peeling off the layers of the onion in 'bless me' sessions while they make no attempt to grow in maturity. And this is a mere caricature of a form of listening to God and to others which can produce prolific growth in personality.

But, as David Watson used to remind us, the antidote to misuse and abuse is not no use but right use. And in a day and age when the ministry of inner healing is being brought into disrepute there is an urgent need to pay attention to its right use and to be aware of the dangers so that we can avoid them.

I was turning these things over in my mind when I

travelled from Dover to Calais recently. My husband and I had driven through thick fog to reach the ferry terminal but as we stood on the deck waiting to depart, the sun shone on the white cliffs of Dover even though the rest of the country was still enshrouded in milky-white mist.

As I drank in the crisp autumn air, I watched while the ferry was cast off. It was no longer tied to the harbour. On the contrary, it was free to venture across the English Channel. But it would not have moved unless someone had started the engine and determined to set sail. 'But even when the ferry docks at Calais, that is not the end of the voyage,' I thought to myself. 'When we arrive in France, a whole new part of the adventure begins. There we have to learn how to drive on the "wrong" side of the road and remember to speak a different language. And that's rather like the ministry of inner healing. When Jesus comes to a person in emotional pain and touches, soothes and heals their innermost sores, it is as though the ferry of their life is cast off. They need remain in bondage to the past no longer. But that person still has to pluck up courage to start the engine of their life and set sail for what might seem like an uncharted sea. They will even have to learn the faith language of radar. And when they seem to have reached their destination, there will be more challenges. The work of growing up never stops this side of eternity.'

The *Pride of Dover* pulled out of the harbour and David and I remained on deck until the famous white cliffs became a white speck on the horizon. And I compared our drive through the fog and this calm crossing to the testimony I have disclosed in this chapter. While I was coming to terms with those patterns of behaviour in me which needed to change, it sometimes felt like driving through fog. But that made the new-found freedom, when it happened, all the more liberating. And it saddened me that a ministry which is so full of potential for people's growth and God's glory should have been brought into disrepute because practitioners had remained unaware of the dangers.

The dangers

Now that many of these dangers have been pin-pointed, however, it is my longing that this method of listening and healing may be exercised with more caution and be restored to its rightful place alongside the healing art of listening, whether the compassionate listening of the caring companion or the more structured expertise of the professional – the psychiatrist, the psychologist, the psychoanalyst, or the psychotherapist.

But if this is to happen we must beware of *persuading* people to open themselves to this kind of ministry. When the time is ripe and if it seems to be the appropriate way forward for them, they will know. And they are more likely to take responsibility for their actions if they have reached this conclusion for themselves.

If they do conclude that this may be one way in which they can take a step forward into maturity we need to be aware that it is all too easy for us to get out of our depth in such a ministry. It is important therefore, wherever possible, to work alongside someone competent to counsel and not try to go it alone. We are dealing, after all, not with a machine which is easily replaceable but with the complexities of people who are precious to God. We must not run the risk of causing further damage. And if we do find ourselves wading out of our depth, we must be honest enough to say so and call in someone more skilled than ourselves. This is not an admission of defeat. It is wise, loving and responsible.

We must also beware of encouraging certain personality types to explore this avenue of healing. As David Seamands rightly points out in *Healing of Memories*,[5] inner healing is most effective with people who appear to be out of touch with their emotions; those who have repressed the memories of the past and need help in discovering why their path to emotional and spiritual maturity is blocked. When God touches the imagination of these people, they can be helped to take significant steps forward.

But the highly emotional, hysterical kind of person

who escapes frequently into the world of fantasy and make-believe will not be helped by this ministry. They will enjoy it. But the exercise could degenerate into an act of self-indulgence. This ego trip for them will prove time-wasting for the listener and could drain him of his last drop of energy. No. This kind of person needs the objectivity of skilled professional counselling and they should be referred whenever possible. That is not to say that their friends will cease to listen. It is to say that friends will help them to see that God is a great God. He has many ways of helping people. Sometimes he uses highly qualified professional people, sometimes he uses the amateur listener, and our role is to make ourselves available, to help as we can and to allow him to be God. After all, as C. S. Lewis has reminded us, Aslan is not a tame lion.

And, unlike us, God is never in a hurry. And so we must let go of our neurotic search for quick cures for personality defects and the quest for instant wholeness. God is changing us from glory into glory, it is true. But the change is almost always slow and gradual with the occasional spurt for our encouragement. Those to whom we are ministering the love of Christ through inner healing, therefore, may need us to stay alongside them for many months until they have discovered how they need to change and how to go about making the necessary changes.

When they have found this key and the inner resources to move forward, they will look back with great gratitude that we stayed alongside them for as long as was necessary and they will marvel at the greatness of God who saw them in their brokenness and loved them enough to rescue and restore them.

At least, those were the emotions that welled up in me as I watched the fog-bound form of England recede into the background and set my face towards France. But that fog reminded me too that God does not always come to the rescue in the way we would like. Sometimes he entrusts us with pain. Even the bewildering pain of depression.

Listening to the Depressed

My doctor in Cambridge warned me to watch out for signs of depression. 'If someone had been scheming to give you a nervous breakdown, they couldn't have done a better job,' he observed when he examined my back and head injuries on my return to England and when I had told him about my father's death. 'Any one of the traumas you've suffered in the past five years could have triggered off a depressive illness. Now this,' he warned again when he came to see David and myself on a subsequent occasion.

This doctor was a caring Christian whom I admired. I knew he was not gunning for God with these comments. Even so there seemed no need to take his words seriously. I was a committed Christian, after all. In those days I imagined that people who were strong in the faith could not suffer from an emotional disorder, so although I heeded his advice to be careful I failed to spot the tell-tale signs of the predicted illness when they began to flash their amber light.

Even with the wisdom of hindsight I cannot discern how or when the depression started. What I do remember is that, whereas in the first year in Nottingham I threw myself into all the church activities with zest, during the second year I began to withdraw. I recall weeping with exhaustion one Sunday lunch-time just before a church picnic. Sensing that I was particularly fragile that day, a concerned friend encouraged me to stay at home instead of picnicking and even stayed with me, denying herself the pleasure of an afternoon out in the sun. And I recall collapsing in an exhausted heap after catering for a luncheon party in the church hall on another occasion and feeling very angry and sorry for myself, especially since it was Friday – our day off.

But as far as I remember, both times I pulled myself together and busied myself in the home and parish once more. It was some months later that I burst into tears in the middle of the parish prayer meeting and took myself and everyone else completely by surprise.

David had been telling everyone our 'joke' about the plague of mice which had taken up residence in the loft of the rectory while we were on holiday. We had summoned the rodent operative but he had been pessimistic. He doubted whether the mice in the house or the rats in the garden could be controlled. 'They build up an immunity to poison,' he said philosophically. 'You have to learn to live with them in a city centre like this.'

We did. And one morning, we found a mouse dead in our bed. I thought I had felt it wriggling between the sheets during the night but David had told me not to be silly. It was all in my mind, he said. During the night however he had rolled over on to the poor little creature and killed it with the weight of his body. We had laughed at the time. But now, as he was sharing this with everyone and they were laughing, I began to tremble as the tears refused every attempt I made to control them. I had only experienced this kind of physical sign of stress once in my life before – the night I arrived home from Yugoslavia still suffering from the shock of the car crash.

Scratchings and scrabblings at night and clearing up mouse droppings during the day became a way of life. At the same time, as explained in Chapter 9, I was seething with resentment that the privacy of my home was constantly being invaded by a secretary who seemed to have taken over the place I felt was mine – alongside my husband. And though I managed to hide much of my negativity from others, and though the depression was still largely masked from myself, my condition was growing worse. The mice on top of everything else were proving too much.

A bad bout of flu caused me to cave in completely. It dragged on and on and resulted in post-viral depression from which I seemed unable to recover. Eventually it drove me to my doctor. I hated the stigma of that word 'depression' when my doctor used it. Even more I hated the thought of taking the anti-depressants he prescribed. 'Just a crutch', he assured me, 'to help you over the hump.'

Anti-depressants! I dared not admit to anyone that I had a bottle by my bedside. I felt so guilty. And a complete failure – as a clergy wife, a mother and a Christian. And I felt angry with myself for being feeble enough to be incapable of coping.

At the bottom of the pit

I took the anti-depressants for a few days. But they made me feel zombie-like all day. Life was bad enough without feeling 'woozy' from one pill to the next so I determined to stop taking them. I decided that I would work through this crisis without medication. These were early days. My faith had not yet grown dim. I believed firmly in Betsy ten Boom's triumphant testimony: 'There is no pit so deep but God is deeper still.' If necessary I would prove this for myself and I did not need doctor's pills to help me do it.

By refusing to take the anti-depressants I was taking a calculated risk. I could have cracked completely. But, as Jack Dominian, Director of the Marital Research Centre at the Central Middlesex Hospital and Head of the Department of Psychological Medicine there, reminds us so helpfully, this is a choice which the depressed person must be allowed to make for himself. Depression, he claims, is a normal, necessary experience. By 'a necessary experience' he means that some depressions seem simply to be 'a kind of human radar which scans the reality of life and gives our appropriate response'.[1] He goes on to explain that the frozenness of depression may be the only way a given personality can negotiate the changes which are taking place, adapt to them and learn how to cope effectively with them.

Looking back, it would seem that this was what was happening to me. And I was not depressed for twenty-four hours a day and seven days a week, month in, month out as some people are. Mine was what some psychiatrists call a recurrent depression. I would experience episodes of deep darkness bordering on despair which would last for weeks but these would be punctuated by remissions, comparatively normal periods when I could be beguiled into believing that the crisis had passed.

Whenever I was enjoying a respite, I would look up the notes I made at St John's about depression and read the books recommended during this counselling course. The subject of depression now held a fascination for me. There were so many questions in my mind which clamoured for an answer. What *is* depression? What causes it? What is the purpose of it? Can you be totally committed to Christ and suffer from depression?

What depression is

No book offered a succinct definition of the illness we call depression. They all claimed that depression means different things to different people.

Some people, for example, complain of feeling depressed when they are down in the dumps or low in spirits or suffering from an attack of the Monday morning blues. Others claim they suffer from depression for a few days each month. They are using the word depression and pre-menstrual tension synonymously. Yet others use the same word to describe the disappointment they feel because the purchase of a house has fallen through or the sadness which seeps into them when their budgerigar dies.

This is depression in its mildest form. Uncomfortable

but not a serious sickness. This kind of depression is a temporary, passing mood.

Some people however suffer from chronic depression. This may develop only slowly but linger on for two years or more with no remission. For such people everything is literally de-pressed – flattened: their emotions, their ability to appreciate beauty in any form, their capacity to tune in to the still, small voice of God, their ability to give love and receive it. Everything is numb. Grey. They feel lonely, fragile, frightened. As Harry Williams describes it, they feel boringly, saddeningly and terrifyingly alone. Eventually the black cloud does lift but while it hangs over them it feels as though they are condemned to this listless, lifeless existence for ever, and, for some, life no longer seems worth the struggle and they become suicidal or at least live with a persistent death wish.

Another kind of depression is known as psychotic depression. In psychotic depression, the patient's reaction to a severely disturbing set of circumstances impairs his ability to test reality or to function normally. Psychotic depression can last for a very long time and is particularly frightening because it can bring about a complete change of character in the sufferer. Someone who normally copes well with many demands and who enjoys being stretched may, over a period of several weeks, become increasingly irritable and tired, pessimistic and agitated, anxious and irrational. Their outlook on life becomes consistently gloomy and as the gloom thickens their behaviour may become bizarre causing distress to their relatives and friends.

Some people describe depression in rather more spiritual terms. They use words like 'wilderness experience', 'stripping', 'refining', 'pruning' to sum up what they mean by this melancholia. This experience is so much like the dark night of the soul with which the mystics were familiar that it is almost impossible to distinguish between the two.

Then there is that general feeling of discontent which permeates some middle-aged people and which we now call 'the mid-life crisis'. This too can be a form of depression.

Not all psychiatrists view depression with alarm. It is simply a scream of the psyche, some claim, an indication that an area of life is being neglected and needs urgent attention. It is a message the person in pain seems to be reluctant to hear. It is work to be done, lessons to be learnt, the pathway to growth.

In other words depression has many faces, it afflicts the young and the old, the rich and the poor, the successful executive and the unemployed, the Christian and the pagan. It is no respecter of persons. And it can be viewed with dismay or with courage; from man's perspective or from God's.

Causes of depression

But what causes it? The textbooks suggest that the causes are as varied and complex and nebulous as the definitions.

Psychiatrists, I discovered, speak of two kinds of depression. Reactive depression and endogenous depression. Reactive depression, as the label suggests, occurs when a person is coming to terms with a significant loss which is perceived as unpleasant, harmful or devastating: the loss of a spouse through death, separation or divorce, the loss of a job through retirement or redundancy, the loss of reputation through scandal, gossip or immorality, the loss of 'what might have been' through discovering that one is infertile or that a much loved friend or colleague or pastor is moving from the area.

Endogenous depression, on the other hand, comes from within. Its cause cannot easily be traced. The root may never be revealed and the depressed feelings may linger, like a dark shadow, year in and year out.

I recognised that, when the cloud of depression descended on me, it was reactive depression that I was suffering from and so I probed more deeply into some of the possible contributing factors. I discovered that psychiatrists have claimed that depressed feelings often follow some of life's crises like a car crash – particularly if injuries are sustained and more especially if particular parts of the body have been affected: the head, back, eyes, hands, ears, to mention a few.

That made me a front runner for depression, I realised, and in a macabre sort of way it helped to know that there was some concrete, acceptable predisposing factor contributing to my inability to control the gloom which frequently crept into the crevices of my psyche. I took courage from Jack Dominian's claim that in such instances 'sadness is a proper and inevitable reaction which acts as a stimulus to make up for the loss'.[2] It interested me that in developing this theme he suggested that it was depression that often stimulated the healing of the wound and that, until the necessary healing and adjustment had taken place, depression was like a much needed protective layer.

People who had suffered the trauma of an early loss in infancy and who have not had their needs met at this most formative stage of their life were likely to clothe themselves with this protective layer of depression later in life. That was the conclusion some experts had reached after careful research into patterns of behaviour among depressed people. When such people were exposed to stress, it was suggested, they were likely to be prone to depressed feelings because every new stressful situation would seem like a recapitulation of that earlier experience when a psychic wound was inflicted before the personality had developed the resources to combat such an assault.

Some professionals went so far as to claim that the early loss of a loved object – particularly the mother – was the basis of all subsequent depression. This need not be the permanent loss through death. It can be the temporary loss of a prolonged separation through, for example, enforced hospitalisation.

Adults who have been subjected to this degree of pain

in infancy, and particularly in the first six months of life, may well re-experience and re-enact this early dread and loss when they nose-dive into depression in later life.

I found these theories particularly intriguing in the light of the childhood memories which had surfaced for me and which are described in Chapter 9. I noted with interest too that many believe that changes in status and environment are thought to contribute to depression in some people. Again, I mused, I was well qualified to fall foul of this melancholia. David and I had had seven homes in ten years. With each move came the challenge of new responsibilities and the loss of familiar surroundings and firm friends. Perhaps it was little wonder that the load-bearing beams of my life were groaning a little.

Furthermore, as Myra Chave-Jones reminds us so helpfully: 'We are inevitably influenced by our surroundings . . . If we live in an emotionally cold environment where we do not seem to be cared for and supported, it is very easy for us to begin to feel undervalued and useless – a quick road to depression.'[3] I thought rather ruefully of the rectory where we lived. Although we had loved it in the early days, the strain of living there was now considerable. It was completely isolated, set as it was in a concrete jungle on Nottingham's inner by-pass. Tramps and drunks called frequently, either to beg for food or money or simply to hurl abuse, and often I would be in the house alone with the children when this happened. Every bus route in the city passed our front door so noise and dirt were a constant problem. And the house had been built over the church hall so whether we were attending a church function or not, the sound of hymn singing would percolate up through our floorboards giving us no rest from parish functions. All of this was imposing its own strain before the problem with the vermin and the saga of the secretary added to the pressure.

And there were the 'vibes'. The house was built over a cemetery and opposite a college where there is the usual occult activity among the students. A few yards up the road there was a meeting hall of the theosophical society. We seemed to be surrounded by evil. Even now, when I go to the church hall I still tune in to that darkness and can be overwhelmed by it. It persuades me to believe that some depression is caused by the principalities and powers of darkness which Paul reminds us of in Ephesians 6:12.

In addition to all this Myra Chave-Jones suggests that, in some people, a hereditary factor might make them susceptible to depression. Such people, she claims, inherit certain genes that predispose them to the illness. My mother, I remember, suffered from depression after Ray enlisted for National Service and again when she became a semi-invalid. My grandmother too suffered several nervous breakdowns and had to be hospitalised. I wondered whether I had inherited a susceptibility to depression from either of them but since there was no way of being certain there seemed little point in dwelling on this factor though I valued the insight.

I also appreciated Myra's reminder that chemical imbalance clearly causes depression in some. This is what triggers off post-natal depression, menopausal depression and, to a lesser extent, pre-menstrual tension. Stress and strain also puts a person under the kind of pressure which might cause them to collapse like a hot air balloon which has run out of fuel. I noted how such physical exertion resulted in Elijah's exhaustion and subsequent depression. And I loved the way God listened, cared for and restored his suffering servant.

But I was especially interested to read that the oldest and most widely accepted explanation of depression seems to be that it almost always involves inverted anger, that is, anger turned in against oneself. A person may seem very sweet and placid on the surface, but underneath their emotions resemble a seething volcano of unexpressed, unacknowledged rage. This frozen rage is thought to be one of the most common causes of depressed feelings. Someone may have been hurt in the past by a teacher or a parent or a relative or they are being hurt or humiliated in the present by an authority figure or peer or colleague who has upset them in some way. Rather than admitting the anger and ventilating it in a healthy way and safe place, they turn it against themselves, blaming themselves for being feeble, a failure or pathetic, and adding insult to injury by piling guilt on top of anguish.

I suspected that frozen rage might lie at the root of my depression. David would sometimes express his hurt and bewilderment that he seemed to have lost the sweet wife he married and exchanged her for a volcano which was liable to erupt at any moment – especially when he and I were alone together.

Christian *and* depressed?

Making a study of the subject in the way I was attempting to do helped me to understand the dynamics of depression and therefore helped me to understand myself. The realisation also crept up on me that it is perfectly possible to be a committed Christian *and* to suffer from depression; that having a firm faith in God is no insurance policy against this dis-ease of the emotions nor even an inoculation against it. I began to see, too, that though I was coping without medication this refusal to resort to anti-depressants would not be appropriate for everyone. Some people need a crutch to help them limp through this wilderness. Just as aspirins cure headaches and antibiotics combat infection, so drugs are sometimes used by God to bring about the cure of a depressive illness caused by chemical imbalance.

I learned too that many great men of God had been entrusted with this mysterious sickness of the soul. In addition to Elijah whom I have already mentioned in this chapter, there was the Psalmist. He summed up my feelings and experiences so succinctly that whenever I felt really low it was to the Psalms that I would turn. These were some of the verses I underlined at the time because they brought me a sorrowful sort of comfort:

Be merciful to me, O Lord, for I am in distress;
    my eyes grow weak with sorrow,
    my soul and my body with grief.
My life is consumed by anguish
    and my years by groaning;
my strength fails because of my affliction,
    and my bones grow weak.

                                    (Ps. 31:9,10)

My tears have been my food
    day and night . . .
all your waves and breakers
    have swept over me.
                    (Ps. 42:3,7)

Job too seems well acquainted with the darkness which
was pervading my entire being:

For sighing comes to me instead of food;
    my groans pour out like water . . .
I have no peace, no quietness;
    I have no rest, but only turmoil.
                            (Job 3:24,26)

When I lie down I think, 'How long before I get up?'
    The night drags on, and I toss till dawn . . .
so that I prefer strangling and death,
    rather than this body of mine . . .
If I have sinned, what have I done to you,
    O watcher of men?

                                (Job 7:4,15,20)

Then there was J. B. Phillips. Unable to shake off the
symptoms of depression, he had been forced to resign
from his first living and go into hiding in Swanage where
he corresponded with other depressives: Leslie Weatherhead was one. In a letter to Jack Phillips, this great
preacher who used to thrill huge congregations each
Sunday with his preaching confesses: 'I feel concerned
about what you describe as depression because I went

through hell thirty years ago. I had over two hundred hours of "analysis" and finally emerged, but it took years . . .' He goes on to confess that he found a certain drug 'an enormous help'. 'I still take one before a Sunday at the City Temple; a challenge which still makes me "anxious".'[4] And there was William Cowper, so becalmed by depression that when offered a responsible post in the House of Lords he succumbed to an anxiety state and was so agitated that he tried several times to kill himself. This was the description he wrote of himself: 'I am like a slug or snail that has fallen into a deep well.'

I learned that many of the world's geniuses had suffered similarly: Isaac Newton, Beethoven, Darwin, Van Gogh, Tolstoy, Spurgeon and Martin Luther. Their inner turmoil did not block their creativity. On the contrary, their suffering seemed to contribute to their greatness. While J. B. Phillips was depressed he translated the whole of the New Testament into a powerful paraphrase. While William Cowper was depressed he wrote some of his best hymns and poems. And while C. H. Spurgeon was depressed he preached some of his finest sermons.

How the depressed person feels

This taught me that I must not waste suffering. Instead I must learn to use it. Even so this did nothing to alleviate the pain when I nose-dived into the tunnel once more. The feelings were always the same – or at least a variation on a miserable theme.

One of the most frightening things was the tightness around my head. It was as though someone had clamped an iron frame round my skull. This would bite into my flesh first and then into my brain. It seemed to be obstructing my ability to think clearly. My mind was befogged. Confused. To think became too much of an effort.

To make matters worse, my energy level seemed to have ebbed away. In its place a debilitating lethargy would sweep over the shore of my life and refuse to go away. Because my mind seemed so sluggish, the quick actions and reactions of others felt like a slap in the face. Cruel. Insensitive. Unloving.

Laughter jarred. Singing grated on the exhausted nerves. And because life seemed such an effort and so unlivable, the tiniest mistake anyone made, like allowing the soup to boil over or leaving the door open on a cold day, triggered off an angry reaction from me which filled me with self-loathing and caused the offender to retreat in self-preservation.

Even ordinary household chores seemed to take too much effort: 'I go into the kitchen. The dishes are all there, piled up, dirty, I haven't the energy or inclination to wash them or tidy the house . . . I can't bear to see people laugh or even see them looking well. I feel so jaded in comparison. Lord, I'm feeling dreadful. When will all this end?' That is what I wrote in my prayer journal.

And because everything seemed so grim, the slightest disappointment seemed capable of knocking me off balance and plunging me into a deeper experience of despair.

Even the sun failed to cheer me. 'The sun is shining but everything is dark – very dark. Help me, Lord, please.' In fact when the sun shone I felt worse. Its shafts came as a sharp reminder that normally I respond to them with gratitude and enjoyment. But now, all enjoyment seemed to have evaporated – even from the pleasures of reading, listening to music and walking in Derbyshire. 'I can't concentrate on anything for long; can't enjoy a book. I'm not interested in television, can't feel you [God] there.' Life seemed an ever-darkening shade of grey: joyless, hopeless, dreary.

'Everything hurts' is a phrase that punctuates my prayer journal at this time as I expressed to God the loneliness that was pervading my spirit. 'Will I ever feel energetic again? I'm so lonely, Lord. Desperately lonely. If only there was someone who would come and sit with me, watch me cry, hear my efforts to communicate and tell me that I'm not going mad. I feel as though I'm going mad, Lord. Is there anyone you could send?'

There were people around, of course. But since I hid

much of this pain behind my usual smiling countenance they could not be expected to detect that I was wandering around in an inner wilderness. And as I admitted to myself in my prayer journal on one occasion: 'I have wrapped myself round in barbed wire and I sit in its terrifying tangle.' No one could reach me. But if they had been watching they would have seen that church services brought so much pain to the surface that I could scarcely cope. While the music group sang quietly and sensitively during the services of Holy Communion, I would kneel in my pew and weep silently: tears that seemed to flow from some deeply hidden part of myself; tears which were, I knew, a language but a language I had not yet learned to interpret.

These tears seemed such a nuisance. An embarrassment. I would be sitting in the hairdresser's using up all my energy in the attempt to project my normal coping image when suddenly my eyes would fill with tears that looked like pools which threatened to overflow down my unusually pale cheeks. 'If only I could stop crying' was a wish I made frequently.

Insomnia also set in. I would go to bed and toss and turn and turn and toss until two or three o'clock in the morning – even before that night when the mouse met his death in our bed.

But perhaps the worst thing was the guilt and self-loathing. Here was I, a graduate, called by God to serve him alongside my husband in the full-time ministry, a committed Christian, falling apart at the seams. Surely I should be able to pull myself together? Surely I should not feel like this? Whatever must God be thinking about me? Deep down, that is how I reasoned with myself.

Richard Winter, in *The Roots of Sorrow*, claims that when a person is suffering from depression it almost always happens that he is suffering from four or more of the following nine symptoms:

loss of appetite or weight loss
sleep difficulties

fatigue
agitation
retardation (being slowed up)
loss of interest
difficulty in concentration
feelings of guilt
a death wish or thoughts of suicide.[5]

The most alarming moment came for me when I had been staying on my own in Derbyshire one weekend. I missed my bus home by seconds and the frustration spilled over into anger. While I waited impatiently for the next bus to come, I sat in the sun on the banks of the river Derwent and longed for the courage to throw myself into its swollen waters which were heaving their way downstream. After that, the death wish was a recurring one which filled me with terror on the one hand but gave me an escape route, at least in my fantasies, on the other.

Work to be done
I was one of the fortunate ones. As I have explained, mine was a recurrent depression, not a psychotic one. During the short intermissions I could think rationally, read, pray and sense the presence of God. And I was fortunate enough to see a purpose in what was happening to me, at least some of the time. In one of the early remissions, I remember reeling from the shock of what I was going through and talking to God about it. Two passages of scripture and a particular prophecy reassured and strengthened me at this time. First God seemed to remind me that soon after his anointing by the Spirit at his baptism, Jesus was driven into the wilderness where he was tested. This testing, I discovered, was not designed to break the Son of God but rather to strengthen him for the ministry that lay ahead, in the same way as metal must be tested before it is usable. In my strongest moments, even when I was crawling through the endlessly long and dark tunnel of depression, I remembered

this and clung on to the hope that maybe this was what was happening to me.

The second scripture came in the form of a promise from Jesus, which again I clung to when the going was tough. 'Simon, Simon,' Jesus had said to his beloved disciple, 'Satan has asked to sift you as wheat. But I have prayed for you' (Luke 22:31–32). Those words 'I have prayed for you' brought such comfort. So much so that I wrote on a piece of paper, JESUS IS PRAYING FOR ME NOW, and stuck it on the wall of my prayer room so that I would be reminded of God's holding hand even when I could no longer feel or experience it.

And the prophecy which I sensed God had given me takes my breath away even now as I unearth it from my prayer journal:

> Just as nature is about to be stripped bare, the petals will fall from the roses, the leaves will flutter from the trees and the earth will lie hard and bare, so I will strip you. You will lie exposed, naked, in all your vulnerability.
>
> But you must not mistake this stripping for wrathful activity. This is not the stripping of vindictiveness or revenge; it is the stripping of great love. With the nakedness of your winter comes my promise that just as the Spring-time will bring the re-clothing of nature in all its freshness, newness and vitality, so your clothing will be accomplished by me. Your new garments will exceed, in beauty and in usefulness, anything you have previously experienced.
>
> Do not be afraid, neither be dismayed for I am the Lord, your God, and I am covenanting my presence to accompany you wherever you go. Go, therefore, in peace, for I am with you.

Unfortunately there were times when I was afraid. Terrified. There were times when I forgot these precious promises. Times when all hope of recovery disappeared. As I have admitted, there were times when I felt I must be on the verge of madness.

Helping the depressed person

It was then that I discovered that 'just listening' really is a ministry of healing. I recall one Sunday morning when I was in too much inner turmoil to risk darkening the doors of a church. But being alone in the house gave me more time to think than was helpful. The darkness over-whelmed me, the tears flowed and despair held me in such a vice-like grip that I scarcely knew how to live with the emotional pain. The helplessness prompted me to pick up the telephone and dial the number of a friend who happened to be a clergyman. To my astonishment, he was not at church. I was so relieved to hear the sound of a human voice that for several minutes I just sobbed. I do not remember what I blurted down the phone. What I do remember is that it was incoherent. Even so, this perceptive, caring friend responded: 'It sounds as though you're in great darkness. Would it help to come round and talk about it?'

This friend lived out of town so it was not possible to meet that morning. We arranged, instead, that I would go the following day.

When I put the phone down, nothing had changed in one sense. I was still faced with the challenge of driving through the darkness of an emotional pea-soup fog in which I had lost my bearings and in which I had lost my nerve, and yet in another sense everything had changed. Someone had registered my pain, heard it, assured me, through this offer of his time, that I still mattered.

I have sometimes watched a person suffer an asthma attack and gain almost instant relief from the atomiser they draw from their pocket and spray into their mouth. This selfless offer had a similar effect on my emotions. I pulled myself together, dried my eyes, washed my tear-swollen face and cooked lunch for the family.

I am not saying that my husband neither listened nor cared. He did. But it often happens that the people the depressed person loves most become trapped in the irrationality of the threads which weave themselves like a web around the depressed person. There are several reasons for this. One is that because the only thing the depressed person wants is that a miracle cure should be found which will free him from this tangle, if the loved one cannot wave the magic wand or say the perfect prayer which will produce this miracle, the depressed person feels let down and angry and might even lash out in verbal violence. Another is that the relative or close friend who is on the receiving end of this verbal abuse may begin to assume responsibility for the depression and believe 'It's all my fault'. Two people then spiral downwards, hook each other's pain and become incapable of helping one another.

This is what happened to us. Even though David absorbed much of my anger at great cost to himself and even though, particularly when he knew the death wish was tormenting me, he attempted to prove to me how much he loves and values me, his overtures of loving care, filtered as they were through my negativity and pain, had a hollow ring about them. I seemed incapable of making an appropriate response.

So once again Anne Long came to the rescue. Once again she listened – and listened – and listened. Even when the record seemed stuck in a groove and played the same tale of woe over and over again Anne listened. Every depressed person needs someone like that; some-one who will not tire of listening to their main topic of conversation: themselves. Someone who will assure them that, even though they, the listener, may have nothing useful to say, they are prepared to stay in the darkness with the person suffering from depression until they emerge eventually from the tunnel's end. David Augsburger describes this patient listening well:

> When hearing is done as an act of caring, it is a healing process. The exact nature of this process will remain forever a mystery, a gift of grace for which we become profoundly grateful as we see it occurring, before which we are rightfully humble as we know we have, in small measure, participated in it . . .

In caring-hearing, the hurt is opened, the festering bitterness of resentful illusions, the burning of angry demands, the numb frozenness of grief, the staleness of depression are allowed to drain. The light is allowed to pour in, sterilizing the infections and stimulating cells of hope and trust to begin new growth.[6]

New growth

'To begin new growth.' While the hoar frost of depression coated my body, mind and spirit, I was conscious only of the frozenness of this emotional winter time. And yet, as in winter we can stand staring in amazement at an ice-caked landscape and become aware that the hush conceals the silent sounds of hidden internal growth, that the naked trees and fallow fields are not being killed but being renewed; so during the long winter months of my depression I too was being renewed.

Renewed? No. More accurately, I believe I was experiencing a kind of new birth.

Carlo Carretto's insights, which I had read while I was depressed and recorded in my prayer journal, have helped me to catch a glimpse of what was happening during this time of constriction and darkness.

God is making me his child, claims Carlo Carretto. He uses 'the cosmos and history to make a divine environment for my birth':

Now I am like an immature foetus, midway between my past and future, between the things I know and those I do not know.

It isn't a comfortable situation.

In fact it hurts.

I suffer from incompleteness, from blindness, from yearning . . .

And it is dark because it is the womb, and it is painful because it is gestation, immaturity.

This is the way God makes us, forming us by matter, making us by events, moulding us by history, as a mother builds a child with her milk and warms it with her love . . .

The gestation of a child lasts for nine months. Our gestation as sons of God, a whole lifetime . . .

[But] God is my father and looks after me. God is my father and loves me.

God is my father and wants me to be with him forever.

If God is my father, I no longer fear the darkness, since he is living in the darkness too and at the appropriate time will turn the darkness into life.[7]

'I suffer from incompleteness, from blindness, from yearning . . .' 'I am like an immature foetus.' Those phrases sum up precisely how I felt as I travelled through that relentless tunnel of depression.

Tunnel of depression? Perhaps Carlo Carretto is right? Perhaps that tunnel which seemed so dark and unwelcoming for much of the time was, after all, none other than the womb of God in which he was re-creating me? Perhaps it may be likened to Frank Lake's dynamic cycle (page 181).

As I think back now to those years of mental and emotional suffering, I see that there are certain parallels to the experience of human birth. But whereas in my infancy, because of my mother's blindness, as explained in chapter 9, I had been denied the evidence of my mother's unconditional love, now as I travelled round the dynamic cycle for a second time – as an adult – God had poured his love into those yawning gaps compensating the love I had lacked the first time round. Contemplative prayer, the prayer of listening to God had played a major part in this profoundly healing experience.

As I had relaxed in his presence, he had come to me. As I had opened myself to an inflow of his grace, he had impregnated me with the gift of his healing Spirit. Even when I had been unable to feel his presence, he had been there, in the tunnel with me, dwelling at the core of my being. As I abandoned myself to him, even when I had been unable to feel his presence, or perhaps more accurately, particularly when I could not feel his presence, he had come to me with the outstretched arms of accepting, unconditional love. And as I had attempted to dwell in him, he had sustained and nourished me: through his word, through stillness, through meditation. When all was dark I could no longer feel him near, but when the depression lifted and the senses sparked to life again, I would become aware that he had been in the tunnel all the time; that he indwelt the very core of my being.

What amazed me most was that he bore the full brunt of my anger. I filled pages of my prayer journal with letters to God which expressed the pain and the anger, the frustration and fear that dogged me. Those tirades are punctuated by messages of love. For even when my feelings were numbed as with frost-bite, God continued to communicate to me that he loved me *with* the depressed feelings. I cannot record that I always believed what I heard at the time. But what I can say is that God was so acting on the raw material of my life that, slowly and gradually, I was discovering that in him I have both worth and status. And when he saw that the time was ripe because I was ready, he brought me to the mouth of the tunnel from which I emerged re-created. Made new. Renewed. Re-energised. Ready to achieve for him, not out of compulsion or neurosis but out of a joyful sense of well-being and with a new understanding of what Jesus might have meant when he said to Nicodemus: 'You must be born again.'

I had no idea when I set out to search for wholeness that the route would lead through this tortuous tunnel of depression, but looking back I believe that every step of that journey was worthwhile. That is not to say that God has now finished with me; that I have reached that much desired state: wholeness. Maturity. No. The learning continues, albeit a little less painfully most of the time. Meanwhile I am left holding the treasures which came from that particular path of personal darkness – not least the richness of the lessons that I learned.

11

One Spoke of the Wheel

One of the lessons I learned through my own limited experience of depression was the ability and desire to stay alongside others who suffer the seeming indignity of the temporary change of character, loss of control and absence of the felt presence of God which depression brings in its wake. People who have never groped their way through this particular fiery furnace seem to find it difficult to understand the anguish sufficiently to sit, month after month, with a depressed person. Only those who have been through a similar crisis appear to find deep within themselves the resilience and the resources both to understand and demonstrate their ongoing care. Mary Craig puts the situation well:

> Is it really paradoxical that when we are distressed we turn to the friend who knows what distress can be like? We don't quite know why, but there doesn't seem much point in going for sympathy, the deep-down, understanding kind, to those other friends whose paths have always been smooth. It is as though human beings lack a whole dimension and cannot come to maturity until they have faced sorrow.[1]

Because God entrusted me with this prolonged darkness, met me in it and gave me the resources to work through it, and because I emerged to enjoy a greater degree of wholeness than I ever thought possible, I now count it a privilege, when God asks it of me, to sit alongside others who are being bruised and buffeted in ways which I understand all too well. This patch of personal darkness, I see in retrospect, furthered my growth in that much needed fruit of the Spirit, compassion.

Almost as soon as I emerged from my own dark tunnel I seemed to be drawn to others who were squealing with the pain depression inflicts. And in attempting to help them I learned that, just as there are do's and don'ts which need to be applied to helping the bereaved, so there are do's and don'ts when it is a depressed person who presents himself to us.

Some do's

I discovered, for example, that when a person starts to send out distress signals – they are unusually listless, unkempt, untidy, lacking in energy, irritable, anxious or weepy, or complain of being 'down in the dumps' more than usual – it is wise to take prompt action. And I try to take as my model the way God coped with Elijah when he collapsed in the desert exhausted and depressed (1 Kgs 19).

So the first thing I do is to listen: sensitively and attentively. And just as God gave Elijah the complete freedom to pour out the full gamut of his feelings, so I try to receive the gift of the person's anguish and anger, his tears and his turmoil or the frozenness which prevents him from feeling or expressing even a fraction of his inner emotional pain. I remember so well the gratitude and relief that came to me through those who sacrificed time in this selfless way.

And I take another cue from God. Just as he demonstrated his love and acceptance in practical ways, so I try to put myself in the skin of the depressed person and provide appropriate practical help. A mother with a home to run, small children to look after and the family to feed, for example, will almost certainly feel overwhelmed by the volume of practical tasks to be done. I have learned not to ask 'Is there anything I can do?' nor to offer empty promises like 'Ring me if you think of any way I can help.'

Instead I prefer to visit the home and, while chatting to this friend or neighbour, sum up the situation for myself. If the sink is full of dirty dishes I wash them without making a fuss about it. If the children are fractious I might suggest that we all go for a walk together or that, while mother has a rest, I take the children to the park. Or if she is struggling with the shopping or the cooking I might help her make a shopping list or suggest that we go to the supermarket together. Or I might bring some ready-cooked casseroles which can be stored in the freezer and heated through when most needed. Although my own experience of depression now lies in the dim and distant past, I have not forgotten the relief I felt when, on numerous occasions, members of our congregation arrived on my doorstep with a ready-made meat pie or chocolate souffle or batch of mince pies which were just what was needed to save me doing what I seemed to have no energy to do: cook for the family.

But I have to remind myself that, though I take God's accepting, practical love as my model, I am not God and there are limits to the amount of help I can give. For one thing, I am aware that depression is infectious. What I mean is that, for me at least, if I sit hour after hour with someone who has nose-dived into depression, some of their darkness seeps into me. I know therefore that common sense demands that I assess just how much time it is wise to spend in pouring love into the bottomless pit of this person's life. And if the situation threatens to be a long-term task, I recognise that the need for other helpers is clear and urgent.

As I listen and give practical help therefore I try to discern whether medical help may be required. If the depressed feelings seem to be dragging on it is always wise to encourage the sufferer to see a doctor. If necessary I go with them to the surgery. The doctor's practised eye may discern that drug therapy would help. Except in situations where the cause of the depression is chemical imbalance, drugs will not cure the depression, but for many people, including Christians, they stabilise the emotions, giving the sufferer the resources to learn the lessons this bout of depression is trying to teach. If the doctor and the depressed person both believe this crutch to be the correct one, I would not advise the patient to refuse medication. Neither would I dissuade them from seeking help from one of the so-called 'talking therapies' – psychotherapy or psychoanalysis – if their doctor prescribed such a course of action. It often happens that such professional people, skilled and trained as they are in understanding the human psyche, can help the depressed person to discover just what it is that they are needing to learn and how best to translate theory into practice.

At the same time I would be listening to God to try to discern what further part he is asking me to play in this person's life. If the symptoms are the forerunners of chronic or psychotic depression, I know that this could last a very long time. There have been occasions when I have sensed that God has asked me to make a colossal commitment to a depressed person. On such rare occasions I have found that I have been given almost supernatural strength to cope. But normally I am aware that I am just one of many helpers; that I can be of most use when I discover what my part is and how it dovetails with the contributions of others. I try to be ruthless with myself; to ask some pertinent questions: 'What can I offer realistically in terms of time and care and love?' Then I offer that and no more, aware that if I offer more I might go under myself and end up helping no one – least of all my own family.

When it becomes clear to me that I am to play a major role in this person's life, like offering counselling or prayer ministry over a period of time, or when I sense that I am being asked to listen to the person's pain week in, week out, I try to ensure that I am supported in four ways: by a group of people who are holding on to me and the entire situation in prayer, by supervision from someone more skilled in understanding the dynamics of depression than I am, by the assent and love of my husband, and by ensuring that I take sufficient time for rest and relaxation and personal prayer so that my own resources will not dwindle to the size of a puddle but can be replenished constantly and be the reservoir God intends them to be. The people who pray for me have no need to know the name of the person I am seeking to help, so confidentiality is not breached in seeking their support. And of course to further ensure that confidentiality is maintained, I ask the depressed person's permission to seek guidance from another counsellor as seems appropriate.

Availability

When I have summed up the situation and decided how involved God is calling me to be, I know that the hard slog is just beginning because I am still near enough to my own years of suffering to recall my greatest longing: 'If only there was someone who would sit with me in the pain – not necessarily to say anything but just to hold my hand and receive my jumbled thoughts and feelings.' By far the best way we can help a person suffering from depression is simply to make ourselves available to stay alongside him in his darkness, prove our love by our faithfulness even when this self-sacrifice is thrown back in our face, spurned or doubted, and by listening over and over again to the same sad tale of woe, the same angry outbursts, the same lack of confidence, the same dreary outlook on life and the same lack of self worth.

This requires patience, stamina, the ability to interpret for the depressed person the sights and sounds of this foreign land through which he finds himself stumbling and the willingness to sit with him in this darkness until the end of the tunnel is reached, remembering that this could take a very long time.

'The ability to interpret the sights and sounds of this foreign land'. One of the sounds will almost certainly be anger because, as we observed in Chapter 10, frozen rage lies at the root of much depression. I have been trying to learn, therefore, to receive a person's anger as a gift and to handle it with care. Anger itself is not a sin. If it were, St Paul would not have written, 'Be angry and sin not.' No. Anger is a natural, neutral response to certain adverse circumstances. It is usually a reaction to fear or frustration. Unless it is defused skilfully it can be used to crush, accuse and blame people and thus be used sinfully. But equally it can be converted into a useful tool. It can point the person to the source of the fear or frustration so that they see clearly where changes must be made.

In receiving the gift of a person's anger therefore, I am listening not only to the angry gestures and the venomous words, but to the base line of the encounter, trying to discern precisely what it is that has triggered off this volcanic eruption. It often happens that the molten lava has to be poured out before these fears and frustrations are discerned. But when these too have been voiced, it is sometimes possible to take prompt and practical action and relieve some of the suffering.

Many of my own fears and frustrations, for example, centred on the rectory, which has since been condemned as 'uninhabitable' by the Church Commissioners. Almost as soon as we moved from that house the depression lifted, at least for a while. I have seen a similar dramatic change take place in others suffering from stress. When the crushing circumstances have been removed, they appear to make a miraculous recovery.

But I try to bear in mind too that an angry person often distorts the truth even though they remain firmly fixed in the opinion that their perception is accurate. My husband reminds me that when I was depressed, if I felt displaced for some reason nothing would dissuade me from the view that he had been guilty of neglecting me or had been particularly insensitive. I needed someone else to confront me, albeit gently, and to help me to see these false beliefs for what they were. Errors of judgement. And I needed someone else's help to discover how to replace falsehood with truth. So in listening to a person's wrath, I try to hear the underlay of terror, to receive the trapped feelings, to accept the person with their rage, to focus more on the hurt than the wrath but, when the time is ripe, to help them to explore whether there are other ways of viewing the situation and other ways of dealing with it. In other words I try to help them to use their anger constructively and not destructively.

Suicide

I also listen for signs which reveal that the depressed person might be feeling suicidal or that they are plagued by the presence of a persistent or recurring death wish: that feeling Elijah expressed so well when he confessed to God: 'I have had enough, Lord . . . Take my life.'

It helped me to be able to confide such feelings in two trusted friends and their healing response stays with me still. One, a clergyman to whom I confessed that, like Elijah, all I wanted to do was to curl up and die, startled me by saying: 'Promise me that if you ever feel like taking your life you will phone me first.' The other, a close friend, simply empathised: 'I didn't know you lived with a death wish too,' she whispered with tears of compassion in her eyes. And she gave me a long, lingering, gentle embrace, wept with me and made a similar request: 'If you should ever contemplate trying to take your life, please phone me first.'

On both occasions the care and concern expressed by these friends penetrated my gloom and I felt cherished.

Jack Dominian helps us to understand that it is almost to be expected that a depressed person will, from time to time, long for an escape route, which may mean that his mind turns in the direction of death:

> The thought that life is too dreadful to go on living crosses the minds of both those who are miserable due to their life situation and of those who have crossed over to the state of depressive illness. In the midst of the various causes of acute unhappiness the desire for relief by ceasing to be is not by itself an unreasonable or surprising reaction.[2]

He goes on to explain that many people live, from time to time, with this kind of death wish but few of them go so far as to contemplate suicide:

> At some moment, however, the real possibility of the removal of oneself occurs to one. From the moment that the act of self-destruction is seriously contemplated as a way out of the predicament . . . such a person, or those to whom the information has been communicated, should ensure that help is sought without further delay.[3]

These words of warning are important, I find. We must always take suicide threats seriously and do all in our power to protect the person from harming himself.

Some don'ts

Just as there are ways of supporting the depressed person, so there are ways which are guaranteed to injure him deeply. One is to tell him, if he admits to suicidal feelings, 'You ought to be ashamed of yourself.' He probably is. And his admission is a cry for help which needs to be met with love and tenderness, not condemnation.

It is equally damaging to say to someone who has plucked up the courage to admit to feeling depressed: 'You shouldn't feel like this' or 'You've been overdoing it, that's what's wrong with you' or 'Pull yourself together'. No one asks to fall prey to the sabotage of depression. When they do they need, not condemnation but listening love. Tenderness.

And sticking-plaster prayers may prove equally painful. By this I mean the kind of prayer prayed by a Christian who understands little of the dynamics of depression, who when faced with a tearful or despondent person believes that the whole complex problem can be unravelled through one prayer or the laying-on of hands, and instead of staying alongside the hurting person expects them to be 'zapped' into wholeness. Such so-called prayer ministry can leave the person deeply distressed, even believing, if no relief comes from it, that they must be beyond help since even prayer fails to pierce their gloom.

No one tried to exorcise me when I was depressed but friends of mine who have suffered from depressive illnesses have been subjected to hours of inappropriate so-called deliverance ministry which has done more harm than good and brought God's ministry of healing into disrepute. There may be occasions when the deliverance ministry will play its part in releasing the depressed person from his tangled emotions. But we must beware of seeing demons under every bed and take advice before jumping to the ready conclusion that the depression is demonic in origin. As people helpers we need to hold two things in tension: the awareness that sometimes there is a Satanic strand contributing to depression, and the realisation that to over-emphasise or exaggerate this possibility is to give Satan more prominence than is appropriate or accurate. Depression needs skilled and sensitive handling if the person is to emerge from the tunnel to enjoy the wholeness which is his, by right, in Christ. And though, from the desperation of their need and the longing for someone to find a quick solution to their pain, they may scream for any kind of prayer or counsel on offer, the wise helper will discern when to pray and when simply to listen, to love and give practical support. The wise helper knows that God, in his infinite wisdom and love, does not always remove our pain instantly. Sometimes he gives us the resources to grow through it, learn from it and thereby enjoy his gift of maturity.

While he is still stumbling along the road that leads to this much desired state – maturity – the depressed person's view of himself will almost certainly reach a low ebb. The temptation then is to try to jolly him along, to try to prove that his perception is clouded, to try to boost his morale by praising and complimenting him. And very often such encouragement will fall flat on its face because our friend will be unable to drink in the implications of what is being said. The helper may then be deflated.

There is a way of giving praise and encouragement which the depressed person might be able to receive. It is to give it in the form of a question: 'Can you see that you did that well?' or 'Does it make sense that you handled that relationship with confidence?' They will turn the memory over in their mind slowly and might even respond: 'Well, yes. I can see that. Yes. That is encouraging.' The encouragement may not last long but it will have brought a glimmer of hope. Whereas if a well-meaning person were to attempt to give gushing praise and applause, it would almost certainly be met with disdain and the response: 'They're trying to convince themselves that I'm better than I am.'

The need for a team

There are no quick cures for depression. And maybe we should not even seek for one because if the lessons are learned thoroughly, depression could be the best thing that ever happened to this person. C. S. Lewis puts the position superbly:

> Imagine yourself as a living house. God comes in to rebuild that house. At first, perhaps, you can understand what He is doing. He is getting the drains right and stopping the leaks in the roof and so on. You knew that those jobs needed doing and so you are not surprised. But presently He starts knocking the house about in a way that hurts abominably and does not seem to make sense. What on earth is He up to? The explanation is that He is building quite a different house from the one you thought of – throwing out a new wing here, putting an extra floor there, running up towers, making courtyards. You thought you were going to be made into a decent little cottage: but He is building a palace.[4]

But while the rebuilding is in progress, the living stones of the depressed person's life need scaffolding to keep them from disintegrating. And no one person can hope to form a structure secure enough to bear this heavy burden on their own. Others must be involved. To admit this is not a sign of weakness or failure on our part but common sense. Gaius Davies, a consultant psychiatrist in London, put the situation well when he made the claim that what is needed to support, not just the depressed, but other people in pain also, is a team of people, each contributing their own unique expertise, each co-operating with the others, each intent on supporting the person until *God's* refurbishment has been completed.

Roger Hurding, another Christian psychiatrist, explains why this cluster of helpers plays such an important part in the life of broken people and he helps to put their problems in perspective.

Man made in the image of God, he claims, was created an essential unity of mind, body and spirit. He was a fully integrated person: his thinking, feeling, creating, intuitive, doing, worshipping, relating and 'simply being' faculties in perfect working order and each in harmony with the rest.

Diagrammatically, man before the Fall looked like this:

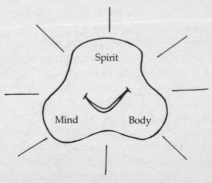

In God's image: WHOLE

But with the Fall came catastrophe. This image was shattered. Man now looked more like this:

Image broken: EVERYMAN

Left to himself he would stay in this state of fallenness and suffer the pain inflicted by imbalance, immaturity and a poor sense of identity for the rest of his life. But if he is exposed to God's love expressed through Christ, his Word, his Spirit and his love incarnated through human carers and counsellors, he will be so transformed that he will be able to enjoy a renewed sense of well-being: balance, maturity, an increased sense of identity and self-worth. He will then look like this:

Balance, Maturity. Sense of Identity

Not perfect. Not fully mature. That happy state will be enjoyed only on the other side of eternity. But enjoying an increased sense of wholeness.

These diagrams have captured my imagination and caused me to dream a dream for the church where I worship and for other Christian communities who are seeking to touch the sores of people who move within their orbit. I have replaced C. S. Lewis's picture of the house with another image: the wheel of a bicycle. Diagrammatically, it will look like this:

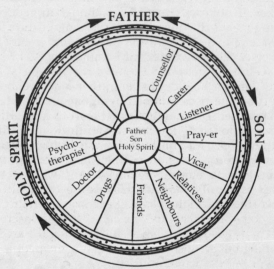

The spokes of the wheel

The mystery is that, within each broken Christian, God the Father, God the Son and God the Holy Spirit have taken up residence. To use the language of St Paul the mystery, the hope of glory, is that Christ is *in us*. Or to quote the language of Jesus, we are indwelt by the three members of the Trinity. But we are also assured that we are *in* Christ. In God. So every damaged personality (and that is each of us) is enfolded in the Trinity and indwelt by the Trinity. But every Christian is also a part of a whole bevy of fellow believers: the body of Christ. My dream is that each member of the body of Christ should discover their gift and use it to the full. When this happens, even though the damage may be severe, the wheel of a person's life may wobble precariously but it will still turn. In this diagram the wheel is supported by a web of spokes who are the burden bearers – the kind of community modelled to me by the residents of Roberts Road which I described at the beginning of this book. In any truly caring community, there will be a similar complex web of spokes. In our own church, even though its geographical setting means that members of the congregation live at a considerable distance from one another, we are setting ourselves the task of creating community. As I write, we are seeking to discern who the 'love therapists' are. By 'love therapists' I mean people who care enough for others to offer practical help when needed: Hoovering, cooking, gardening – those prepared to love with their sleeves rolled up. It has been a sadness to me to discover that fewer people volunteer for this hidden ministry of caring than for the more 'glamorous', up-front tasks of counselling and prayer ministry. Love-in-action, it seems, is the cinderella of today's ministries.

We are also seeking to discover those in whom God has invested a special ability to listen. We are conscious that each of us needs to go on and on learning the art-form of listening but we also recognise that some people have a flair for this particular ministry.

From a large group of listeners, some counsellors are emerging. Some of these have already received counselling training through their secular profession: social workers, probation officers, and Marriage Guidance Counsellors. If no such training has been received we offer basic guidelines to those who appear to be competent to counsel.

But we are aware that it is possible for any counsellor to wade out of their depth and so we have the ear of qualified psychologists, psychiatrists, psychotherapists and psychoanalysts who will advise and supervise when the occasion demands. Similarly other therapists give their support when it is needed: doctors, physiotherapists, occupational therapists and solicitors, to mention a few.

Alongside these other spokes of the wheel, we place the 'prayer therapists'. These are people who will make themselves available to intercede with or for the person in pain. Some of these therapists will have had experience in the ministry of inner healing which I have described in Chapters 8 and 9. Some of them have little experience in listening to people's problems and no experience in counselling. What they bring to people in pain is the gift of faith that God will intervene in some way. When they pray with a person presenting a particular need, they will listen to the description of the problem with one ear and attempt to listen to God with the other ear. They will bear in mind the picture of the person redeemed by Christ but not yet whole (see diagram 3) and they will be leaning heavily on God, relying on him to show them through a word of wisdom or discernment just how he wants to minister to the dents in that person's personality or body or spirit which is causing trouble at the moment.

If the person asking for help is clearly clinically depressed or bereaved, they will pray 'a holding prayer' and refer them to someone more experienced than themselves who can offer appropriate counselling. In some instances, when this seems to be the correct procedure, they might simply pray for the person and the professionals who are attempting to give more long-term help. On other occasions, when the problem is less complex, they might ask God by his Spirit to work in this person's life in any way he chooses. On such occasions, they might look for signs that God's Spirit is at work in the person's life. Because the Holy Spirit is sometimes described as wind, if the person's eyelashes flutter as though they were being blown by the wind while they are being prayed for, the prayer therapists take this as a sign that the perplexed or hurting person is being touched by God in some way. Or, because the Holy Spirit is described as fire, they are not surprised when the person they pray for glows with heat or if their own hands start to burn as they lay them, prayerfully, on the person's head or on injured parts of his body.

And we have seen God work miracles through these untrained people-helpers. By a miracle, I mean a work of healing which cannot be explained in human terms. But, equally, like many others, I have had the distressing task of attempting to piece together the parts of people who have received inappropriate ministry from well-meaning prayer therapists who have made a wrong diagnosis: mistaking, for example, a panic attack for demonisation.

At the same time, I have stayed alongside emotionally immature and hurting individuals who have been brought into wholeness through the talking therapies and drug therapy. But, equally, I have known of some who have remained untouched by psychiatry but who have been wonderfully helped by inner healing or prayer ministry.

For these reasons, the more involved I become in the task of reaching out to hurting people, the more I echo the words of the hymn writer when he wrote: 'God moves in a mysterious way his wonders to perform.' God is mystery. The ministry of healing is a mystery. A mystery is something too complex for the human mind to fathom.

Even so, if we are to be responsible to our calling to be compassionate as our Father is compassionate, we have to try to understand and I, for one, am grateful that, over the years, I have had the privilege of working alongside several professionals who have spent years acquiring learned people-helping skills. But I am grateful, too, that I have also worked with several 'novices' who bring nothing to an encounter with a troubled person other than an awareness that God wants to touch this person's life in some way. Both have challenged me. The professionals challenge me to go on and on learning all that is to be learned about the complexity of the human personality. The novices challenge me to open myself more fully simply to be used by God as and when and how he chooses. Meanwhile God seems to be challenging me to place my dependence in him but to go on with the learning.

And this dresses me down to size. Humbles me. And it has brought me into the realisation that because God is using a whole variety of people in a whole variety of ways to bring wholeness to an individual, I can be content to be just one spoke in the wheel of a person's life. I need never masquerade as the Messiah. Omnicompetent. I need not even make apology for my limitations. On the contrary, I can feel comfortable working within them; content to leave other parts of the burden bearing to those with different expertise.

That is not to say that we can be cavalier or irresponsible in the way we help others. Of course not. We need to learn the discipline of accountability to each other. Loose spokes are dangerous. They cause punctures and even accidents. Christians can cause similar casualties if they insist on operating in isolation. Whether we are listening or counselling, praying for people or offering practical help, we need therefore to keep in touch with the others and with the indwelling Christ so that our goal is achieved – the wheel of the person's life functions freely once more.

Qualifications of a 'spoke in the wheel'

'What kind of qualities are you looking for in people who offer to be spokes in your wheel of caring?' That is a question I am asked frequently. All kinds of characteristics have crowded into my mind in an attempt to answer it.

First and foremost, I look for people who will incarnate the love of Christ. Most of us, from time to time, find that we are rather like the small boy who, for a special treat, went on holiday with his father. Lying in the dark and in that strange bed, he felt alone and frightened. His father, sensing the fear, attempted to reassure him with the comforting thought that there was no need to be afraid because he was not by himself. God was with him. 'Yes,' replied the boy. 'But just for tonight I would like to have a God with skin on.'

And people who incarnate the love of Christ become those much needed 'Gods with skin on' which provide us with the props that are essential to our well-being when we are heavy hearted. The kind of people I have in mind are those who so respect the bruised and bleeding of this world that even in the midst of their pain they offer them warmth, sensitivity, understanding, concern, unconditional love and the Christ-like compassion we focused on in the first chapter of this book. These are the kind of people of whom it is often said as it was of the scientist and priest Teilhard de Chardin, 'Just to speak to him made you feel better; you knew that he was listening to you and that he understood you.' These are the people who bestow, even on the broken-hearted, a sense of their full worth as children of God.

Secondly, I look for people who will learn to listen to God as well as to other people. This ability to tune into the Father heart of God is essential for several reasons. First, as Francis MacNutt reminds us, the creature is dependent on the Creator for the wisdom to know how best to fulfil his role of 'God with skin on'. For, 'just as a doctor looks for the right diagnosis, the Christian helper is seeking discernment – which is the right diagnosis in the realm of prayer.'[8] This discernment comes in a variety of ways, as explained in *Listening to God*. Sometimes it comes in the form of a picture, sometimes through one word which may seem meaningless to the helper but which will cut ice with the person in pain, if, indeed, it has come from God. Or it might come quite naturally in the form of the wisdom to know which questions to ask and which to withhold, when to speak and when to keep silent and in what way one should pray. Unless we listen to God, we shall never graduate from anything higher than our own assessment of a person's pain. But what is really needed is God's perspective. When we have this, we can determine whether the dark valley the person seems to be travelling through has been caused by sin which needs to be confessed and cleansed or whether it is a sickness which needs a healing touch from God or whether it is a mysterious treasure to be seen as a trust from God; the kind of darkness encapsulated in the immortal words of Francis Thompson:

> Is my gloom after all
> Shade of his hand?
>   (The Hound of Heaven)

Such in-tuneness with God comes most easily to those who have learned to keep silence. And this silent attentiveness before God is important for another reason. Rathbone Oliver, a psychiatrist as well as a priest, puts the situation well:

> The extent of your power to help will depend not on your knowledge of psychiatry, or even on your knowledge of dogmatic or moral theology but on the assurance you bring to human souls that you yourself have been with Jesus . . . People, unhappy, anxious, self-tormented people, are drawn toward real holiness as moths are drawn to a candle.[6]

In other words, what hurting people crave is not the paucity of human help but rather a touch of the divine love, wisdom or healing through God's human agents: his people helpers.

Would-be people helpers need to learn the art of listening to God because none of us has within ourselves the divine love which penetrates and communicates, which heals and consoles or challenges and confronts. But God will add these resources to us. And he will do it while we creep into him ourselves, make a deliberate attempt to lay on one side our preoccupation with our

own needs and insecurities, fears and unresolved ten-
sions and add to us sufficient resources to stay alongside
broken people. Without this love much of the time we
spend with hurting people may well be wasted.

And there is a fourth reason for learning to listen to
God. It is here too that we receive forgiveness and
cleansing for the sin which would block us from being
effective channels of God's power and holding, healing
love.

Allow God to be God

People who are aware of the need to depend on God
for discernment and resources are those who are most
likely to allow God to be God. This, too, I believe to be a
quality which should be sought by anyone attempting
to help others in the name of Christ. I say this because
of the tragic polarisation I detect in certain circles. What
I see happening is this. Some skilled psychiatrists,
psychoanalysts and other professionals who have
spent hours studying the complexities of the human
psyche are falling into the trap of assuming that they hold
the monopoly when the task in hand is that of straighten-
ing bent minds or healing hurt emotions. Very often, of
course, God does use them as his chief instrument of
healing to hurting people. On the other hand, as Gerard
Hughes reminds us, God is a God of surprises. And
sometimes he chooses to by-pass the insights of the
well-qualified professional and chooses instead to bring
peace to one of his heart-broken children through the
prayer of faith offered by an amateur who has never even
trained in counselling. But such professionals are not the
only ones who wear the blinkers. Many prayer therapists, I find, are equally short-sighted and have been heard
to claim that unless a person has clearly been touched by
God's spirit, the help given to the hurting person has
been invalid and ineffective. This claim is naive, inaccurate and arrogant. It results in the failure to discern that
sometimes our prayers do not produce the crop of instant

cures we anticipate, because on many occasions, God chooses to touch individuals in need through the slow, gradual growth which is effected through psychiatry, drug therapy or counselling. The mystery of God is that he flatly refuses to be tied down by our methodologies. He is a God of variety.

Effective helpers will be those who not only rejoice in whatever method God chooses to bring wholeness to his hurting child, they will be those who have a theology of pain, suffering and death as well as a theology of healing. By this I mean that they will not fall into the trap of demanding that the person being helped should receive instant healing but rather will discipline the clamouring voices inside themselves that demand a miracle every time and learn instead that in the economy of God, pain sometimes has a purpose and that the ultimate healing is, in fact, death itself. One reason I look for people who will allow God to be God is that such people have discovered the unique contribution which other people can make and, instead of feeling threatened by the presence of others, co-operate with them humbly and gratefully in the way I have already outlined in this chapter. So the psychiatrist will support and maybe even supervise someone whose main contribution will be prayer ministry, maybe through the prayer for inner healing; or the counsellor will work alongside the general practitioner, the physiotherapist and the psychologist who are also seeking to bring a certain person into wholeness. Each will make their unique contribution to the person being helped. And in doing so each will learn from the other.

Proficiency, accountability and personal growth

And I look for three more qualities in people who volunteer to be spokes in the wheel of caring. One is proficiency. To become a really effective helper of others demands hard work and a lifetime of learning. While the learning continues, there is a need for each helper to be accountable to others for the way they handle another's hurts. This means that, just as a gifted conductor will draw out the best from a choir or an orchestra, so a gifted, dedicated director of pastoral care will be needed to draw out the full potential of those whom God calls to care in the way I have described. And if this potential is to be realised, each helper will catch a glimpse of the need, not only to be proficient and efficient, but they will make it their quest to grow in personal maturity. This will usually mean that there will need to be someone who will help them to continue to grow in self-awareness, someone before whom they can spread their work load and who will comment on it, someone who will help them to discover how and where their own resources are to be replenished so that they live balanced, healthy lives and avoid burnout.

Who is equal to this task, some readers might ask. And the answer is no one. At least, not in their own strength. But then, we are not asked to serve God in the energy of the flesh but rather we enjoy the privilege of being empowered and energised by his life-giving Spirit. And it is as the indwelling Spirit courses his life through our veins that spiritual fruit matures: love which according to one Harvard professor, is 'incomparably the greatest psychotherapeutic agent . . . something that professional psychiatry cannot by itself create, focus or release',[10] joy, peace, patience, goodness, gentleness, kindness, self-control (Gal. 5:22). The very qualities I have been underlining.

Being one spoke in the wheel of the life of a person in pain, far from being the glamorous ministry people often mistake it to be, is tiring and draining. As Anne Long used to remind her students, it costs 'not less than everything' of the people helping. Human spokes therefore need plenty of patience and plenty of stamina.

But there are rewards. One will be ours to enjoy when the Lord returns. Matthew describes it powerfully:

When the Son of Man comes in his glory, and all the angels with him, he will sit on the throne in heavenly glory. All the nations will be gathered before him, and he will separate the people one from another as a shepherd separates the sheep from the goats. He will put the sheep on his right and the goats on his left. Then the King will say to those on his right, 'Come, you who are blessed by my Father; take your inheritance, the kingdom prepared for you since the creation of the world. For I was hungry and you gave me something to eat, I was thirsty and you gave me something to drink, I was a stranger and you invited me in, I needed clothes and you clothed me, I was sick and you looked after me, I was in prison and you came to visit me.' Then the righteous will answer him, 'Lord, when did we see you hungry and feed you, or thirsty and give you something to drink? When did we see you a stranger and invite you in, or needing clothes and clothe you? When did we see you sick or in prison and go to visit you?' The King will reply, 'I tell you the truth, whatever you did for one of the least of these brothers of mine, you did for me.' (Matt. 25:31–40)

Anything? Hoovering, cooking casseroles, 'just listening', counselling? Yes. Anything. And, if my testimony is an accurate gauge, there is another, more immediate reward. It is the pure joy of watching someone you have been helping crawl out of their joyless chrysalis, not as the caterpillar they once were, but the beautiful butterfly God always intended they should be. Free.

12

Listening to Joy

For as long as I remember I have been able to weep with those who weep. Life in Roberts Road seemed to equip me for that. But the realisation dawned on me as the counselling course at St John's drew to a close that I seemed ill equipped to rejoice with those who rejoice. When people were in pain, I slipped very easily into the role of helper. But when it was joy they were wanting to share with me, I felt ill at ease, on the fringe, uncertain of what was expected of me.

This bothered me. So in the third term at St John's I shared my concern with the small group of ordinands and their wives who were part of the same 'growth group' as me. 'This is the area in which I'd most like to mature,' I confided.

I had expected these young people to look shocked when I made this confession. I imagined that the problem was peculiar to me. Instead their eyes expressed empathy and understanding and several heads were nodding as I said my piece.

That term I set myself the task of trying to discover the reason why I was so ambivalent about listening to joy. How *did* one rejoice with those who rejoiced with as much care as one wept with those who weep? What was the secret? While searching for answers to such questions, I asked God to do a further piece of transforming work in me; to set me free to listen to joy with genuineness.

Louis Evely's books, *Joy* and *Suffering*,[1] put the problem into perspective for me and helped me to discover one reason why some people receive sorrow more easily than joy.

This Jesuit priest claims that the inability to receive joy is a universal problem; that though Jesus made us depositaries of his joy and though Christianity is a religion of joy and though God has filled his world with joy, Christian people have not yet learned to cherish this priceless gift. Man has missed his entry into joy, he claims. We are much more inclined to mourn with Christ than to rejoice with him. We are better disposed to be sorrowful with Christ and to share his sufferings than his joy.

At first these claims astonished me. We at St John's, it seemed, were not alone in our problem. I read on.

After the crucifixion, Louis Evely reminds us, a few faithful friends lingered at the foot of Christ's cross. But on the morning of the resurrection, no one was present to witness him bursting the bonds of death or to watch while the angels rolled the stone away. Consequently part of Jesus' post-resurrection task was to convert each of his friends so that they could receive the reality of his joy. But he had to take them by the hand, one by one, and teach them how to receive this joy.

How to receive joy

While I continued to pray that God would convert me in this way, I thought carefully about some further observations of this Jesuit author.

Jesus had already taught his disciples one part of the secret of receiving joy, he explains. It starts with prayer. In the words of Jesus: 'Ask and you will receive, and your joy will be complete' (John 16:24). Now Jesus goes on to show that there is a flip side to this coin. If they are to find themselves in harmony with joy, they must learn to lay aside their preoccupation with themselves.

This is one of the lessons the risen Christ seems to be trying to drum into the minds of the disciples on the road to Emmaus. In his encounter with them, Jesus' first task was to strip them of the prejudices and presuppositions which clouded their perception so that, eventually, their hearts were ready to receive Christ with joy. He deals similarly with Thomas's doubts. When these have been removed the scales fall from his eyes and with joy he cries: 'My Lord and my God.' And, perhaps most movingly of all, we are permitted to eavesdrop as Jesus stands on the shore of the Sea of Galilee and converses with the great deserter, Peter; the one who, that very morning, had resolved to return to his former lifestyle: fishing in the Sea of Galilee. And Jesus takes from his mind the sting of the memory of that night in Caiaphas' palace when Peter denied all acquaintance with Jesus and, in its place, he puts joy: the joy of the awareness that he is still loved and capable of loving; that he is not only usable but recommissioned.

'Yes. Louis Evely is right,' I said to myself. 'Before I can hope to receive joy from another, I must be stripped of my preoccupation with self, be prepared to let go of those things on which my security seems to depend and abandon myself afresh to God. I'll never be able to receive joy with genuineness while another's good news seems to threaten my security.'

I was beginning to see that the block was selfishness on my part. I thought of the occasion when a close friend of mine announced her engagement. She had talked to me at length about her relationship with the young man she was in love with. And through these conversations our closeness with each other had deepened. But when, eventually, she made her commitment to her husband-to-be, I realised that the dynamics of our relationship would need to change. I would have to step back. In time, after she married, I would lose her because she would move away from our area. And because her joy threatened my security, though I made all the right happy noises about being glad for her and though I congratulated him, I had not received their joy with the care I would have received their pain if they had announced that they were separating.

I reflected that I sometimes showed a similar ambivalence when a counselling relationship came to its natural conclusion. I thought of one such relationship in particular. A certain closeness had developed between myself and the girl I had been helping. Over the months, as we worked together, God touched her life in remarkable ways which thrilled and encouraged us both. But this meant, of course, that the time came when there was no more need for counselling sessions and since we are both busy people, our paths no longer crossed. She would write to me from time to time to tell me how God was continuing to touch her with his healing hand. And though I was happy for her, and though I wrote to express my joy, I was aware that there was a hollowness about this so-called joy. It was not a deep emotion. Only superficial. And, again, the problem was self-centredness. I could not really rejoice with her until I had relinquished the selfishness which would have liked to cling to her friendship.

'Detachment! That's the secret!' I recorded in my prayer journal. 'If I am serious about learning to listen to joy, I have to learn the discipline and art form of detachment: detachment from self and detachment from the earth-boundness which still persuades me that my security finds its source in people and possessions rather than in the God who smiles on me constantly with affection and who has sealed his loving promise: "I will never leave you or forsake you."'

I took comfort from Louis Evely's claims: 'Joy is slow to stir in us',[1] true joy is attained only gradually – by degrees.' And, I was later to discover, it does come. It came for me as I learned to listen to joy in much the same way as I listen to pain: attentively and with the attitude of mind which determines: 'I'm going to receive this person's gift and handle it with care.'

After I had made this resolve, I learned to read the language of the eyes of the joyful person – to watch them sparkle. Similarly I learned to listen to the tone of the voice as it struggled to contain its excitement. I learned to watch, too, the radiance of the face, to drink its joy and to take this joy deep down into my spirit and sip its nectar. And God gave me so many opportunities to practise these new skills. He continues to give me the privilege of listening to joy.

I am particularly aware of this as I write this chapter. It is December – the time when I write the annual news-letter for our friends. And as I look back over the year and try to decide what to write, I am aware that these last twelve months have been crammed with special joy, not because there has been an absence of pain but because true joy – the kind which comes from sorrows overcome – has dotted my path in the same way as shy primroses dot the hedgerows in spring.

I think, for example, of the occasion when my husband and I were enjoying Cantonese cooking in a Chinese restaurant in China Town in Brisbane, Australia. 'This makes me homesick for Singapore,' I admitted as we ate. Almost before the words had left my lips, I noticed a man smiling at me through the restaurant window. I could scarcely believe my eyes. He was a Singaporean; a friend who, on one of my visits to his country, had begged me to pray for him because he and his wife had been told they were infertile and they both longed for a child.

I did pray. A few months later his wife had written to share their good news. She was pregnant. When the baby was born they sent me a photograph of her which still smiles at me from my kitchen wall.

And now, here they were, grinning from ear to ear and walking through the restaurant door to greet us. As they placed their miracle baby into my arms, it was as though I was handling joy in a physical form. It was a moment of intense and pure joy.

Later that evening, as we talked to these friends in our hotel room, this joy spilled over into heartfelt thanks-giving to God that he had allowed our paths to cross so mysteriously; that we had all 'happened' to be in the same restaurant in the same town at the same time. I gave thanks too, for the fulfilment of Jesus' promise: 'My joy shall be in you and your joy shall be full.'

But joy has also come in less tangible forms. It came in Malaysia one summer when my husband and I enjoyed a reunion with ex-members of our congregation who have now returned to their native land. One of the first people to greet me was a girl I had tried to help when she was a student in Nottingham. She reminded me of the dark days of depression she encountered and of the talks we used to have. And I read the gratitude in her eyes and saw the smile of thanks on her lips and felt the warmth of her embrace, and I found myself receiving and internalising, not only her love and gratitude, but also the joy which seemed to bubble from her. It was another wonderfully joyful moment.

But perhaps the most moving of them all came in the context of a Communion service in a sleepy village in my homeland: England. The service was being conducted by a pastor who, when he had nose-dived into the dark tunnel of depression, had given my husband and me the privilege of staying alongside him in the seemingly-interminable darkness. But just as J. B. Phillips had translated the entire New Testament when he was depressed, and as William Cowper had written some of his most profound poetry and hymns from the dark pit of depression, and as Leslie Weatherhead was capable of enthralling thousands by his preaching even while he was gripped by depression, so this pastor's effectiveness for Christ had not been blunted by the darkness but rather this desert had produced abundant growth.

And as I watched him press his thumbs into the brown loaf which was to become for us the bread of heaven, into my mind flooded memories of the countless times I have watched those thumbs being twiddled aimlessly, listlessly and boringly as they expressed the lifelessness which dogged him. And as I watched in wonder as worship lighted up his face, I recalled the many occasions when that face had been overshadowed by loneliness and anguish. As I listened to the quiver of excitement in his voice as he confessed: 'I'm so excited by God's Word,' I thought of the hours I had heard that voice bemoan the seeming absence of God and the inability to concentrate on his revealed Word. And I realised that a miracle was unfolding before my eyes.

The miracle was not that this man had experienced a dramatic healing in the sense that one day he was suffering from depression and the next he was enjoying freedom from darkness. His had been a gradual change. God had used drug therapy, the talking therapies, prayer therapy and love therapy to bring him through the dark valley and into this oasis. But just as I had been given the privilege of staying alongside him in the shadowlands, so now I was being given the even greater privilege and joy of being on the receiving end of his ministry.

'The greater privilege and *joy*.' Yes. It was a moment pregnant with profound joy. Not the shallow, transitory, effervescent kind which, like a will o' the wisp, is here one second and disappears the next but the deep down, lasting kind which you savour and ponder and which prompts you to fall on your face at the foot of Christ's cross in wonder, love, adoration and praise; the kind which brings tears to your eyes – tears of JOY.

That day the God of surprises surprised me by joy. Through the transparency of this humble pastor's ministry, he had shown me what he has been creating in the inner recesses of my being: a deep vein of joy. 'My gift to you through others,' he seemed to whisper. 'As you've struggled to absorb their pain so now be enriched by their joy also.'

Some repercussions

And I have been enriched by joy. As I look back in an attempt to trace some of the ways in which God answered that prayer I made in the growth group at St John's, I am aware that, just as Jesus changed the direction of Peter's life when he taught him to receive the joy of the resurrection, so I received a recommissioning from

God as I learned to tune in to joy. It was while I listened to the joy the engaged couples in our church were expressing that the idea of organising seminars for engaged couples was conceived. And it was while one particular couple shared their secret joy with me – that they were expecting their first baby – that a seed thought was sown which led to my piloting our first Pregnant Parents' Group in the church. Similarly, it was when married couples invited us to rejoice with them that the marriage seminars which had been held in our home had revolutionised their lives that the urge to set up retreats for married couples pushed me into action.

Engaged Couples' Weekends, Marriage Fulfilment Weekends, Marriage Refreshment Retreats for Christians in Leadership, Pregnant Parents' Group; all have one aim: to focus on the joy which God intended us to give and receive in our relationships in the home and to discover how best to enter into this joy.

These weekends and mid-week retreats are fun as well as hard work. They have opened up for me a whole new dimension of listening to others and encouraged me to dream an even bigger dream for our church. Living as we do, in a troubled, sin-stricken world, there will always be a need for the kind of crisis counselling I have described in this book. But prevention is better than cure. And so my longing for my own church and for the church at large is that, instead of pouring all our resources into gluing together the shattered remains of the broken people who come across our paths and perpetuating the myth that the church is a hospital where sick people come to be cured, we tune in, as well, to the joy and resilience of those who are catching glimpses of the abundant life Christ promised. And we speak to this joyful resilience. We teach those who are coping how to enter more deeply into the joy of their Lord, how to develop good nurturing relationships both in the family and beyond, how to anticipate problems and how to handle them when they arise.

We will teach our parents how to find joy in their

children and how to cherish them so that they grow up relishing their uniqueness. Equally we will teach our children how to understand and find joy in their parents; how to show them that they are valued.

We will listen to the joy of teenagers in love and teach them how to handle the bitter-sweet emotions that come as part of the package of puppy love. We will help our engaged couples to prepare for the joy of marriage, teach our married people how to find more joy in one another as the years fly by and show our single people the special joys of singlehood. And we will not stop there. We will recognise that there are peculiar joys which are denied the young but which make themselves available to the middle-aged and the elderly. So we will whet people's appetites through books and videos, seminars and sermons and show them how to savour the joys of middle age, retirement and even old age.

Best of all, we will point them to the source of all joy, Jesus himself, and to that inexpressible joy which will one day be ours when he returns; that day when the sorrows and sadnesses of this life will be replaced with the ecstasy that will be ours when we see him face to face and exchange our earthly ministry for the heavenly one of serving him tirelessly day and night for ever.

On that great day we shall understand more fully the mysteries of our faith, including the mystery which stares me in the face every time I go to my prayer room. There hangs a banner which was made for me by a nun. Against a blue background which symbolises the vastness of the cosmos, she has placed, in white felt, a representation of the glorified Christ. His arms are outstretched in welcome, reminding me that the glorified Christ is also the welcoming Christ. But as I gaze at his hands and his feet, I see the marks of the nails which she has stitched to remind me that though he is glorified, still he is scarred. And on to the felt she has sewn the figure of the crucified Christ – the one who took upon himself our pain and our shame so that we could take upon ourselves his glory; the one who refused to by-pass Calvary but rather chose to go through the agony of Gethsemane and Good Friday to reach the ultimate joy: Easter day.

Sometimes I feel drawn to this figure because of his aliveness and splendour. At other times it is his vulnerability which compels me. And therein lies the mystery. Joy and pain intertwine. This side of eternity they are bedfellows. Both are essential parts of our humanity.

As I come to the final paragraph of this book, I hear a carol coming from the radio. It is one I learned when I was a child in the Sunday School in Roberts Road – before Barry Hart died:

> What can I give him, poor as I am
> If I were a shepherd, I would bring a lamb
> If I were a wise man, I would do my part
> Yet what I can I give him, give my heart.

> (C. Rosetti)

'Give my heart.' Even when I sang that as a child, my heart would be strangely warmed. For years I used to think that that warmth was all that was needed because I was simply required to give my love, my adoration, my worship and my praise. But now I see that it means all of that and much more. For Christ calls us to give to him the compassionate heart that prompts us to serve him in others. He calls us, too, to give him our listening heart – the heart that listens to God and to others; that is sensitive to sorrow but is equally quick to tune into joy.

Notes

Preface
1. Quoted in *The Prison of Love*, ed. Catharine Hughes (Sheed and Ward, 1972), p. 25.
2. Peter Dodson, *Contemplating the Word* (SPCK, 1987), p.1.

Chapter 1
1. Henri Nouwen, Donald P. McNeill, Douglas A. Morrison, *Compassion* (Darton, Longman and Todd, 1982), p. 4.
2. ibid. p. 27.
3. ibid. p. 16.
4. ibid. p. 18.

Chapter 2
1. Gary Collins's phrase.
2. See Gary R. Collins, *How to be a People Helper* (Regal Books, 1976), pp. 33–4; id., *Christian Counselling* (Word Books, 1980), pp. 24–5.
3. Henri Nouwen, Donald P. McNeill, Douglas A. Morrison, op.cit. p. 32.
4. ibid. p. 24.
5. John A. Sanford, *Ministry Burnout* (Arthur James, 1982), Introduction.
6. F. B. Meyer, *The Shepherd Psalm* (Marshall, Morgan and Scott, 1953), pp. 28, 30.

Chapter 3
1. in Henri Nouwen, *Reaching Out* (Fount, 1975), p. 60.
2. ibid.
3. Katharine Makower, *Follow My Leader* (Kingsway, 1986), p. 116.
4. H. R. Niebuhr, source unknown.

252   *Listening to Others*

Chapter 4
1. For a fuller discussion, read John Stott, *Issues Facing Christians Today* (Marshalls, 1984), ch. 1.
2. ibid. p. 9.
3. Alan Burgess, *The Small Woman* (Pan, ch. 1. 1957), p. 111.
4. ibid. pp. 143–44.
5. John Stott in *Alive to God Notes*, SU (October/December 1987).
6. id., *Issues Facing Christians Today*, op.cit. p. 14.
7. ibid. pp. 21–22.
8. See ibid. p. 9.

Chapter 5
1. Henri Nouwen, *Compassion*, op.cit. p. 13.
2. As explained in Joyce Huggett, *Two Into One* (IVP, 1981), Preface.
3. Myra Chave-Jones in a talk given at St Nicholas's Church, Nottingham, September 1986.
4. Anne Long in a handout given to the students at St John's College.
5. Norman Wakefield, 'Learn to be a listener!' *Counsellor's Journal*, CWR, vol. 4, No. (1981), p. 10.
6. Michael Jacobs, *Swift to Hear* (SPCK, 1985), p. 124, 125.
7. John Stott, in Myra Chave-Jones, *The Gift of Helping* (IVP, 1982), Foreword, p. 8.
8. Gary Collins, *How to be a People Helper* (Regal Books, 1976), p. 58.
9. Roger Hurding, *Restoring the Image* (Paternoster Press, 1980), p. 17.
10. Michael Jacobs, *Swift to Hear*, op.cit. p. 28.
11. David Augsburger, *Caring Enough to Hear and Be Heard* (Herald Press, 1982), p. 25.
12. ibid. p. 29.

Chapter 6
1. John Powell, *Will the Real Me Please Stand Up?* (Argus, 1985), p. 113.
2. Myra Chave-Jones, *The Gift of Helping* op.cit. p. 39.
3. John Powell, op.cit. p. 147.
4. ibid. p. 142.
5. ibid. p. 145.

6. Gary Collins, *How to be a People Helper*, op.cit. 1985 ch. 3.
7. Abraham Schmitt, *The Art of Listening With Love* (Abingdon Press, 1977), p. 169.
8. Myra Chave-Jones in a talk given at St Nicholas's, Nottingham.
9. John Powell, op.cit. p. 162.
10. Agnes Sanford, *Sealed Orders* (Logos, 1972), pp. 112, 114.
11. Joyce Huggett, *Listening to God* (Hodder and Stoughton, 1986).
12. Michel Quoist, *Prayers of Life* (Sheed and Ward, 1963), pp. 91, 92.
13. Catharine de Hueck Doherty, *Poustinia* (Fount, 1975), p. 20.
14. Abraham Schmitt, *Listening with Love* (Abingdon Press, 1977), p. 9.
15. Roger Hurding, *Roots and Shoots* (Hodder and Stoughton, 1985), p. 35.
16. Mother Teresa, an adaptation of a prayer by Cardinal Newman quoted in Daphne Rae, *Love Until It Hurts* (Hodder and Stoughton, 1981).

Chapter 7

1. Myra Chave-Jones in a talk given at St Nicholas's, Nottingham.
2. John Powell, op.cit. p. 97.
3. Simon Stephens, *Death Comes Home* (Mowbrays, 1972), p. 66.
4. Colin Murray Parkes, *Bereavement: Studies of Grief in Adult Life* (Pelican, 1972), p. 189.

Chapter 8

1. Gary R. Collins, *Christian Counselling* (Word Publications, 1980), p. 411.
2. Francis MacNutt, *Healing* (Ave Maria Press, 1974), p. 181.
3. Derived from a model created by Frank Lake.
4. Francis MacNutt, op.cit. p. 183.

Chapter 9

1. Francis MacNutt, op.cit. p. 170.
2. ibid. pp. 183–4.

3. Frank Lake, *Clinical Theology* (Darton, Longman and Todd, 1966), p. 140.
4. John and Paula Sandford, *The Transformation of the Inner Man* (Logos, 1982), p. 19.
5. David Seamands, *Healing of Memories* (Victor Books).

Chapter 10
1. Jack Dominian, *Depression* (Fontana, 1976), p. 149.
2. ibid. p. 150.
3. Myra Chave-Jones, *Coping With Depression* (Lion, 1981), p. 16.
4. Vera Phillips and Edwin Robertson, *The Wounded Healer* (Triangle, 1984), p. 103.
5. Richard Winter, *The Roots of Sorrow* (Marshalls, 1985), p. 25.
6. David Augsburger, *Caring Enough to Hear and be Heard* (Herald Press, 1982), p. 152.
7. Carlo Carretto, *Summoned by Love* (Darton, Longman and Todd, 1977), pp. 23, 24, 55, 56.

Chapter 11
1. Mary Craig, *Blessings* (Hodder and Stoughton, 1979), p. 134.
2. Quoted in ibid.
3. ibid. p. 142.
4. Quoted in Mark Gibbard, *Dynamic of Love* (Mowbrays, 1974), p. 1.
5,6,7: Roger Hurding, *Restoring The Image* (Paternoster Press, 1980), pp. 8–11.
8. Francis MacNutt, op.cit. pp. 195–6.
9. Rathbone Oliver, source unknown.
10. Gordon Allport, quoted in Gary Collins, op.cit. p. 25.

Chapter 12
1. Louis Evely, *Joy* (Burns and Oates 1968), p. 39.

Recommended Resources

The Acorn Christian Healing Trust was founded in 1983 by Bishop Morris and Anne Maddocks. Christian Listeners, led by the Rev. Anne Long, is one of several projects organised by this Trust. It comprises a twelve-session training course – normally church-based. Christian listeners become available to doctors, social workers and other health-care professionals for a ministry of listening in the locality of their church.

Christian Caring was established in 1985 on the initiative of a group of evangelical clergy in Cambridge. It has three main aims: to encourage the establishment of pastoral care support groups in the local churches, to train their members and to provide a professional therapy service for Christians in the locality who are in complex emotional need. Further details may be obtained from The Administrator, Christian Caring, Old School, 61, St Barnabas' Road, Cambridge CB1 2BX.

Care and Counsel was established in 1975 by Myra Chave-Jones. It offers personal therapy and counselling to individuals, couples and families whose emotional problems seem best discussed within a Christian context. All its therapists and counsellors are committed Christians. They organise seminars, courses, conferences and support groups designed to further inform and teach those already engaged in pastoral work.

The Post Green Pastoral Centre is one of the many ministries of the Post Green Community which was established in 1974. It organises conferences and camps, offers retreats, counselling and Spiritual Direction and receives individual guests. Its concern is to provide a caring, loving environment where the needs of the whole person can be heard and met. For further details write to: Post Green Pastoral Centre, 56, Dorchester Road, Lytchett Minster, Poole, Dorset BH16 6JE.

The Clinical Theology Association was formed in 1962 by Frank Lake and is now directed by Peter van de Kasteele. The Association exists to train people in Christian pastoral care and counselling and authorised tutors are currently available in most parts of the UK. Further details are obtainable from The Clinical Theology Association, St Mary's House, Church Westcote, Oxford OX7 6SF.

The Centre for Pastoral Care and Counselling is directed by the Rev. Michael Jacobs. Among other things, the centre provides training for clergy and lay leaders in the dioceses of Derby, Lincoln and Southwell. Short courses and day workshops are arranged which aim to help those involved in listening to brush up and improve their skills. Two audiotapes are available which are best used in conjunction with the book *Swift to Hear*. Further details are available from: The Centre for Pastoral Care and Counselling, Vaughan College, St Nicholas Circle, Leicester LE1 4LB.

Wholeness Through Christ Prayer Counselling Ministry aim to enable the ministry of the Holy Spirit to the whole person. It is a ministry within the churches to Christians who desire to be rid of all hindrances in order to become more effective in their Christian life and ministry. They are offered healing from bondages, fears and inner wounds that have crippled and often hindered their spiritual growth and development, in order to be more effective in serving their local churches and in helping others in need. To become effective in this ministry takes time. Wholeness Through Christ as a Trust, arranges Retreats for the healing of the Whole Person and Schools

of Prayer Counselling for this purpose. It goes on to
provide further personal ministry and training for those
who are being called into a specific Wholeness Through
Christ Prayer Counselling ministry in their local situation.

The Oxford Christian Institute for Counselling was
established in 1985 and has three main aims: to provide a
counselling service in a Christian context for people in
appropriate need in Oxford and the surrounding dis-
tricts; to provide support and supervision for those
involved in counselling on behalf of the Institute and to
provide educational training and study for Christians
involved in counselling. Seminars, talks and learning
experiences are arranged for counsellors and those
wanting to become more effective carers and listeners.
Course members must be supported by their local church
and are selected by interview.

**St John's College Extension Studies Pastoral Counsel-
ling Course** exists to provide lay people and clergy with
an understanding of the way people tick and some skills
with which to minister to them. Teaching includes a
biblical understanding of man, counselling skills and
pastoral care of the depressed and the bereaved. Students are expected to attend two residential weekends
at St John's College and to commit themselves to a four-
to-six month period of home study. The college also
runs an advanced course called Journey Through Life
which is run on similar lines and is for those who have
some grounding in counselling. Further details may be
obtained from St John's Extension Studies, St John's
College, Bramcote, Nottingham NG9 3DS.

Caring Seminars is the umbrella title for the Regional
Counsellor Training Scheme launched by the Crusade
for World Revival (CWR) in 1985 and conducted by
Selwyn Hughes and team. These seminars are held on
Saturdays and aim to equip Christians to help others

with the more simple problems which frequently crop up in the life of the local church. In addition, CWR organise a variety of courses in in-depth counselling at its residential training centre. Further details may be obtained from the centre: Waverley Abbey House, Waverley Lane, Farnham, Surrey GU9 8EP.

Network is a Bible-based, Christian organisation, commissioned in 1986, which seeks to serve the church and the community in three areas: *counselling* of people in need, *training* its own counsellors and others through a programme pioneered by Dr Roger Hurding and general *resources* of library, tapes, local information and short courses for Christians in the Bristol area. Further details may be obtained from Network Christian Counselling, 10 Cotham Park, Cotham, Bristol BS6 6BU.

Recommended Reading

On Listening

Michael Jacobs	*Swift to Hear* (SPCK)
John Powell	*Will the Real Me Please Stand Up* (Argus Communications)
Abraham Schmitt	*The Art of Listening With Love* (Festival Books)
David Augsburger	*Caring Enough to Hear and be Heard* (Herald Press)

Each of the above books contains valuable insights which show the reader how to listen to others more effectively.

On Counselling

Alistair Campbell	*Rediscovering Pastoral Care* (Darton, Longman and Todd)
Roger Hurding	*Roots and Shoots* (Hodder and Stoughton)
E. Kennedy	*On Becoming a Counsellor* (Gill and Macmillan)
Michael Jacobs	*Still Small Voice* (SPCK)
Myra Chave-Jones	*The Gift of Helping* (Inter-Varsity Press)
Gary Collins	*Christian Counselling* (Word Books)
Roger Hurding	*Restoring the Image* (Paternoster Press)
M. Scott Peck	*The Road Less Travelled* (Rider)
Gary Collins	*Innovative Approaches to Counselling* Vol. 1 (Word)
H. Norman Wright	*Self Talk, Imagery and Prayer Counselling* Vol. 2 (Word)
Frank Lake	*Tight Corners in Pastoral Care* (Darton, Longman and Todd)
Frank Lake	*The Dynamic Cycle* (CTA)

On People Helping

Henri Nouwen	*Compassion* (Darton, Longman and Todd)
Gary Collins	*How To Be a People Helper* (Regal Books)
Jennifer Rees-Larcombe	*God's Gloves* (Marshall Pickering)
Henri Nouwen	*The Wounded Healer* (Fount)
Henri Nouwen	*Reaching Out* (Fount)

Inner Healing

John and Paula Sandford	*The Transformation of the Inner Man* (Logos)
Barbara Leahy Shleman	*Healing the Hidden Self* (Ave Marie Press)
Agnes Sanford	*Sealed Orders* (Logos)
Ruth Carter Stapleton	*The Experience of Inner Healing* (Ecclesia Books)
Francis MacNutt	*Healing* (Ave Maria Press)
Francis MacNutt	*The Power to Heal* (Ave Maria Press)
Barry Kissell	*Walking on Water* (Hodder and Stoughton)
Mary Pytches	*Set My People Free* (Hodder and Stoughton)
David Seamands	*Healing for Damaged Emotions* (Victor Books)
David Seamands	*Healing of Memories* (Victor Books)
Agnes Sanford	*The Healing Light* (Arthur James)
Agnes Sanford	*Healing Gifts of the Spirit* (Arthur James)
Anne White	*Healing Adventure* (Arthur James)
John Wimber	*Power Healing* (Hodder and Stoughton)

I would not endorse all the teaching of each of these writers but the books I mention all contain useful insights into the ministry of inner healing.

Bereavement
How to care for the dying and bereaved:

Ian Ainsworth-Smith	*Letting Go* (SPCK)

Colin Murray Parkes	*Bereavement* (Pelican)
John Hinton	*Dying* (Pelican)
Kathleen Smith	*Help for the Bereaved* (Duckworth)
Elizabeth Collick	*Through Grief: The Bereavement Journey* (Darton, Longman and Todd/Cruse)
Edgar Jackson	*The Many Faces of Grief* (SCM Press)
Jean Grigor	*Loss: An Invitation To Grow* (Arthur James)

Not all the above books are written from a Christian point of view but each of them contains invaluable insights into how best to help the grief-stricken person. The last two are designed to be used by groups of people working through their grief together.

Helpful books to give to the bereaved at the appropriate time

| C. S. Lewis | *A Grief Observed* (Faber) |

C. S. Lewis' moving and powerful account of his own feelings as he came to terms with the death of his wife.

| Wendy Green | *The Long Road Home* (Lion) |
| Ingrid Trobisch | *Learning to Walk Alone* (Inter-Varsity Press) |

Two bitter-sweet books which describe how the authors are coming to terms with widowhood.

| Simon Stephens | *Death Comes Home* (Mowbray) |
| Mary Craig | *Blessings* (Hodder and Stoughton) |

Two powerful books which help readers to put themselves in the shoes of parents who suffer the trauma of the death of a child.

| Elizabeth Heike | *A Question of Grief* (Hodder and Stoughton) |

A sensitive, wise and challenging contribution which will be of help particularly to those who lose a friend through death.

Anthologies which might bring comfort to those who mourn

Agnes Whittaker   *All in the End is Harvest* (Darton,
                           Longman and Todd/Cruse)

(A beautiful collection of prose and poems, prayers and
reflections which could be given to a Christian or an unbeliever
at any stage of grief).

Cicely Saunders   *Beyond All Pain* (SPCK)

(Dame Cicely Saunders' own collection of poems and prayers
written mainly by terminally sick patients in the St
Christopher's Hospice where she is Medical Director. Could be
given to believers and unbelievers).

Jolanda Miller   *Facing Life Again* (Inter-Varsity
                          Press)

(Might help some Christians in the later stages of grief. Read it
first to make sure that you feel it is suitable for the person you
have in mind).

Depression
For befrienders and counsellors:

Myra Chave-Jones   *Coping With Depression* (Lion)
Jack Dominian   *Depression* (Fontana)
Richard Winter   *The Roots of Sorrow* (Marshalls)
Dorothy Rowe   *Depression* (Routledge and Kegan
                          Paul)
John White   *The Masks of Melancholy* (Inter-
                          Varsity Press)
Ross Mitchell   *Depression* (Pelican)

Each of the above make their own important contribution to the
understanding of depression.

**Biographies which might help a person suffering from
depression**
Vera Phillips and   *The Wounded Healer - J. B. Phillips*
Edwin Robertson   (Triangle)

Stanley Baldwin	*Bruised But Not Broken* (Kingsway)
Nancy Anne Smith	*Winter Past* (Inter-Varsity Press)
Alexander Davidson	*Through a Foreign Land* (Lutheran Publishing House)
Don Baker Emery Nestor	*Depression* (Marshalls)

JOYCE Huggett

LISTENING TO GOD

*The bestselling companion to
Listening to Others*

This is both a profound spiritual
testimony, and offers practical
help for discovering a new
dimension of prayer. God longs
for his people to have a closer
walk with him and to
communicate with him. Such is
the evidence of the Bible and
Christian history, but many
Christians have only scratched
the surface of the potential of
prayer, easily discouraged by
obstacles and perhaps
uncertainty that God really can
speak to them today.

Joyce Huggett confirms that
God is far from silent when
Christians seek his will and his
voice. Drawing from nine years'
experience of prayerfully
listening to God, Joyce shares
the thrilling discoveries she has
made, offering practical
encouragement and honestly
tackling difficulties as well as the
rewards of this exciting
discipline.